Contemporary Crafts

THE SOURCEBOOK OF CRAFT ARTISTS
GALLERY EDITION

2

THE GUILD®

Kraus Sikes Inc.
Madison, Wisconsin
USA

Published by:
Kraus Sikes Inc.
228 State Street
Madison, WI 53703-2215
TEL 800-969-1556
TEL 608-256-1990
FAX 608-256-1938

Administration:
Toni Fountain Sikes, President
James F. Black, Jr., Vice President
Susan K. Evans, Vice President of Sales
Theresa Ace, Business Manager
Yvonne Cooley, Sales Coordinator
Debbie Lovelace, Operations Manager

Production, Design, Editorial:
Lillian Sizemore, Production Manager
Kathlyn Williams, Production Assistant

Katie Kazan, Editorial Manager
Theodora Zehner, Editorial Assistant

Bill Kraus, Writer
Jorge Arango, Writer

DNP America, Inc., Printer

Publisher's Representatives:
Susan K. Evans
Sharon Marquis
Bastien Atterbury
Martha Johnson
Diane Nelson
Karen O. Brown
Kimberly McKnight

Worldwide Distribution:
Hearst Books International
1350 Avenue of the Americas
New York, NY 10019

::: THE GUILD.
is a registered trademark of Kraus Sikes Inc.

ISBN (softback) 1-880140-14-4
ISBN (hardback) 1-880140-13-6

Printed in Hong Kong

**Special thanks to our
1995 Review Committee:**

Reed McMillan
The McMillan Gallery

Valerie Paterson
American Craft Museum

John I. Russell
Brookfield Craft Center

Jura Silverman
Jura Silverman Studio & Gallery

Gary Yee
Adrien Linford

Cover art:
Fairy Table by Judie Bomberger, hand-wrought, painted steel, approx. 3'H. On top of table: *Hog Mama*, two-dimensional, approx. 20"H. See page 44.

Artwork shown in introductory essays:

Page 7: blown glass vases by David Van Noppen

Page 8: *African Bed* by David A. Ponsler, forged steel,
photo: Daryl Bunn

Page 9: *Arizona Symphony* by Maureen McGuire

Page 10: *Sweltering Sky Kimono* by Judith Content, silk,
photo: James Dewrange

Page 11: *Forest Root Chair* (left) by Daniel Mack,
photo: Bobby Hansson

Page 11: *Sans Hands Chair* (center) by Paul Reiber, cherry,
walnut, gold leaf,
photo: Fess Shirley

Page 11: *Frank Lloyd Wrong Chair* (right) by Barbara Field,
photo: Bernard Wolf

Page 12: *Handie Lamps* by Cheryl Reneé Riley,
photo: David Livingston

Page 12: raku-fired plate and vessels by Carol Rossman,
photo: Michael Dismatsek

Page 13: *Arches of Dawn* by Loretta Mossman, wool tapestry;
patinated bronze buffet by David Reisbord,
photo: Robin Miller

Treasures dreamt of ... *wishes answered.*

The objects found within these pages are the stuff of dreams. They float across our mind's eye in colors and shapes that astonish. They speak to us as certainly as a mother's whisper to a child; they beg to be touched and held, in some cases even worn to the Cinderella Ball. They move us just as definitely as does a Duke Ellington harmony.

It is the sweet indulgences, after all, that remind us of the essentials of living.

Within these pages, we invite you to discover some of North America's best craft artists. This journey of discovery requires only an easy chair. In order to unearth these treasures, you need a fertile imagination for a spade, and a telephone as a magic wand. If there is something here that fulfills a dream, turn to the section beginning on page 127. This tells you where to go to find what you want. In some instances it is directly to the artist; in other cases you will be directed to galleries and stores that carry the work. Telephone numbers are provided for all.

We are here to assure you:
Just as treasures can be dreamt of, wishes can be answered.

Toni Fountain Sikes
Publisher

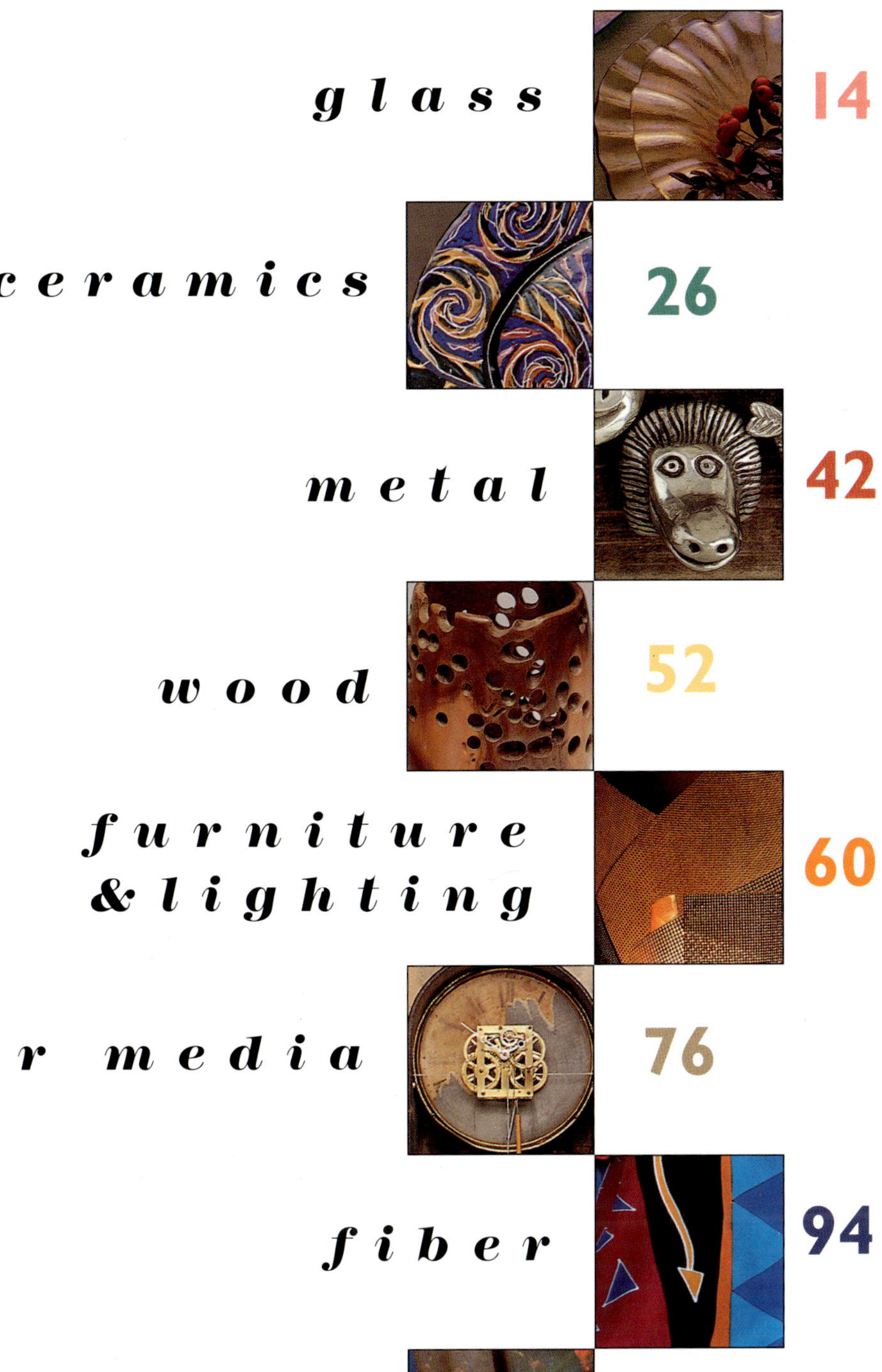

10 *Great Ways* to use

1 DAYDREAMING.   Ever have one of those days when life feels dull? We have a remedy. Thumb through the pages of this book. Think about beautiful works of art for your home. Think about heirlooms for your children, gifts for dear friends. Think about calling the artist whose work you love best. Feel refreshed?

2 QUALITY CONTROL.   This book begins with the assurance that the artists included are reliable and professional. Featured artists in GUILD sourcebooks are juried in on the basis of experience, quality of work, and a solid business reputation.

3 MOTIVATION.   Take time to read our introductory essays by Bill Kraus and Jorge Arango. Kraus writes with insight about the richness crafts bring to our homes and work spaces. Arango explores how our society's concerns influence our interest in crafts. Both speak movingly about the importance of handmade goods in our lives.

4 WORKLOAD REDUCTION.   Making a beautiful environment takes a lot of planning. This portable gallery in a book lets you take hundreds of fine handmade objects into your own home or office 'on trial'—a great way to visualize your more beautiful world.

5 REACH FOR THE PHONE.   If something in this book intrigues you—a shape, a color combination, an unusual use of textures or materials—go ahead and call. Our "Finding the Artwork" section beginning on page 127 includes phone numbers for artists and the galleries that feature their work. They're waiting to hear from you.

6 ABOUT THOSE GALLERIES.   There's no substitute for seeing artwork in person. Our list of galleries includes the very best. Visit those in your hometown often—and take our list with you when you travel.

7 STUDIO SHOPPING.   Some artists work with the doors barred and the phone cord pulled. Others welcome studio visitors—and sales—on a call-ahead basis. A studio visit can be great fun and a wonderful way to learn more about an art form. Use our phone list to inquire about policy and appointments.

8 BECOME AN EXPERT.   Want to learn more about these artists and art forms? Throughout the book, you'll find descriptions and contact information for a host of excellent resource organizations and publications. Each offers information and services for the crafts collector.

9 ARTISTS NOW AND THEN.   Many of the artists whose work you see here are also represented in earlier GUILD publications—look for references on artists' pages. You can order many of these sourcebooks through our main office. Call 1-800-969-1556 for order information.

10 JUST DO IT.   If you've been thinking about collecting North American crafts, but haven't felt quite ready, we have this advice: TAKE THE PLUNGE! You won't be sorry.

Object EXPRESSION

by Bill Kraus

We are what we eat, physically. We are what we read, intellectually. And we are what we collect, aesthetically. The urge to gather and display is universal, and today's craft artists are providing us with a cornucopia of wonderful objects—from the purely utilitarian to the emphatically decorative—that give us more and more ways to satisfy that universal urge. The essence of craft is the celebration of the object. Beautiful, original objects that fulfill functional requirements are the root and heart of this varied field. These objects can be simple and plain or elaborately ornate, but traditionally they perform tasks.

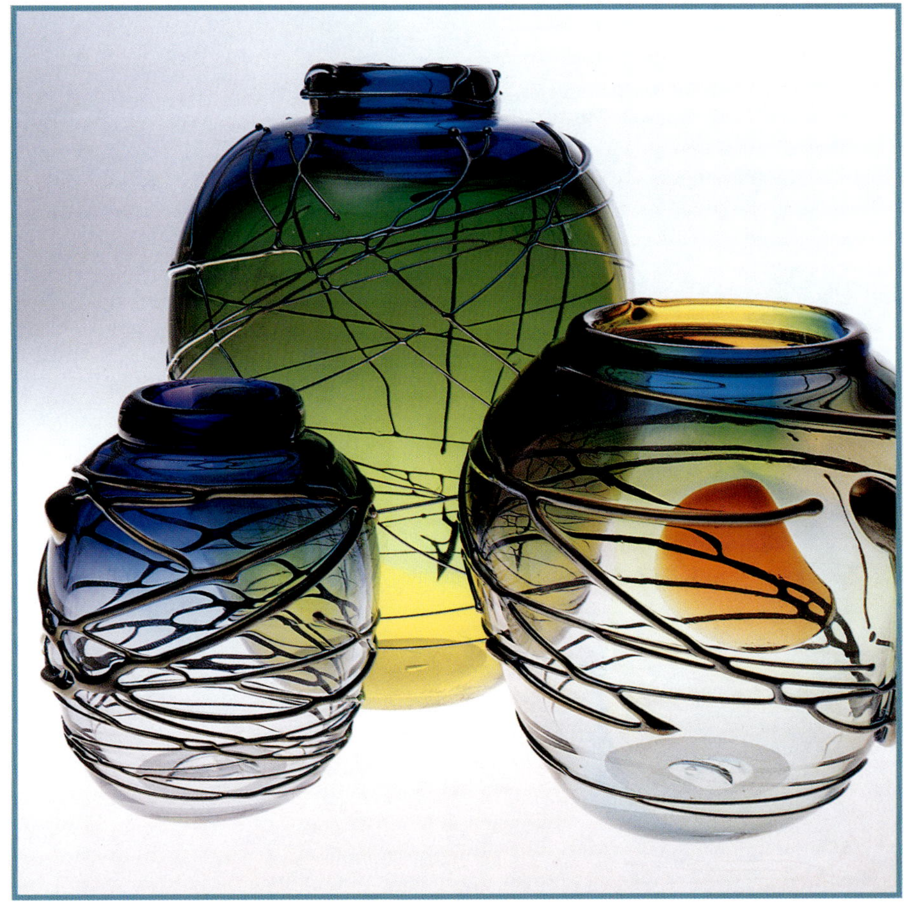

Craft has always implied function; what craft artists are helping us discover is that while the terms 'functional' and 'utilitarian' are close, they are not synonymous. The function does not have to be utilitarian. The function may simply be to be beautiful, to decorate, to enhance a place or a space, to evoke an emotional response.

Collecting breathes life into art, and whatever an object's function is in this land somewhere between utilitarian and decorative, these are very much our things, and they help define us. A space that is filled with objects of every kind, shape, size, color and material reveals volumes about the occupants of the space.

We step into each other's homes and share these objects—full of humor, elegance, maybe even a touch of kitsch. Not only the objects but the aesthetic styles can range from the highly embellished country and folk to austere and classic traditional to high tech and hard-edged minimalism. All styles can live together, complementing one another and reflecting our own personalities.

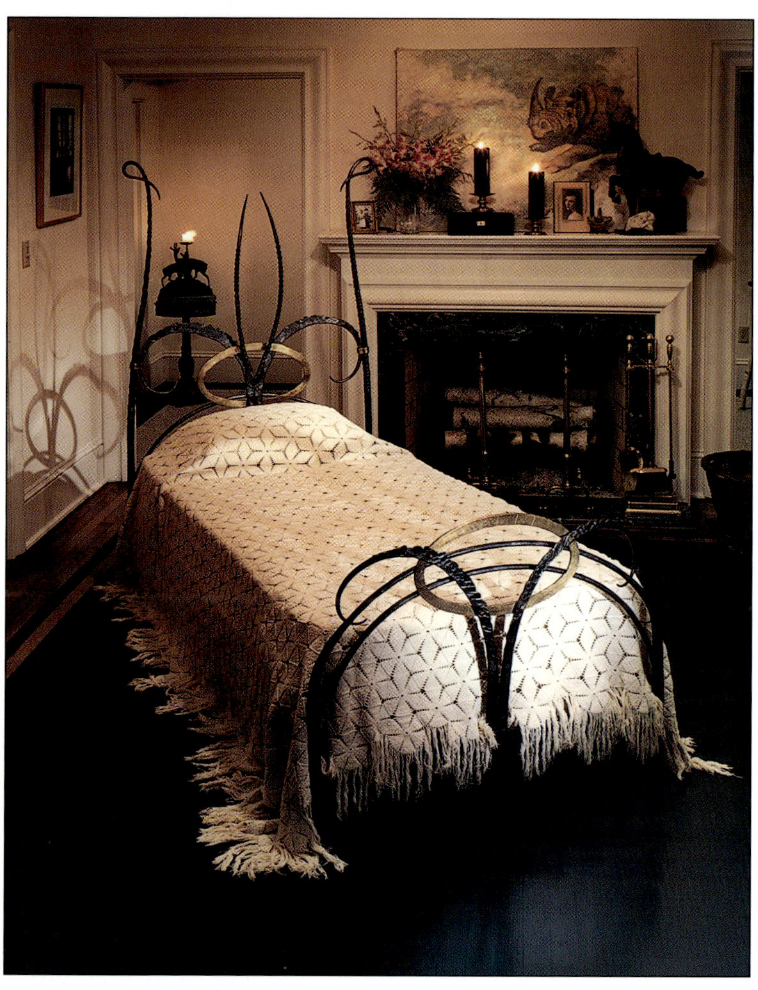

We are also learning that our beloved objects belong everywhere. The things we collect do not have to be on pedestals or under spotlights. Refusing to accept anybody else's idea of 'where things go,' we put our prizes in niches, on busy shelves, in rooms as utilitarian as the laundry or the bath. And then we look at them and use them, or just look at them—and truly live with the things we love.

A ceramic tea cup can make you feel good when you drink from it; the texture, shape, and color are a pleasure to hold and behold.

The mysterious wooden box with hidden compartments holds secrets as well as possessions.

The sculpted glass bowl that sits on the conference room table looks different from every angle, in every light, at every time of day. It does things to the psyche as well as to the room it graces.

◆

WHAT CRAFTS REVEAL
about ourselves

by Jorge Arango

Those who prognosticate about trends in the consumer marketplace are famous for coming up with deceptively simplistic concepts and meaningless jargon. What exactly is 'low tech,' for example? And is it sage green that's in this year … or kiwi … or celadon? America's need for neatly labeling things often reduces complex ideas to tidy little sound bytes that obscure the often valuable research that led these forecasters to their conclusions. In the long run, what is most important about their predictions is not the fact that florals are in or out. It's *why* they are in or out that is instructive, *which* issues of contemporary American life pushed them to the forefront—or the back burner—of the consumer's mind. The why of it is what teaches us something about our society and ourselves. So, when we hear crafts are hot, we should ask why. What social and cultural trends led to this reassessment of the handmade? What combination of these factors is contributing to their desirability?

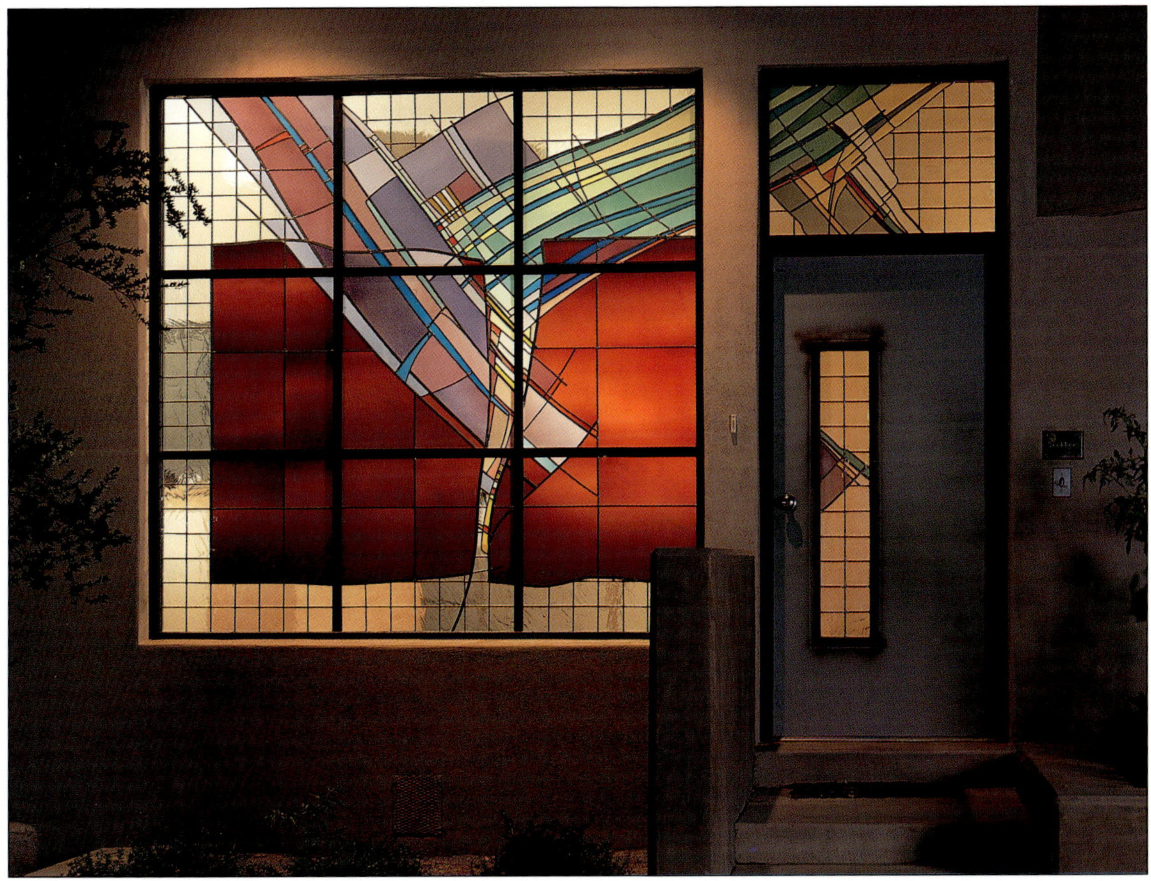

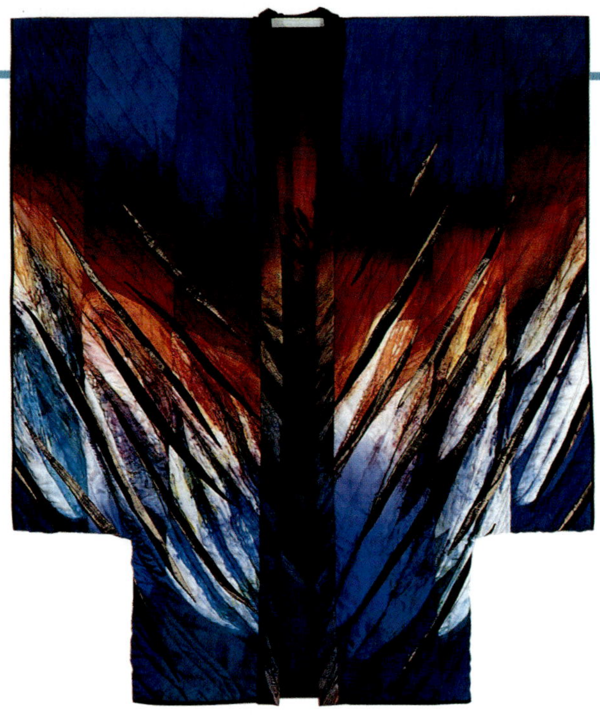

The idea of handwork nourishes the nostalgia we experience as we reflect on our past. How many times have we heard the phrase, 'They just don't do handwork like that anymore'? What's wonderful about crafts is that we can reply, 'Yes, they do.'

This notion of a craftsperson toiling artfully at the workbench recalls a romanticized, simpler time when honest hard work made a person feel whole. There was a transforming power in the craftsman's lifestyle that sprung from pride of workmanship. The sense of integrity behind this noble pursuit has a direct effect on the perceived value of what craftspeople make. It comforts our collective nostalgia to know that this way of life is not lost.

THE MILLENNIUM APPROACHES

The year 2000 is barely six years away. Historically, the turn of any century is a time of soul-searching and reflection, of looking back over the last hundred years and taking stock of where we are and where we want to be. An approaching milestone like the new millennium intensifies that mass self-analysis.

So what do we see when we look at our world at the end of the 1900s? For one thing, we're seeing a lot of similarities to attitudes that gave birth to the Arts & Crafts movement at the turn of the last century. As in the late 1800s, the promises of industry ring hollow. Technology and machines seem responsible for a host of ills: from displaced workers and pollution to a loss of basic skills. Like the great thinkers of the Arts & Crafts movement in England a hundred years ago, modern Americans are rejecting cookie-cutter, machine-made products and longing to re-establish the connection between objects and the real, live people who create them. Products that display evidence of a human element become extremely important. Hand-painted underglazes, unevenly textured weaves, hand-carved details all create, in the consumer's mind, a connection between the product and a person who painted, wove or carved it.

CRAFTS AND THE NEW ECO-AWARENESS

The perceived morality of the craftsperson's lifestyle also jibes well with the righteousness of America's environmental awakening. Craftspeople are viewed as living in harmony with the earth, judiciously using the resources Mother Nature provides—clay, wood, fiber—to create products that are organic and that do not pollute.

Many crafts display processes that reinforce this positive relationship in the consumer's mind between craftspeople and nature. For instance, we can understand how a basket is constructed because we can see the process, the way the fibers are woven together. Because we can see the way it was woven, we can visualize the hands that wove it. And, because the material comes from nature, we tend to feel comfortable with its origins: no intimidating machinery, no nasty by-products. The problem with many manufactured goods, we're realizing, is that we don't understand how they're made. Who knows, for instance, how plastic is created or molded? The only knowledge we may retain about plastic is that it is synthetic and that it doesn't biodegrade—strong negatives in an age concerned with being green.

Craftspeople have recognized this desire in the general public to do right by the earth and have deftly pointed up their use of lead-free glazes, non-toxic paints, natural dyes, and sustainably managed hardwoods. It's impossible to overestimate how empowering it is for a consumer to know that his or her purchase did not contribute to clear-cutting of tropical rainforests, that instead this object came from a tree that was responsibly and selectively harvested.

The eco-awareness that started in the '60s also launched a whole new genre of crafts: handmade products that employ recycled materials. Picture frames made of old buttons, chairs with backs made of old farm tools, baskets made of discarded chicken wire—the draw of these products is two-fold. First, there is the gratification that comes from knowing these found objects were reused creatively rather than dumped in a landfill. Secondly, they are the direct descendants of what we today refer to as folk art. They display ingenuity, resourcefulness and a homey, comfortable charm, all hallmarks of what we see as our great American past.

MULTICULTURALISM AND THE HANDWORK OF OTHER PEOPLES

In the last few decades, Americans traveled abroad in great numbers, experiencing other cultures along the way. Simultaneously, a steady influx of Asians, Latin Americans, Haitians, Middle Easterners and peoples of other cultures entered the American workforce. In our daily lives, we confronted racial and cultural differences, sometimes successfully, sometimes not. At jobs, in schools, houses of worship and neighborhoods we encountered faces that were red, yellow, black and every shade between. And these faces brought with them Native American beadwork, Bolivian backstrap weavings, African kente cloth and colorful Caribbean metalwork, along with a host of other indigenous crafts.

Simultaneously, Americans came to appreciate the rich regional diversities that already existed within our own borders. The proliferation of Southwest style is the perfect example, but regional awareness extended to every quarter of the country—from the handwork

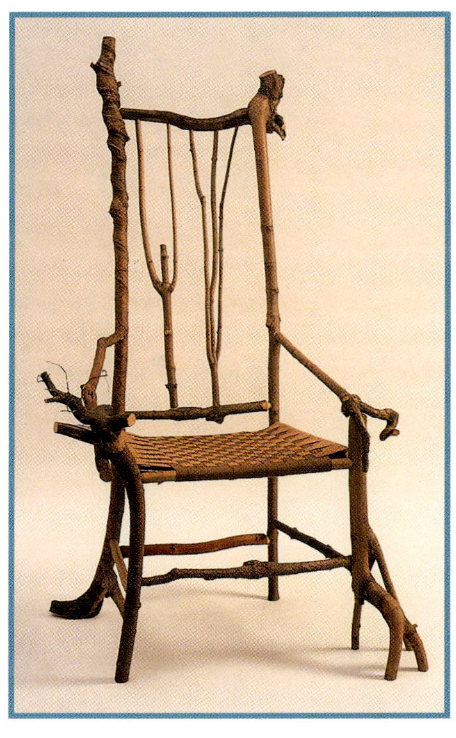

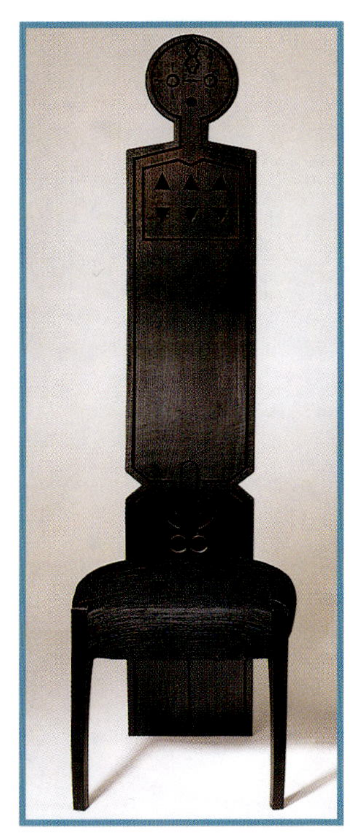

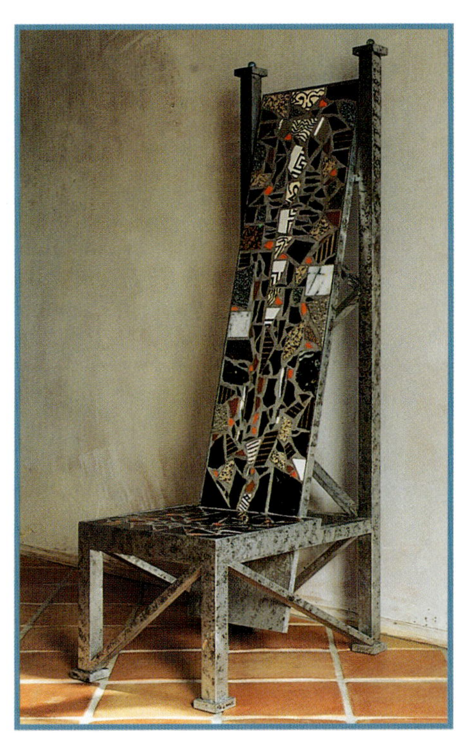

that came out of rural Appalachia to the Inuit arts of the Pacific Northwest, from cornhusk dolls of America's Midwest heartland to the complex stitchery of an Amish quilt. These crafts reinforced the notion that America was not one massive, homogeneous culture, but a melting pot of peoples, languages and traditions. Localities came to realize the unique marketing advantages of promoting local craftspeople as a way of distinguishing themselves from neighboring regions.

To be sure, the road to real, social multiculturalism is a bumpy one. But the fact remains that we are more receptive than we've ever been to the rich visual heritage behind each of the cultures we encounter.

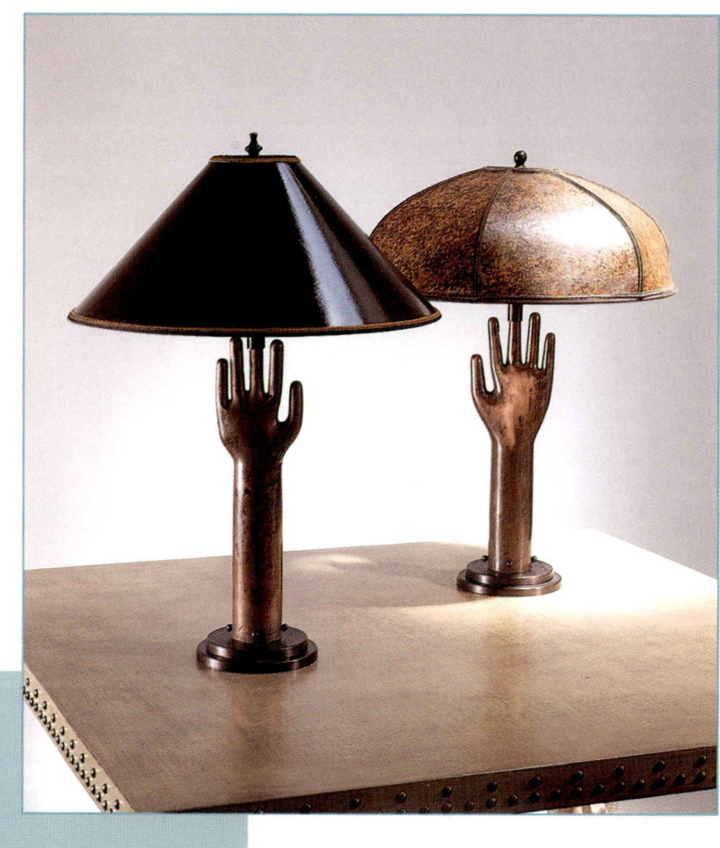

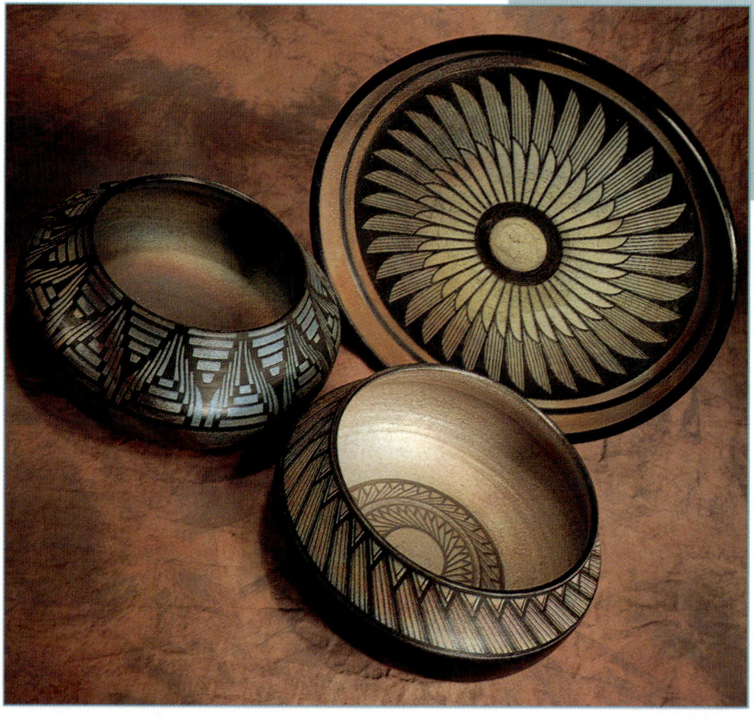

This has given craftspeople who work in ethnic idioms wider access to the market. And it has created a craving for rough, unfinished textures and crude, naive forms that hark back to our primitive and ethnic roots. Even artists working in metal and glass are striving for primitivism as a way to make their work warmer, more familiar. Just look at the amount of sandblasted glass in the marketplace. This treatment creates a feeling of ancient objects excavated from antiquity. And notice the trend in metalworking to brush, oxidize or hammer a surface rather than polish it to a chrome-like sheen. We want the tactility of ancient objects, not the icy perfection that bespeaks a modern technology.

Primitivism pushes many of the buttons that are motivating consumers to buy crafts: It reinforces the nostalgia for purer pre-industrial times; it re-establishes that connection to the artist behind the art; it implies a primal bond with the earth; and, importantly, it suggests ritual and ceremony. It is this last aspect of primitivism that, on an unconscious level, satisfies another great and illusive need: the desire for spirituality in our lives. One of the biggest shortcomings of a largely secular society is that no matter how much can be explained by science and technology, many of life's great mysteries remain just that—mysteries. Civilization's attempts to reconcile these anomalies with the daily realities of life are what gave birth to religion and its rituals and ceremonies.

Most everyone was raised with some sort of religious instruction, be it Judeo-Christian, Protestant, Buddhist or Muslim. So, a person needn't subscribe to beliefs of any particular religion for the mystical nature of its rituals to resonate for him or her. And the objects used to celebrate those rituals become the trigger for those emotions. Many crafts, particularly ethnic ones, do just that. Ceramic shrine structures imply a kind of Zen peace, Native American fetishes suggest that culture's pantheistic beliefs, a bejeweled silver goblet recalls chalices used in Judeo-Christian ceremonies. It's not necessary for us to believe that the particular religion from which

this imagery comes holds the answers to eternal questions. It's the symbolism that's important, the *idea* that is comforting.

Of course, we should always remember the limits of this kind of analysis. The search for easy answers in an increasingly complex world can move us to pin impossible hopes on a single philosophy. The Arts & Crafts philosophers, after all, truly believed that the

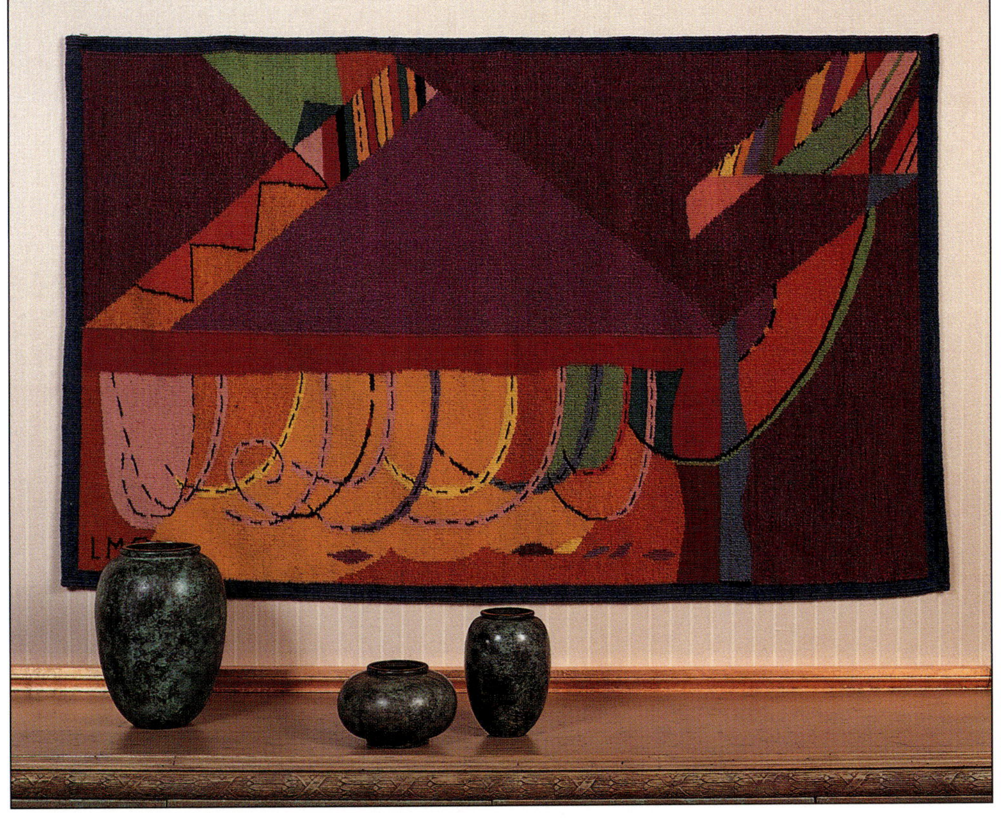

craftsman lifestyle could effect social change. What they came to realize was that, while a noble pursuit, this was not a mode of living available to an entire civilization. We must realize that crafts cannot, in and of themselves, achieve the goals of multiculturalism and eco-awareness. They cannot provide spiritual fulfillment. But crafts can be useful tools for understanding the human condition and for bridging the differences that divide us so that we can arrive at a greater harmony with ourselves and our world.

glass glass glass glass glass gl

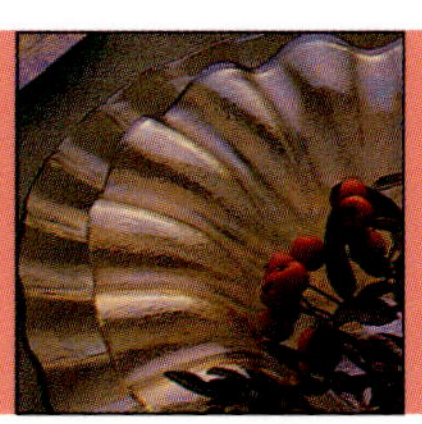

Thomas Buechner III
Vitrix Hot Glass Studio

Inspired by the natural qualities of molten glass, the beauty and timeless grace of Tom Buechner's vessels are a result of two decades of glassmaking. In 1979, Tom co-founded Vitrix Hot Glass, a studio now regarded among America's foremost, not only for Tom's light and elegant forms and his high standard of craftsmanship, but also for the studio's commitment to quality and to the satisfaction of its customers. A full brochure is available.

Also see these GUILD publications:
THE GUILD: 2, 3, 4

A   multibit perfume bottle, ruby, 5"

B   vertical open form, hyacinth, 14"

C   raindrop bowl, cobalt, 13"Dia

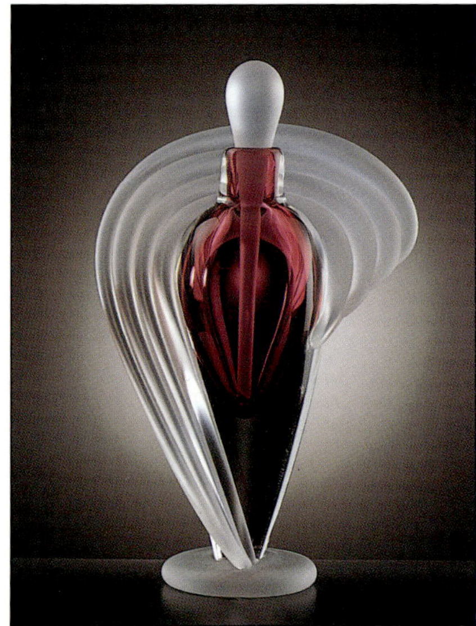

A   Tommy Olof Elder

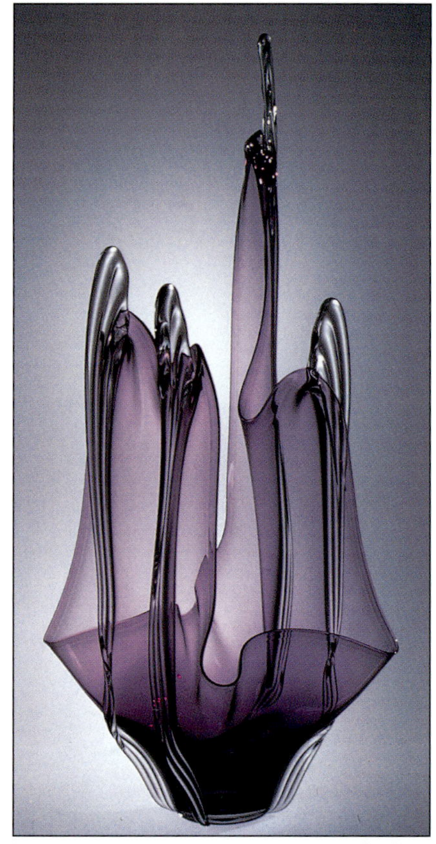

B   Ray Errett

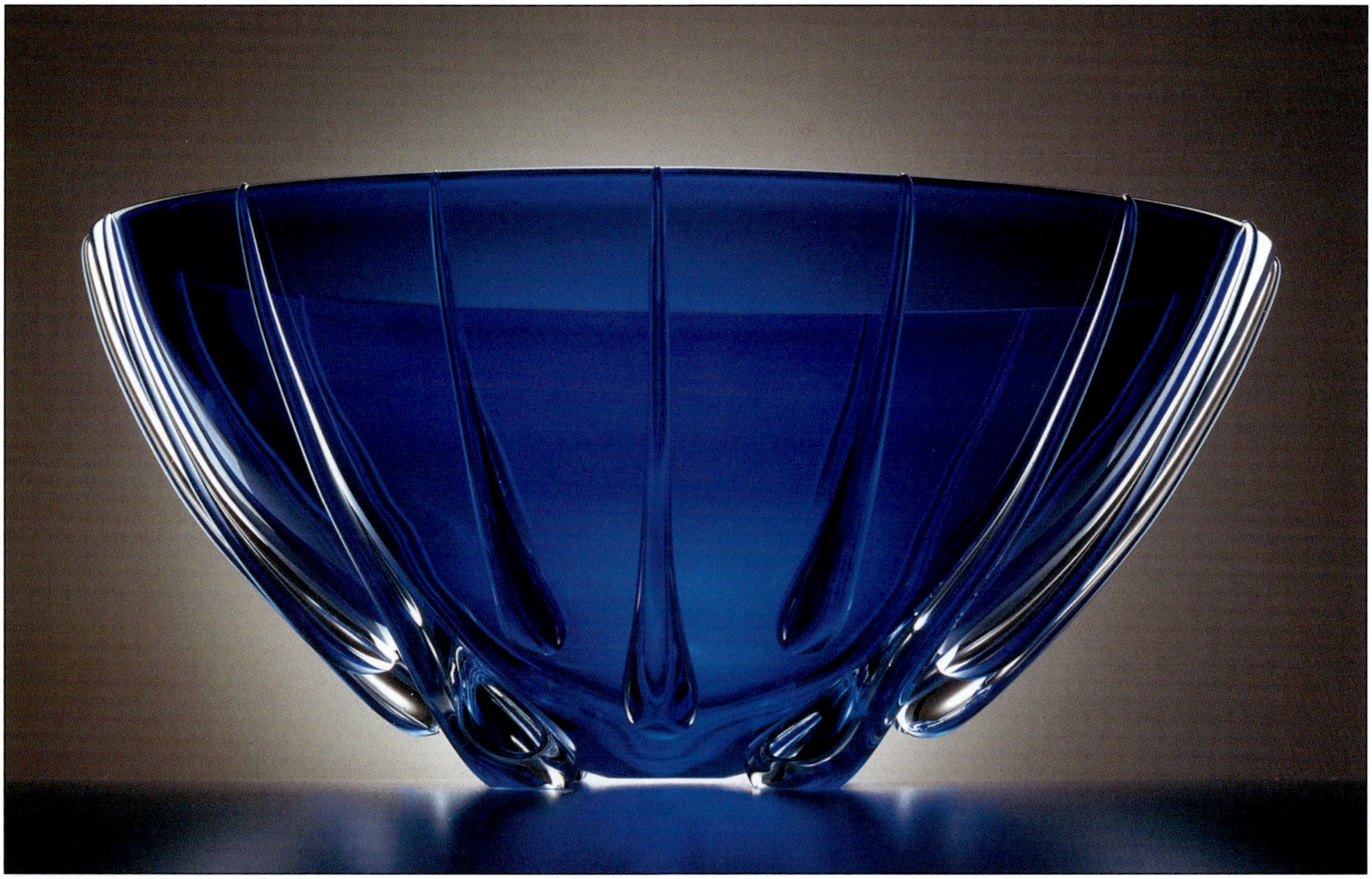

C   Tommy Olof Elder

Jonathan Winfisky
Designer-Glass Artist

Jonathan Winfisky has been designing and producing unique and original blown and cast sculptural glass vessel forms since 1975.

Forms from the *Sculptural Design Series* and the *Madonna Series* are designed to work collectively or individually when displayed in private residences and public spaces.

The *Madonna Series* is a study in intimacy and what makes this energy possible. This grouping explores the transformations which can occur between these forms when arranged in a series.

Larger pieces are available by commission and all designs can be produced in a wide variety of sizes and colors. Please call or write for further information.

Also see these GUILD publications:
The Gallery & Retail Edition: 1
The Designer's Reference: 7, 8

A *Sculptural Design Series,* ©1995, bowl 15", vase 12", fluted vase 8", perfume vial 5½", tapered vase 10"

B *Madonna Grouping,* ©1995, etched glass, 8-12"H

C *Madonna Series,* ©1995, *Crystal Forms,* 18"H

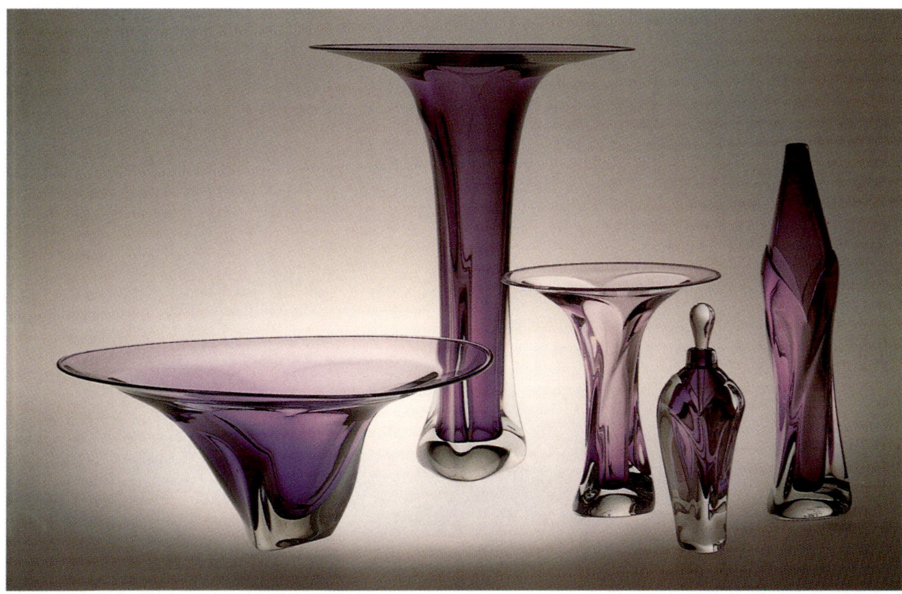

A

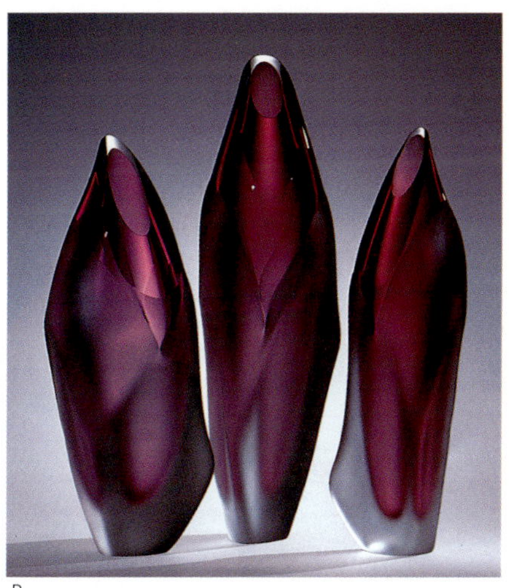

B

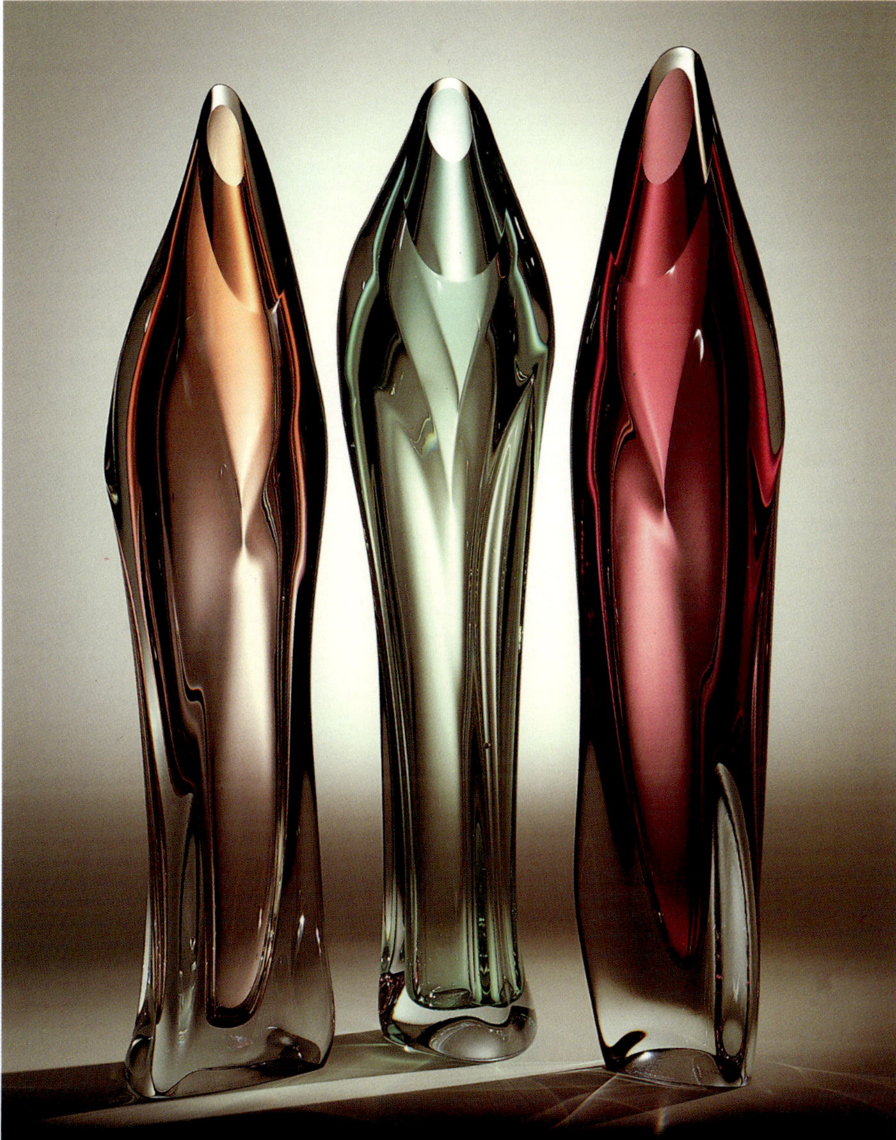

C

Michael K. Hansen
Nina Paladino Caron
California Glass Studio, Inc.

Michael and Nina have been working together for 18 years. Their glass is represented internationally in galleries and in private and corporate collections.

Pictured are hand-blown glass vessel forms and a perfume bottle. A complete catalog is available upon request.

Also see these GUILD publications:
The Gallery & Retail Edition: 1
THE GUILD: 5
The Designer's Reference: 6, 7, 8

A *California Classic Collection*, ginger vase, red, etched designed, *Triangle*

B *Erika Collection*, perfume bottle, white iridescent bottle, etched and painted 'fan' design, with gold

C *California Classic Collection*, fluted bowl, black with silver leaf and silver trailed glass on the surface

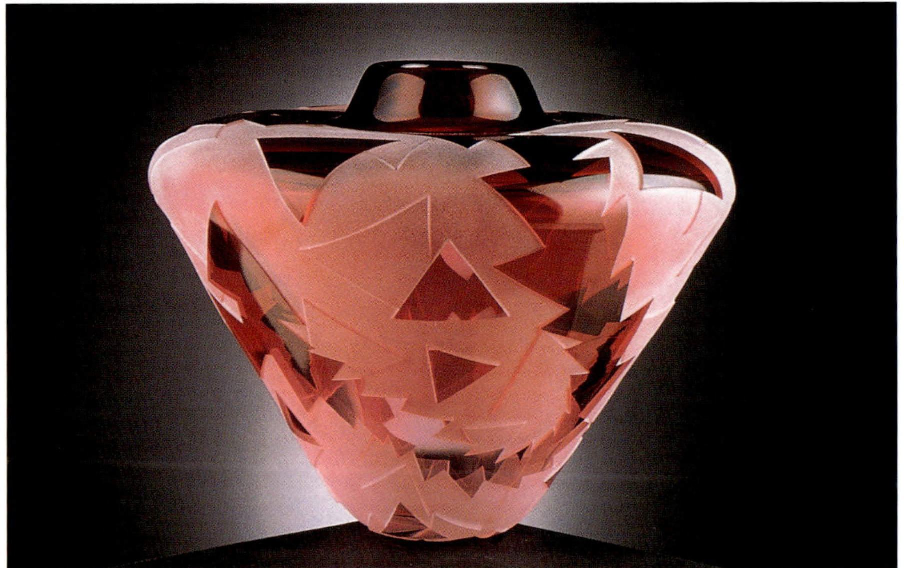

A

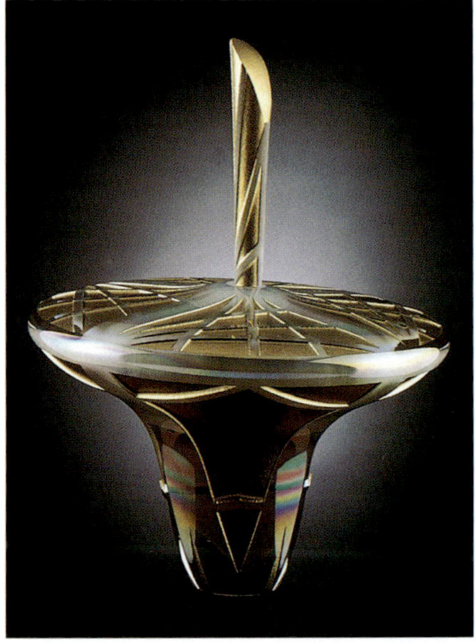

B

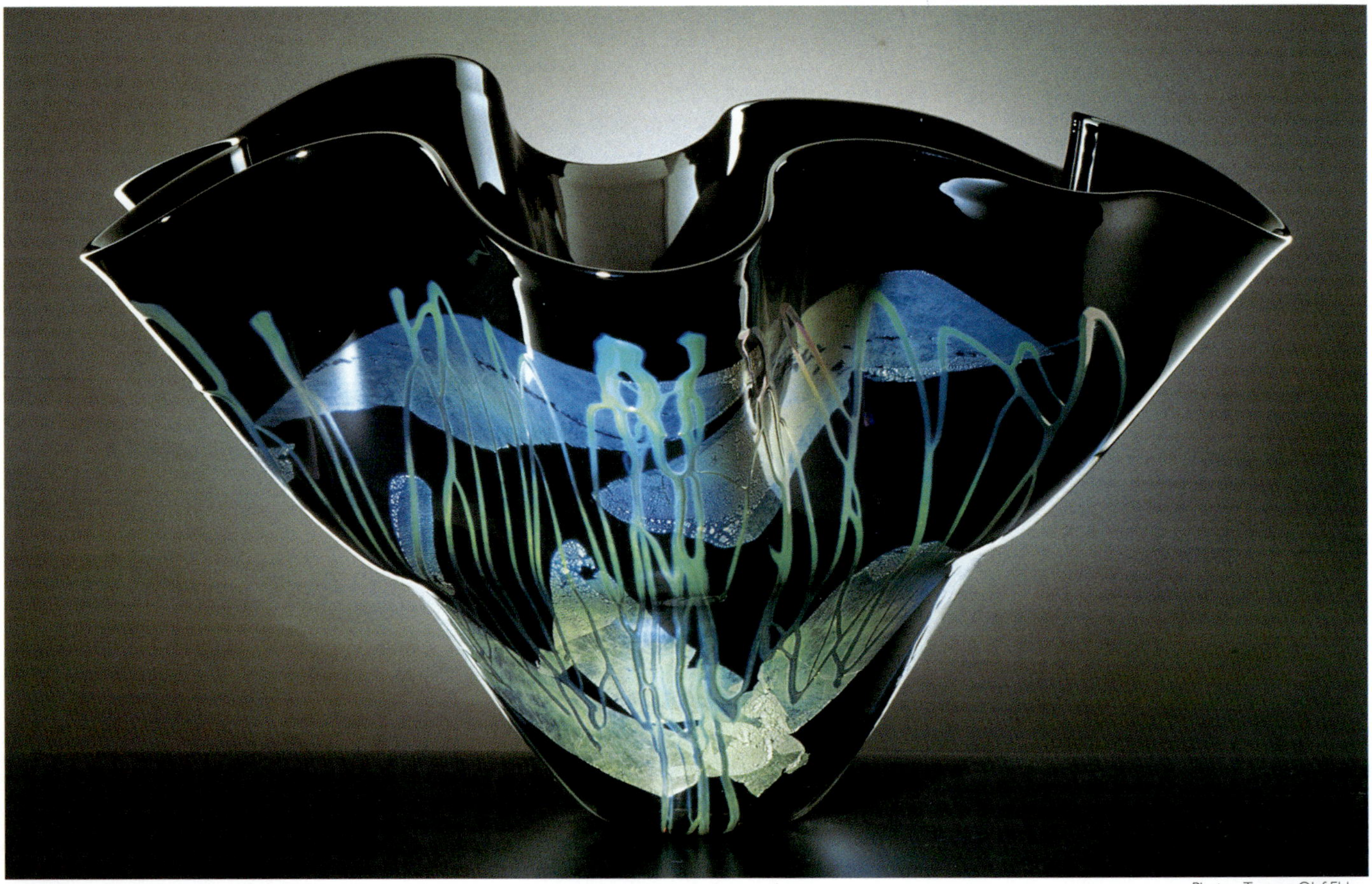

C

Photos: Tommy Olaf Elder

Michele Savelle

Michele's bowls tell stories, each one unique, with imagery derived from many experiences and sources. Most have a humorous angle.

All are fused and slumped glass, with an area of handmade glass in the center of the bottom of each one.

Michele studied at Pilchuck Glass School, shows nationally and teaches in the Seattle area.

Also see this GUILD publication:
The Gallery & Retail Edition: 1

SHOWN: *Adam Goes Exploring*, 16"W x 6"H

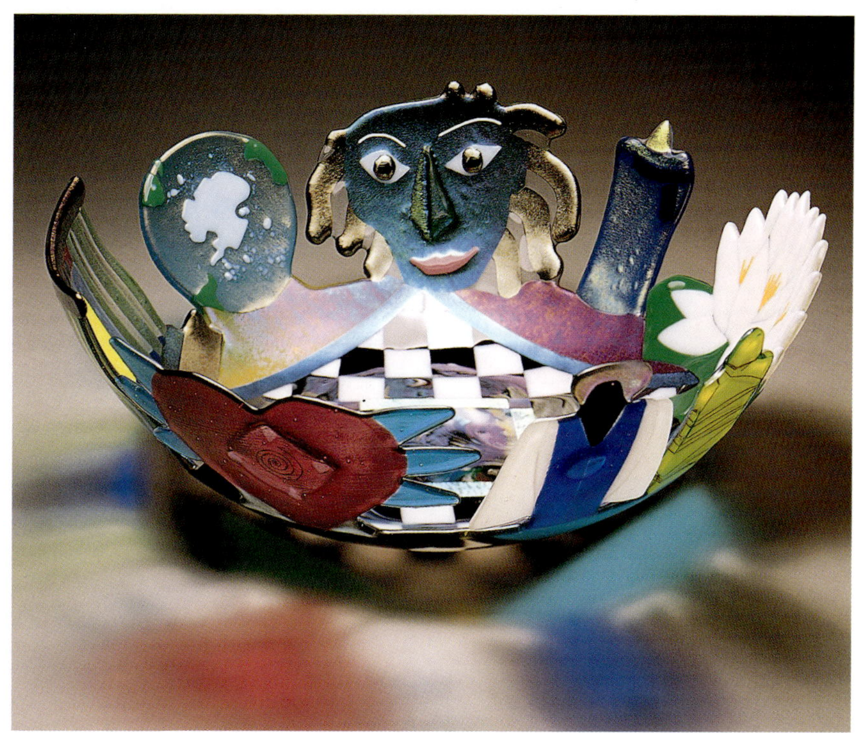

Jon Savelle

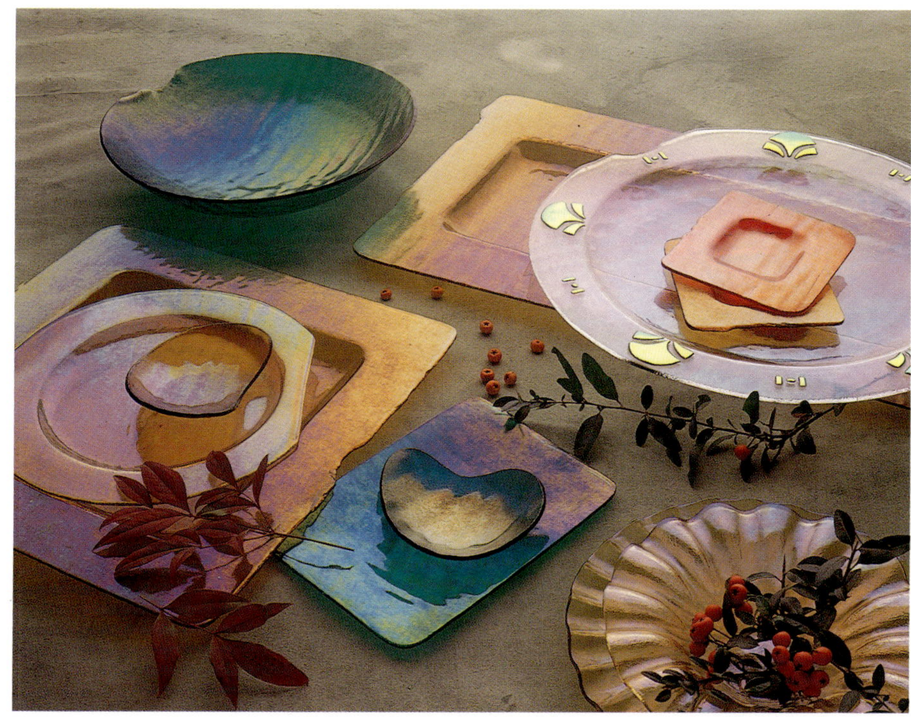

Susan Marie Anderson, Seattle, WA

Mesolini Glass Studio
Gregg Mesmer
Diane Bonciolini

Gregg Mesmer and Diane Bonciolini combined their talents in 1977 by creating Mesolini Glass Studio. Bonciolini's studies at the renowned Pilchuck Glass School in 1980 led to the development of their award-winning slumped glass tableware that is both beautiful and practical. Notably, each signed, dated and numbered piece in this collection is created with glass that is a by-product of the recycled glass industry.

Color kits available for $15. Call or write for current price list and catalog.

Also see these GUILD publications:
The Gallery & Retail Edition: 1
THE GUILD: 5
The Designer's Reference: 6, 7, 8

David New-Small

**New-Small & Sterling
Studio Glass, Ltd.**

David New-Small has been making glass since his first session at the Pilchuck Glass School in 1978. His work is included in the collections of the Corning Museum, the governments of the Philippines, China, Japan and Canada. A *Marine Reliquary* was included in the inaugural exhibition of the Canadian Craft Museum.

His current work reflects his concern for and fascination with the oceanic habitat he explores as a scuba diver.

Also see this GUILD publication:
The Gallery & Retail Edition: 1

A *Marine Reliquary—ARV256*, 1994, blown glass,
   23 cm (9")Dia

B *Marine Reliquary—ARV373*, 1994, blown glass,
33 cm (13")H

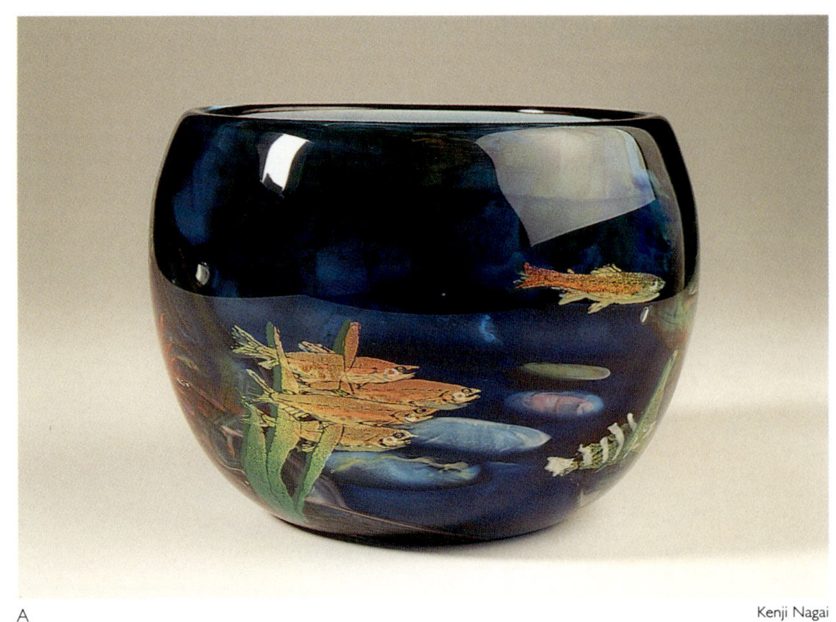

A

Kenji Nagai

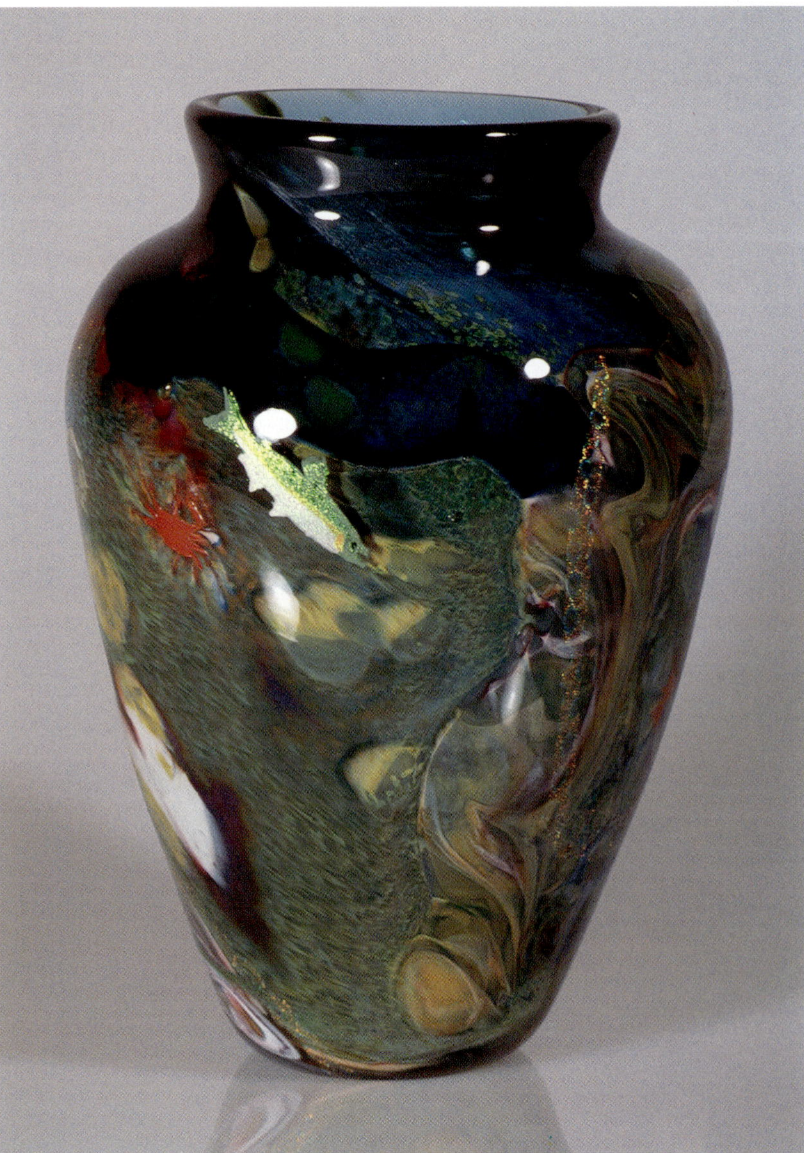

B

Stephan J. Cox

The glasswork of Stephan J. Cox is easily recognized for its understated elegance and simplicity of design. Mr. Cox exhibits and sells his work worldwide and is represented in many private and public collections, including the Corning Museum and the White House. Much of his recent work is deeply carved with diamond tools and sandblasting.

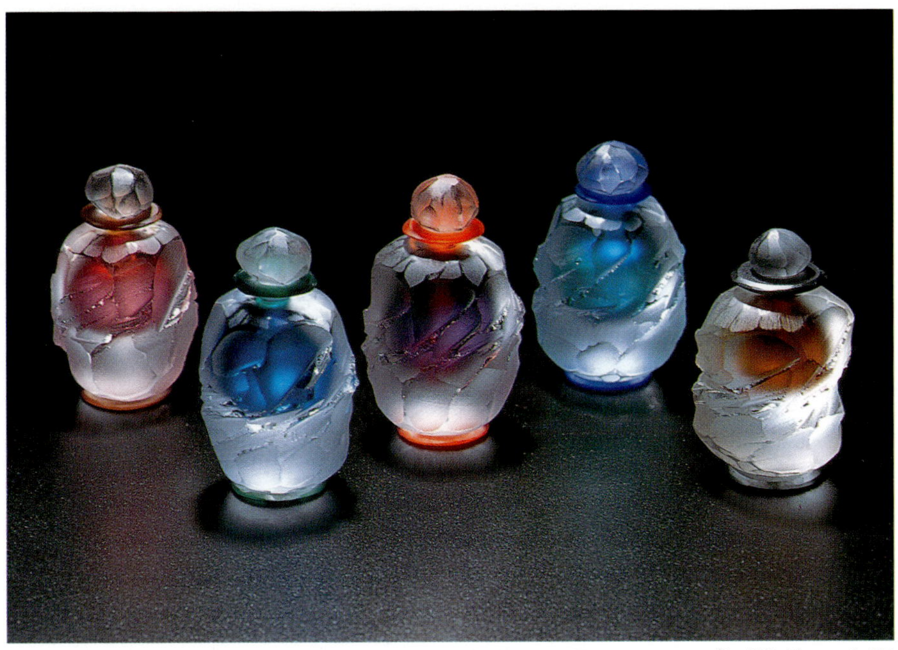

Chiseled Vials, diamond saw-carved glass perfumes, 1994, 3½"H x 2"W

Don Pitlik, Minneapolis, MN

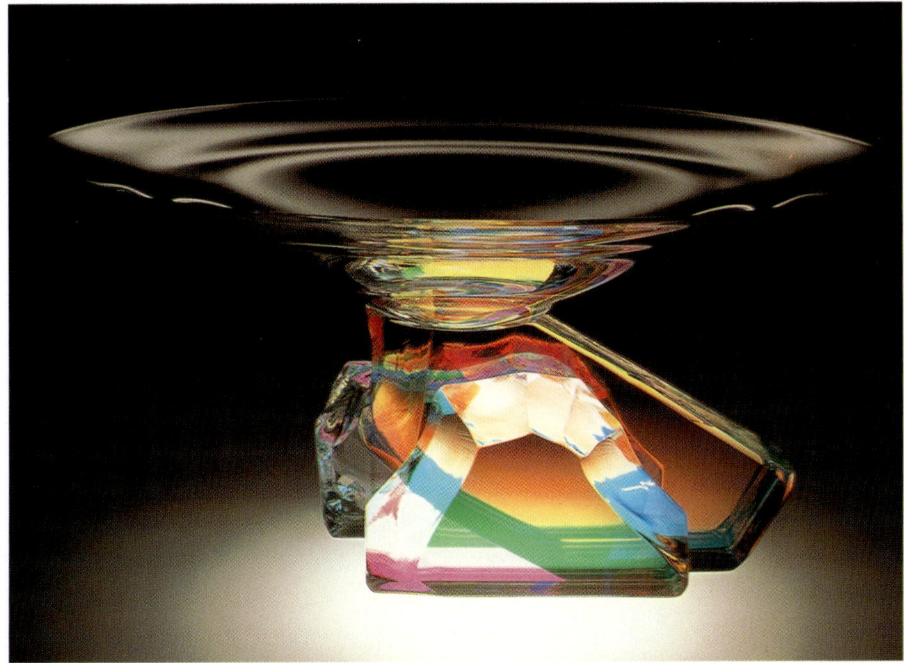

Steven Maslach

Steven Maslach has been working in glass since 1969. The *Dichroic Series* shown is highly kinetic and changes color depending on the angle of light. The work is of blown, cast, chiseled and polished glass, laminated with optical color filters. Designs include functional tabletop pieces, unique vessels and large-scale sculpture.

Museum collections:
Corning Museum of Glass
American Craft Museum
Chrysler Museum
High Museum of Art
Oakland Museum of Art

Kevin Fulton
Glass Sculptor

Kevin Fulton has been blowing glass for 20 years. He specializes in aquatic life-forms, which are available individually or combined in large scenes. He has created several large commissions, including a permanent installation in the Space Needle restaurant in Seattle, WA. He has also designed awards for events and organizations, including U.S. West.

Also see these GUILD publications:
THE GUILD: 4
The Designer's Reference: 6

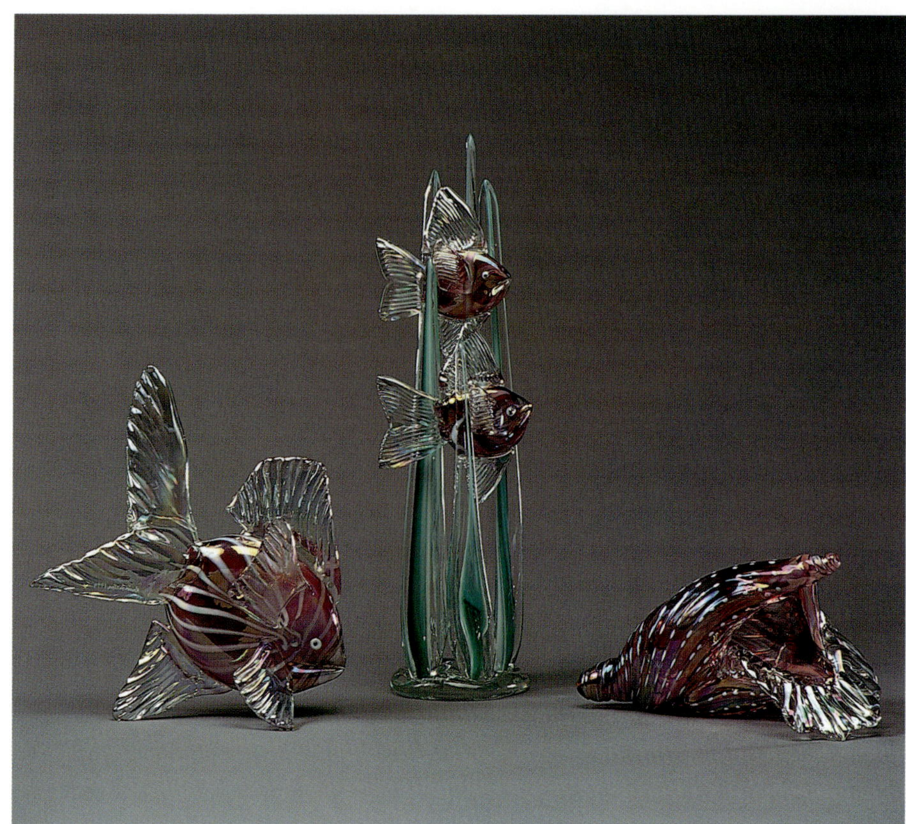

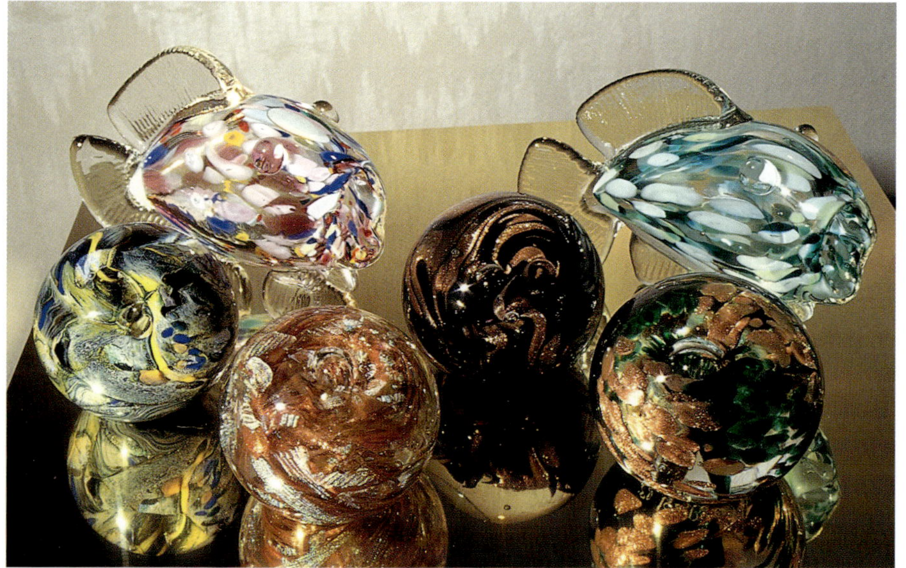

Pat Longacre, Clearwater, FL

Ed Kozlowski, Jr.
Budda Belly Glass Studio

Ed Kozlowski, Jr. began working with glass in 1985 when he took his first lesson at a craft store to learn to do stained glass panels. His worked has progressed over the past nine years to include blown glass, glass beads and fused glass.

Many of Ed's pieces incorporate either dichroic glass or gold aventurine. He enjoys the sparkle and the mystical properties they add to his work.

Ed's paperweights can be found in The Magic Kingdom, Disney World, Orlando, FL, and in galleries and gift shops in the Tampa Bay area. His work has also been sent to Canada, France, Japan, Thailand, South Africa and most of the 50 United States.

Sledd/Winger Glassworks

Nancy Sledd/Mary Lu Winger

Award-winning glass artists Nancy and Mary Lu are nationally known for their unique stained glass room dividers and fireplace screens.

Galleries and shops enjoy an ever-increasing demand for these dynamic creations. Easily displayed, these functional, freestanding screens create a natural focal point in any setting.

Custom orders are welcome.

SHOWN: *Meteor*, 1994, stained glass and wood, 60" × 54"

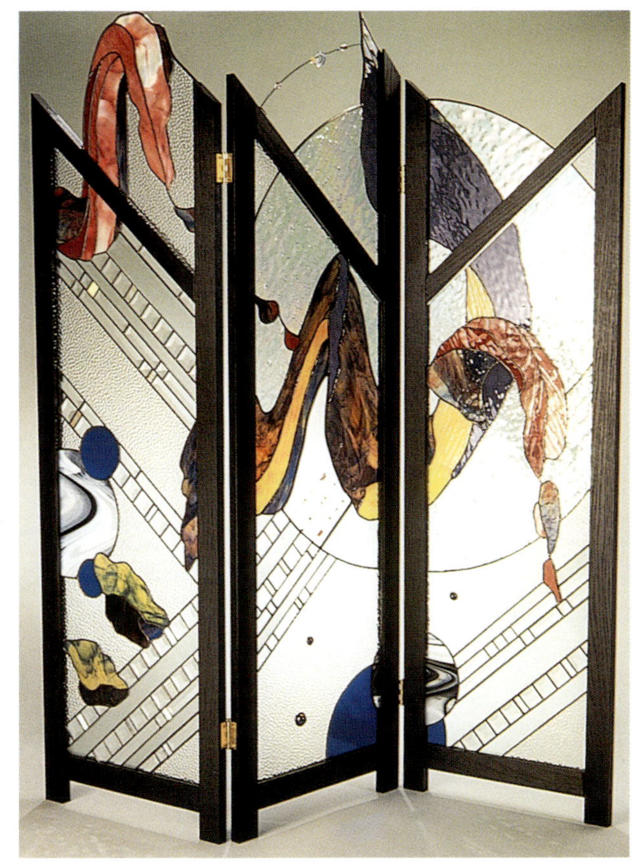

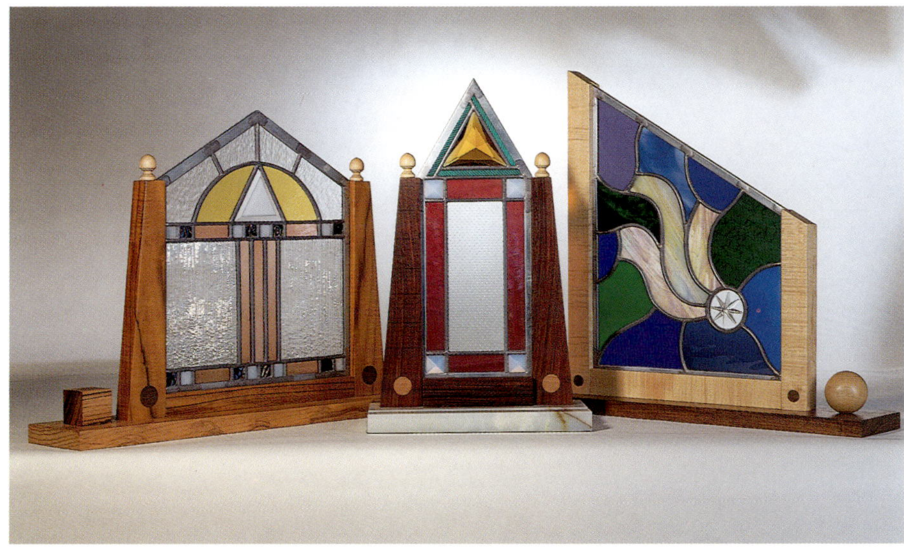

Larry Zgoda

Larry Zgoda Studio

Larry Zgoda has been designing and crafting original, architectural stained glass for over 20 years and has developed a unique, signature style based on geometry and ornament. Presented here are several small-scale (approximately 14"H) autonomous works appropriate for gallery and retail sale. Architonomous (Architecture plus Autonomous) is the label Larry Zgoda places on these free-standing stained glass screens.

Also see these GUILD publications:
THE GUILD: 1, 2, 3, 4, 5
The Architect's Source: 6, 7, 8, 9, 10

PSG'S GLASS ARTIST

28 S STATE ST
NEWTOWN, PA 18940
FAX 215-860-1812
TEL 215-860-9947
$25/year

PSG's Glass Artist is a full-color bimonthly publication featuring articles on the creative use of the glass arts and crafts. In addition to how-to information and artist and studio profiles, each issue contains book reviews, career tips, a home-studio section, and a complete calendar of glass-related events.

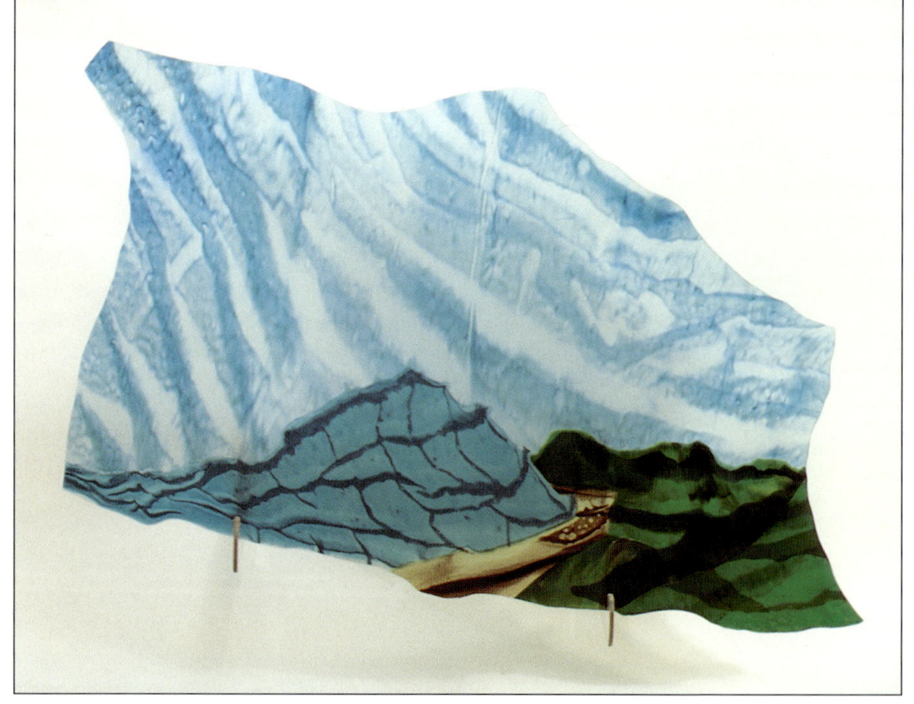

Mark Bleshenski
Markroy Studio

The glass art of Mark Bleshenski captures the feeling of transparent watercolors. Pieces are created entirely of hot-worked glass bent with a flowing curve. Works may be hung on the wall with included brackets, or free standing for tables. Backlighting brings the pieces alive with detail and rich color gradations.

Also see these GUILD publications:
The Gallery & Retail Edition: 1
THE GUILD: 3, 4, 5

SHOWN: untitled wall-mounted piece, 36" x 24"

Sandra C. Q. Bergér
Quintal Studio

With nearly 20 years of diverse glass art experience, Sandra Bergér has a varied repertoire of sculptural and architectural works. Inspired by the pre-Columbian culture, the figures in this limited-edition series embody a Mayan belief in the powerful force of light. Precision engineering and durable execution facilitate shipping, handling and presentation.

Internationally exhibited and published, Bergér has a history of laudable collaborations and lasting relationships with clients, galleries and collectors.

Experienced and professional, Bergér provides worldwide service and timely delivery.

Also see these GUILD publications:
THE GUILD: 1, 2, 3, 4, 5
The Architect's Source: 6, 7, 8, 10
The Designer's Reference: 8

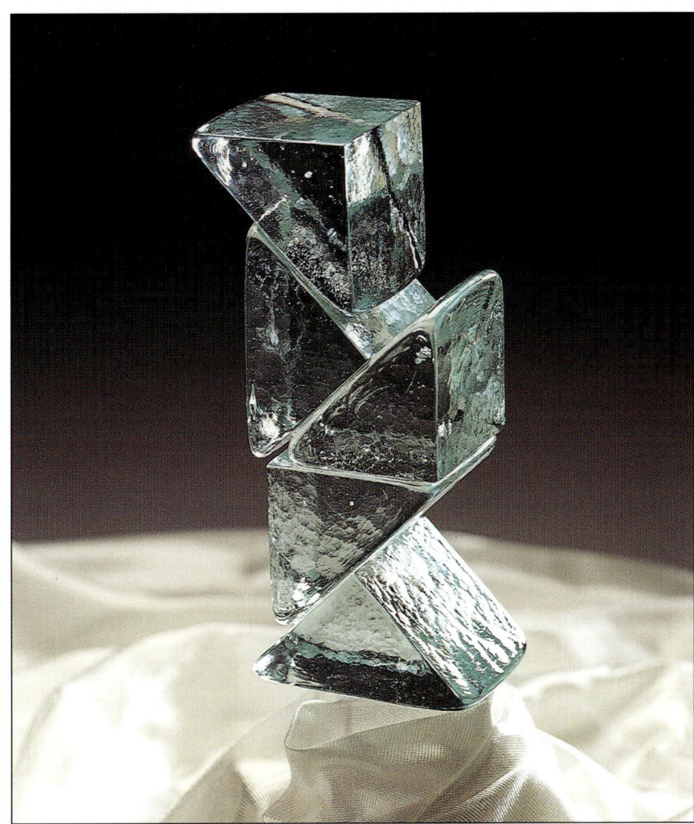

Indian Spirit, 1994, captures the Mayan figure headed to market with a load of goods on his back, solid cast glass, 12"H, approx. 15 lbs.

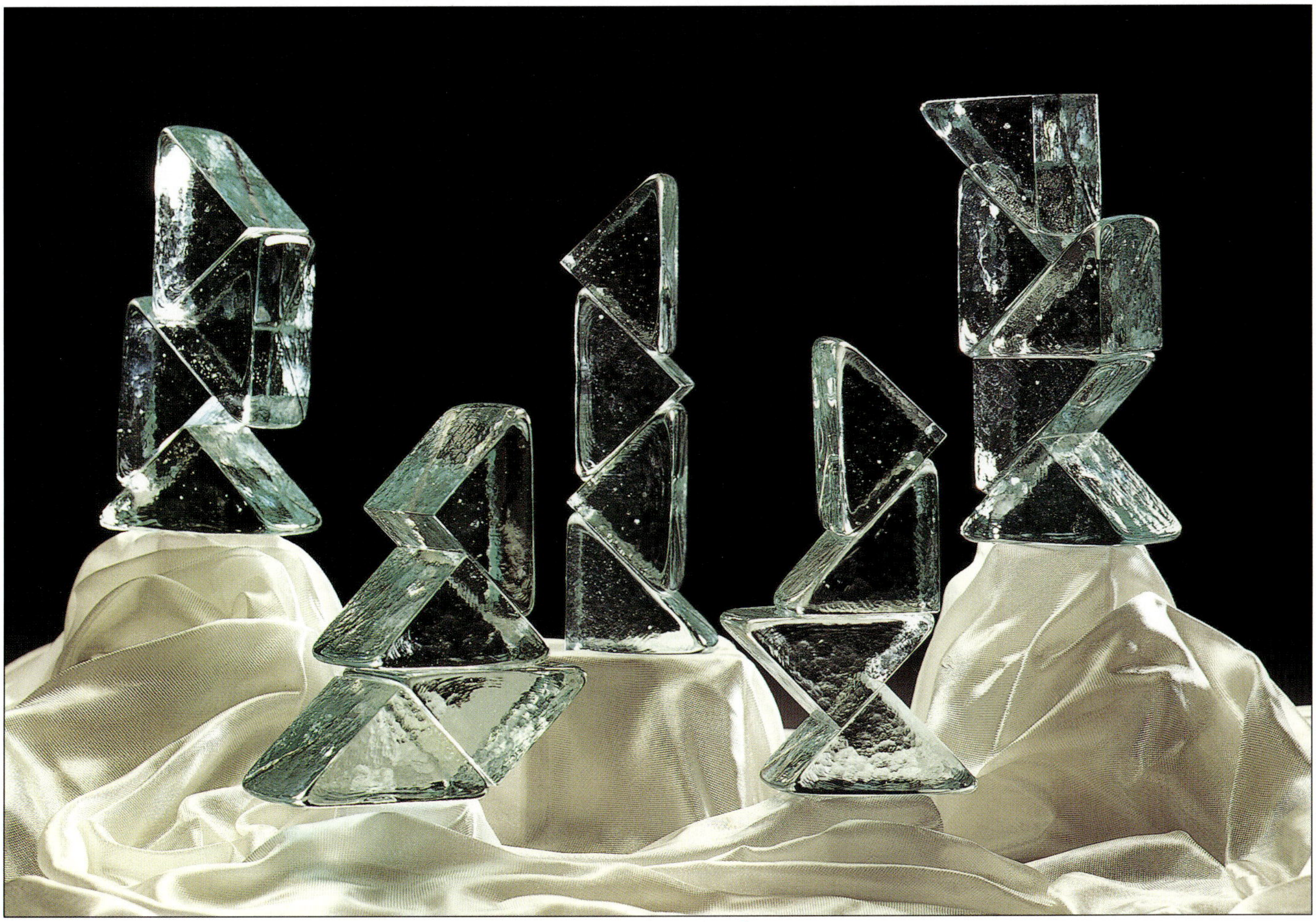

Mayan Ice series, 1993-1994, (left to right) *God of Light, Temple Spirit, Priest, Bird of Freedom, Indian Spirit,* custom-cast glass, 10" to 14"H, each approx. 12 to 15 lbs.

Photos: William A. Porter, San Francisco, CA

ceramics ceramics ceramics cer

ceramics ceramics ceramics

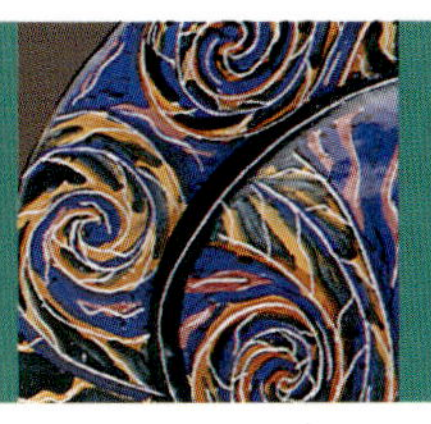

David Terrett Beumée
Porcelain by David Beumée

Specializing in wheel-thrown porcelain pottery, David Beumée produces wares which seek to combine beauty and refinement with an exceptional palette of glaze colors. All work is intended for everyday use. David began his career in ceramics in 1976, and his work was recently featured in *Ceramics Monthly*.

SHOWN: porcelain dinnerware, 1994, with accessory vase and covered jar

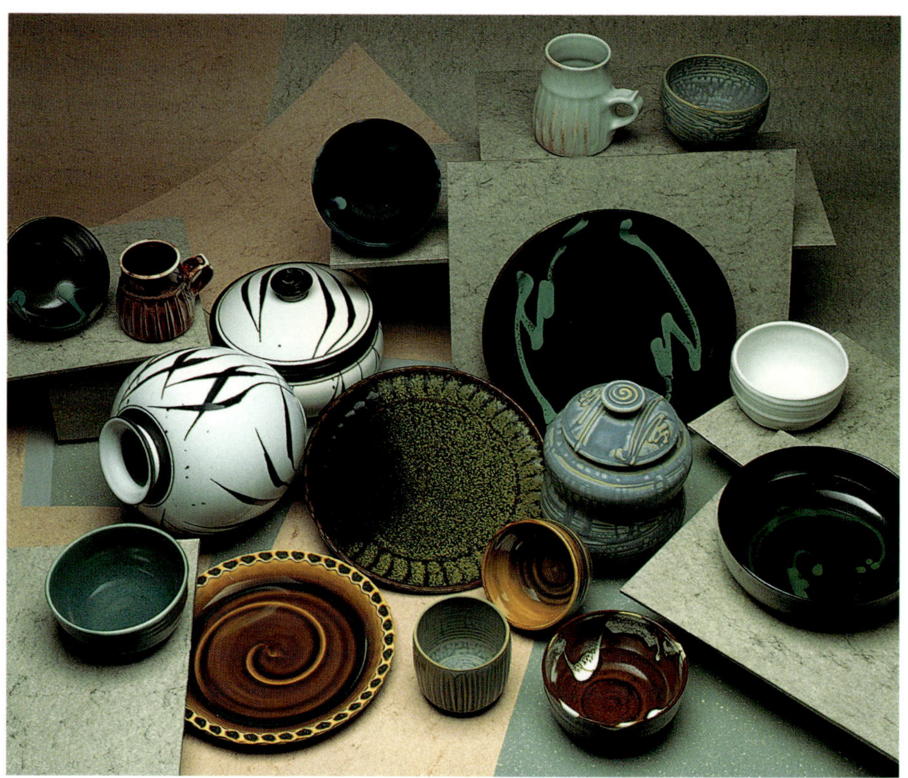

John Bonath

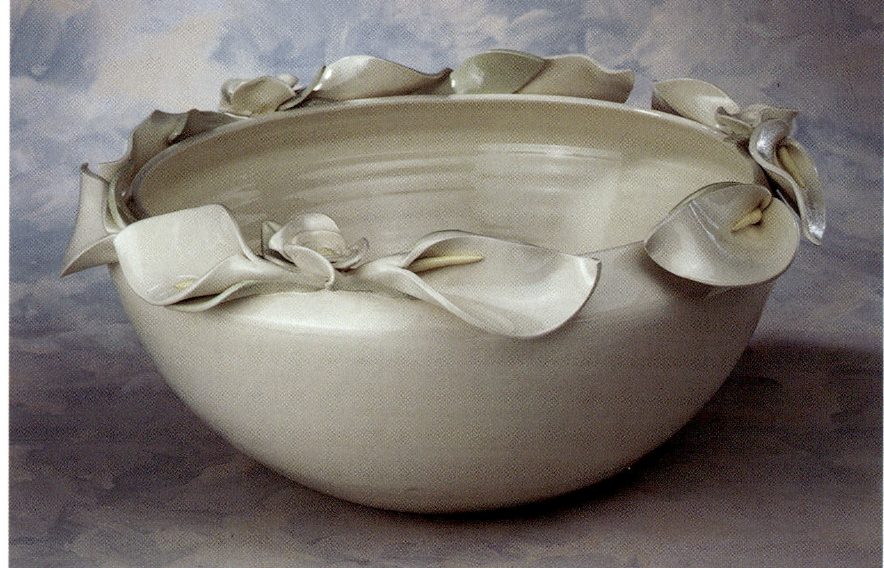

Barbara Bravo
Bravo Original Ceramic Designs

For 20 years, Barbara Bravo's pottery has reflected her love of natural beauty and clay. The flowing floral designs in white earthenware are classic and have been sold in galleries nationwide. The latest addition to her extensive collection, *The Heirloom Series*, has timeless appeal and can be enjoyed today and then passed on to future generations.

SHOWN: *Garland Crested Bowl*

Hoyman/Browe Studio
Querencia Fine Tableware

Querencia [ka-ren-see-ah] n. sp. a favorite place, home, where the heart is.

We have designed our tableware for our family and friends, people who love to eat and laugh, entertain and share. The patterns document the annual cycles of our garden and the bountiful country we live in, from spring flowers to fall harvests. All decorations convey the strength and beauty of hand brushwork.

Our work has appeared in *H&G*, *Home*, *Metropolitan Home*, *American Craft*, and *Ceramics Monthly* and is currently used in many well-respected restaurants by nationally known chefs.

Turning houses into homes for 20 years.

A *Talmage* deco tableware

B *Carmen Miranda* deco tableware

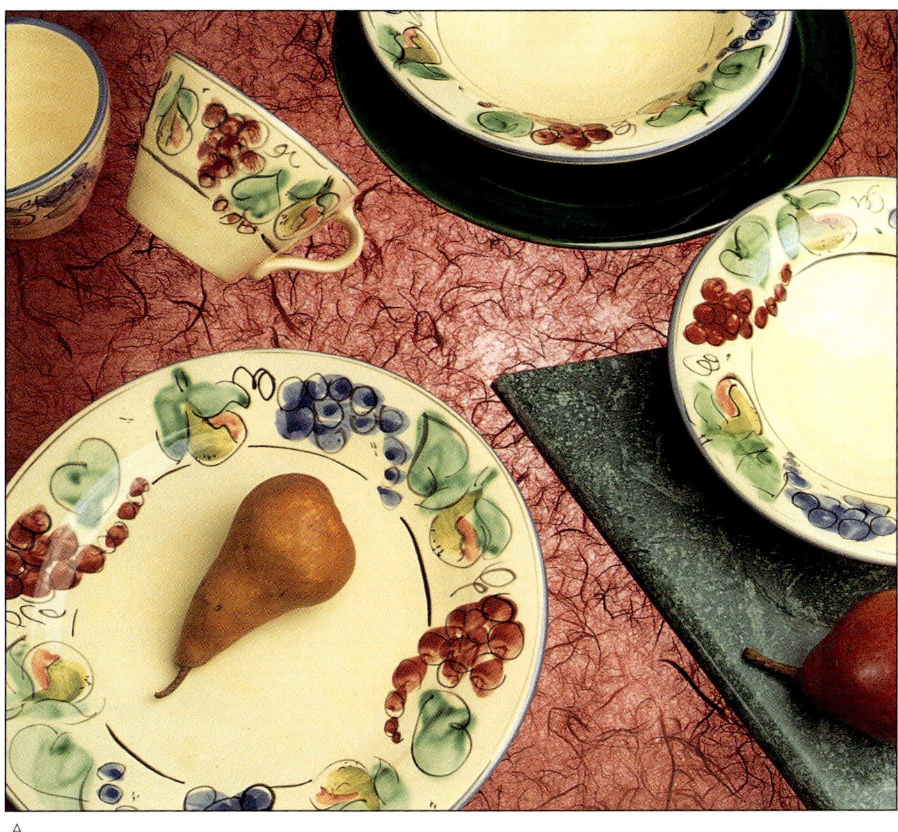

A

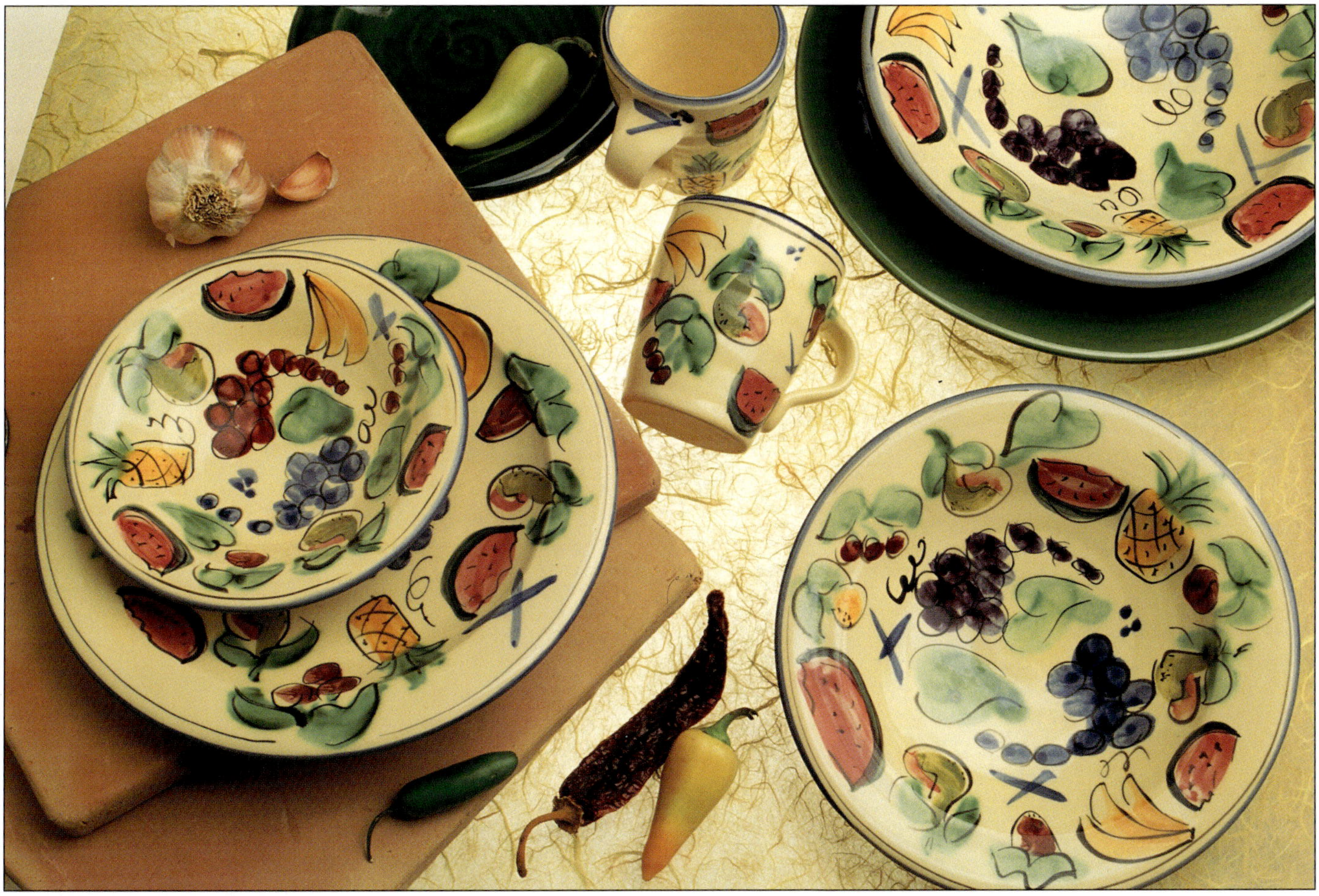

B

R. Bruce Carpenter
3 Crane Ceramics

Having studied in Arita, Japan, Bruce Carpenter creates limited-production and unique high-fire stoneware and porcelain vessels. Indigenous materials are used in the glazes to create simple and direct work. While working within tradition, he is constantly aware of the evolution of his designs. The functionality of the work is used to enhance the beauty of the artistic endeavor.

SHOWN: plate, 42 × 8 cm; *mizusashi*, 17.5 × 16 cm

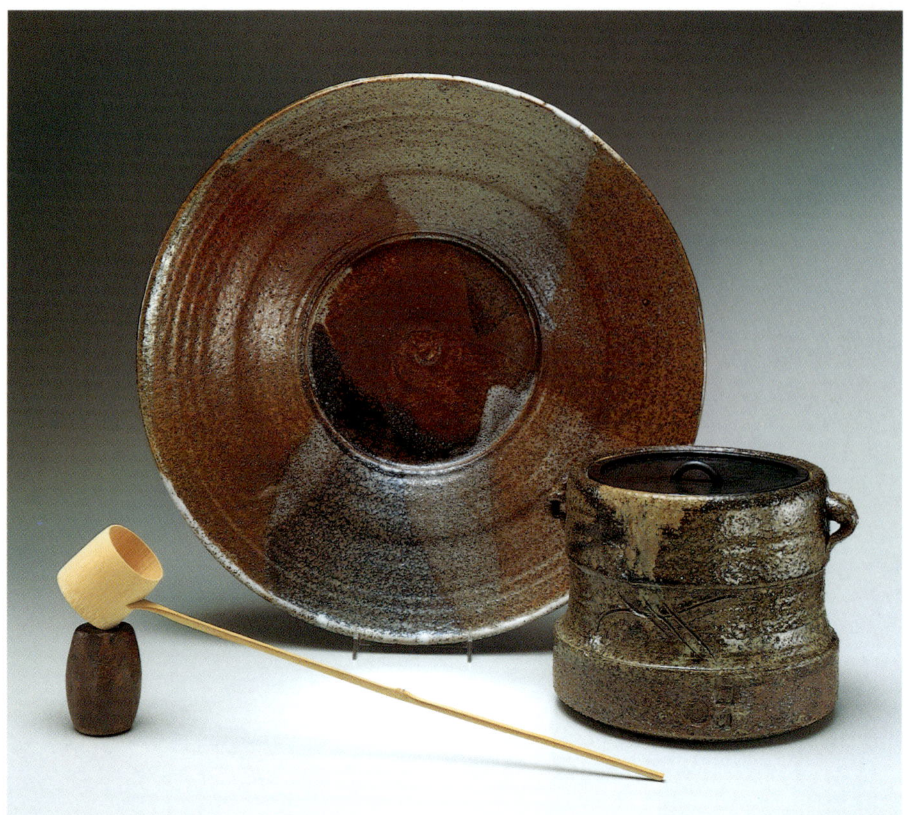

Damian Andrus

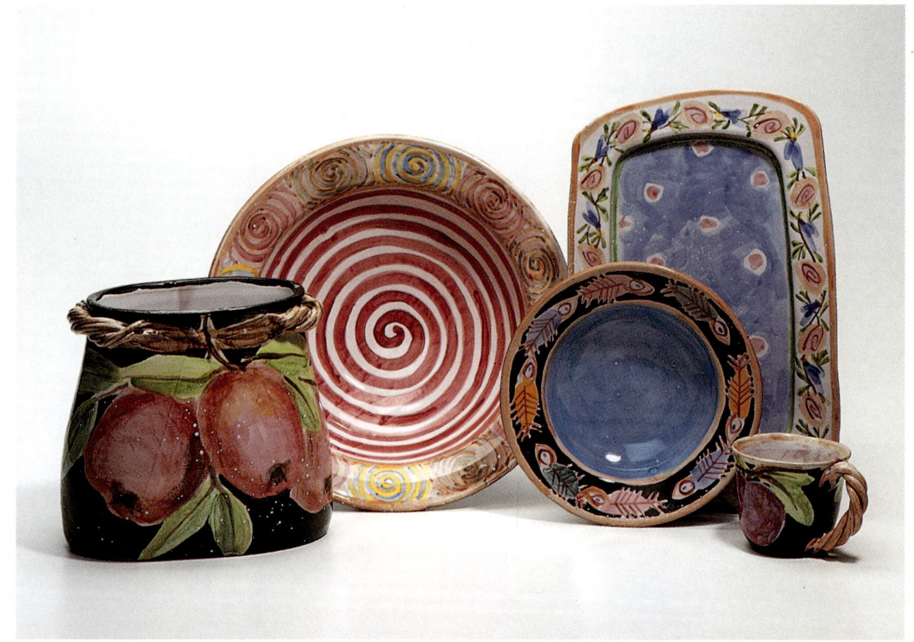

Ann Wheat Pace
Decorative and Functional Ceramics

In her Houston studio, Ann Wheat Pace creates dinnerware, platters, serving bowls, oval pots, trivets and coaster sets using a watercolor technique over red earthenware. The majolica-like, lead-free glazes are dishwasher and microwave safe. The white dots and lines which appear during firing contribute to the uniqueness of each individually crafted piece.

SHOWN: dinnerware and accessory pieces

Dancing Fire Studio

Ann Lynn Whiteside

Works in clay by Ann Lynn Whiteside have evolved into large vessels, 18" to 27" high, with sensuous curves and wild patterns from nature.

Combining design, color theory and abstract patterning, she expresses both her concern for her fellow creatures and her own drive to create.

Each one-of-a-kind vessel is unique in shape and painted design.

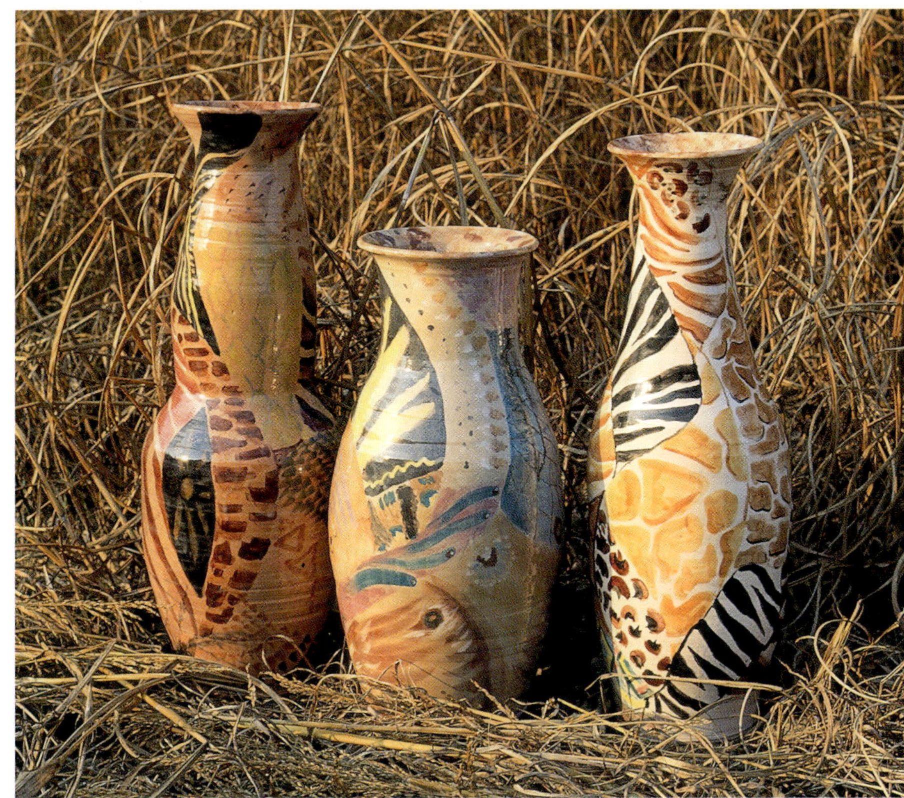

Butterfly, Veldt Fur and *Reptile* in their natural habitat

Craig Tanner

AMERICAN CERAMICS

9 EAST 45 ST #603
NEW YORK, NY 10017
FAX 212-661-2389
TEL 212-661-4397
$28/year

American Ceramics, an art quarterly, was founded to enhance the preservation of ceramics' rich heritage and to document contemporary developments in the field. Articles feature the best and brightest ceramists: rising stars and established luminaries, as well as those early pioneers who transformed ceramics into a genuine art form.

Boots Culbertson
Culbertson Pottery

Natural forms are reflected in both functional and sculptural work from this 25-year-old award-winning studio. From delicate porcelains to whimsical, sculpted stoneware cats, from functional ware to fountains, garden pieces and lamps, each piece is masterfully designed and reduction fired. Production time is four to ten weeks.

Also see these GUILD publications:
The Gallery & Retail Edition: 1
The Designer's Reference: 8

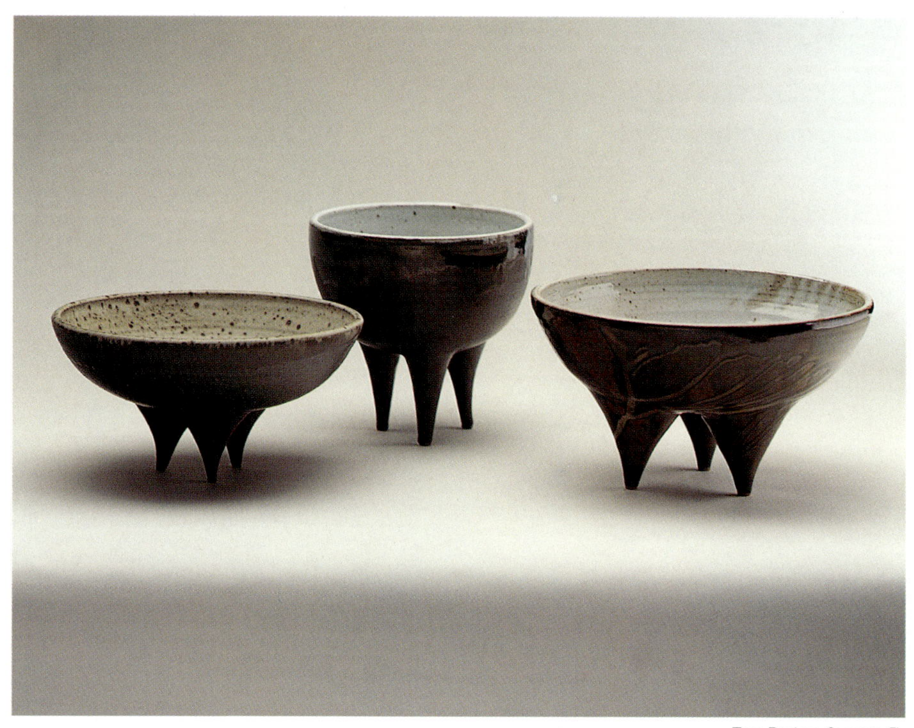

Tom Dodson, Sarasota, FL

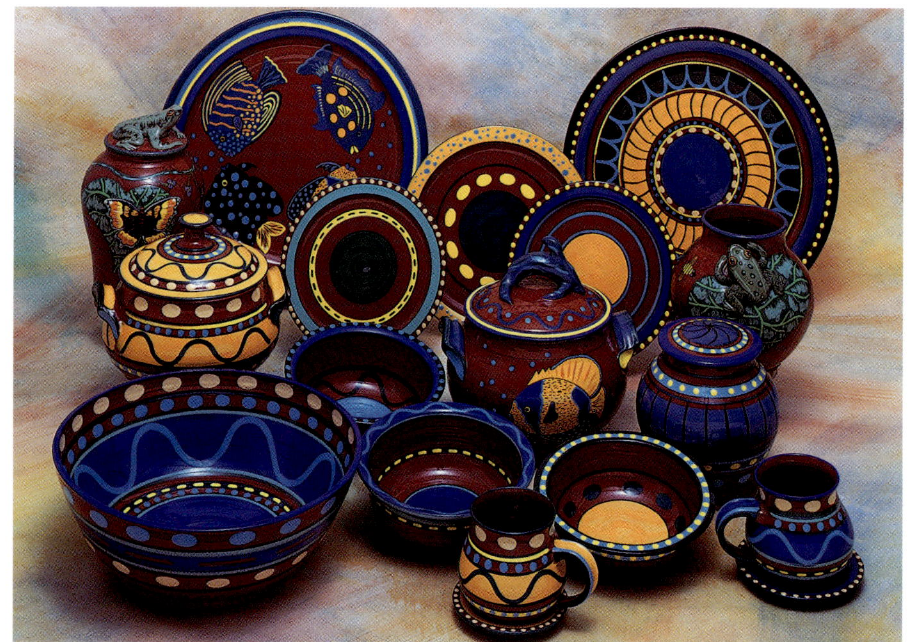

Alec Hemer

RezWare
Ellen Reznick

Hand-painted RezWare pottery is colorful, unique and made to last. Each piece is a signed original design and all are ovenproof and dishwasher safe. Ellen Reznick specializes in a variety of coordinated dinnerware and useful serving pieces. She has been in business for 16 years, selling her products through many fine galleries and stores throughout the country.

Also see this GUILD publication:
The Gallery & Retail Edition: 1

Susan M. Sipos
Object/Art

Majolica ware that is totally handmade and hand painted to order. Each piece is unique, carefully made, and undergoes repeated firings, resulting in works of intricate brilliance.

Her work appears in museums and collections worldwide.

BFA from Cleveland Institute of Art.

MFA from the University of Illinois.

Years of experience: 25.

Work is dishwasher and microwave safe.

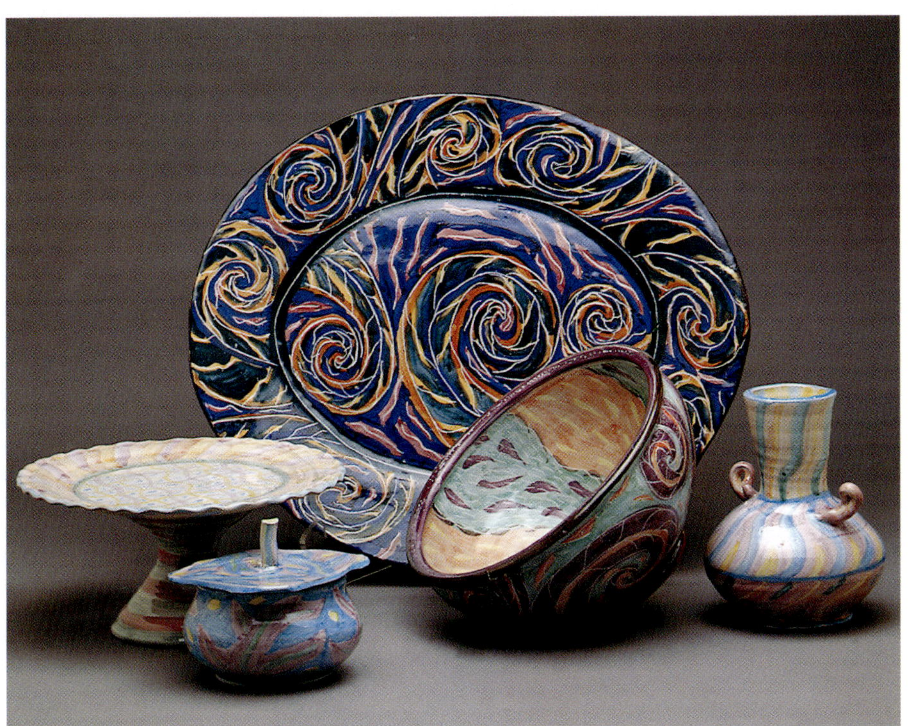

Ernest Wilmeth II

Mr. Wilmeth's thrown clay vessels are made with white stoneware or earthenware. After each piece is formed and dried, it is sanded, then bisque-fired and pit- or smoke-fired to achieve the desired results.

His clay works are in the collections of the Bowne Corporation and the Delancey Street Foundation. He holds life membership to Great Britain's Royal Society of Art and is listed in *Who's Who in American Art*.

SHOWN: clay vessels

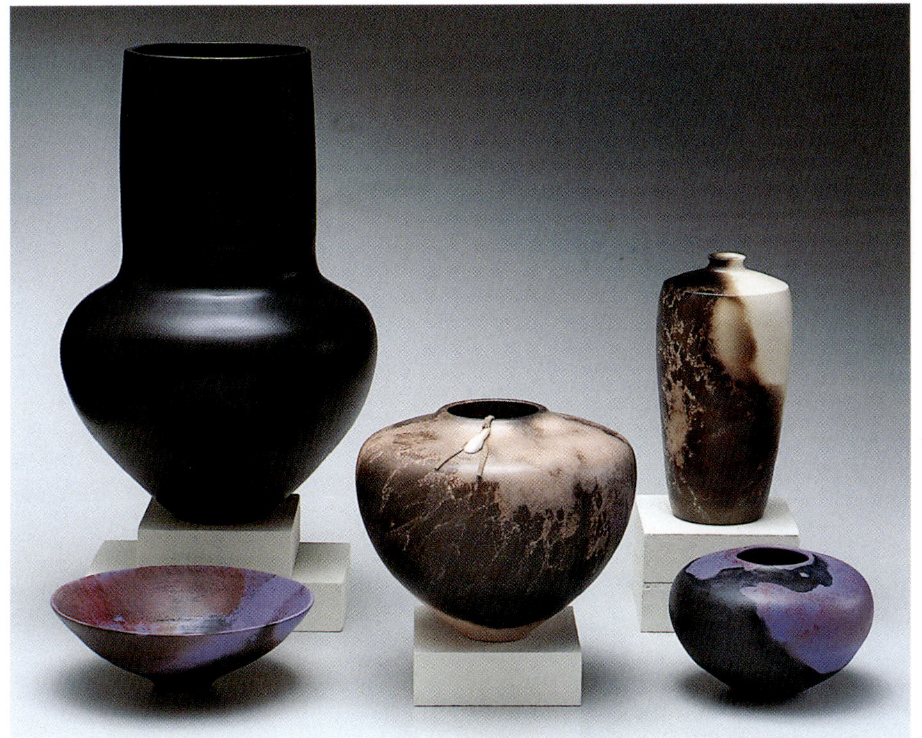

Damian Andrus

Richard Tuck

Richard Tuck's vessels and sculptural stoneware clay work reflect his interest in form and working with the formal elements of mass, volume, line, space, color, and surface texture. His work strives to be in harmony with its environment and have a contemplative nature. Tuck is a traditionalist in that he draws upon the history of ceramics and sculpture for inspiration. His works are variations on vessel and sculptural forms with each being an individual solution.

Tuck's work is represented in private and corporate collections here and overseas.

A *Metafisica Reliquary*, 1994, stoneware, 13" × 6" × 8"

B *Vessel Form*, 1994, stoneware, 14"H

C *Torso*, 1994, stoneware, 16"H

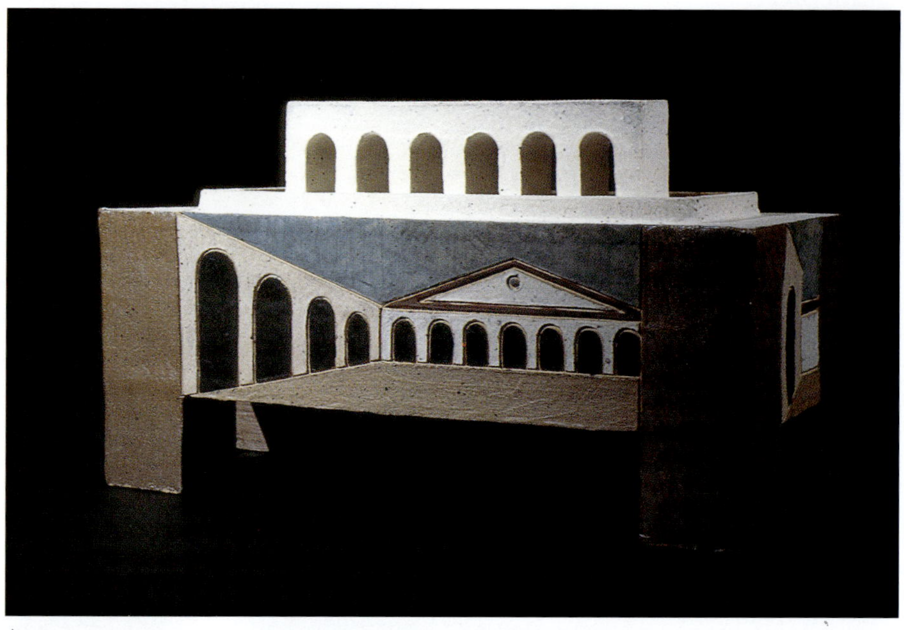

A

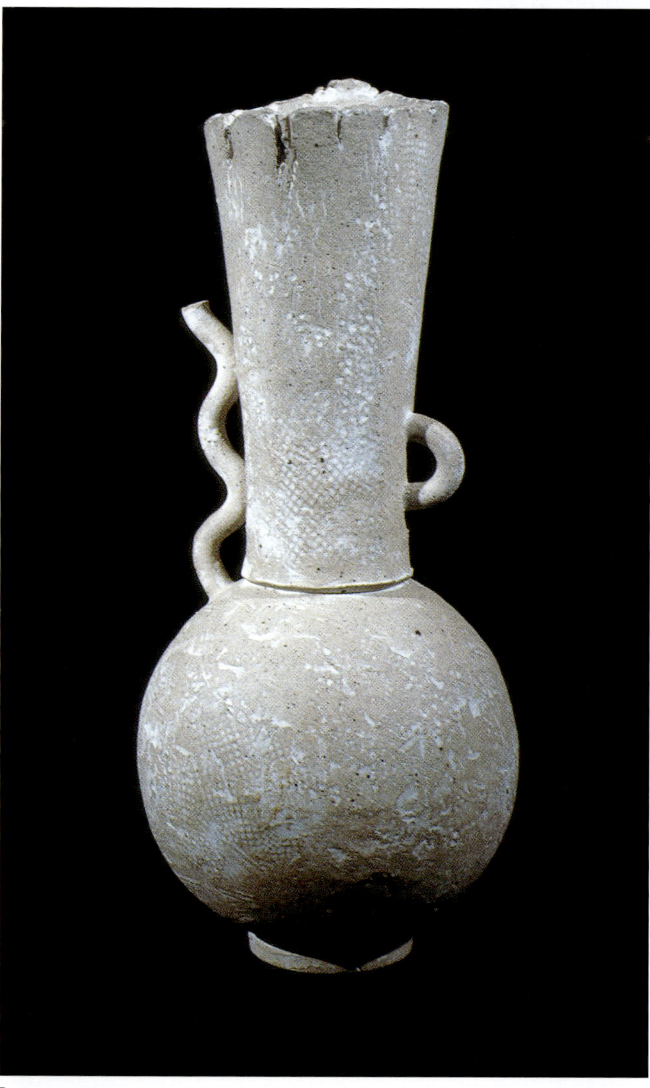

B

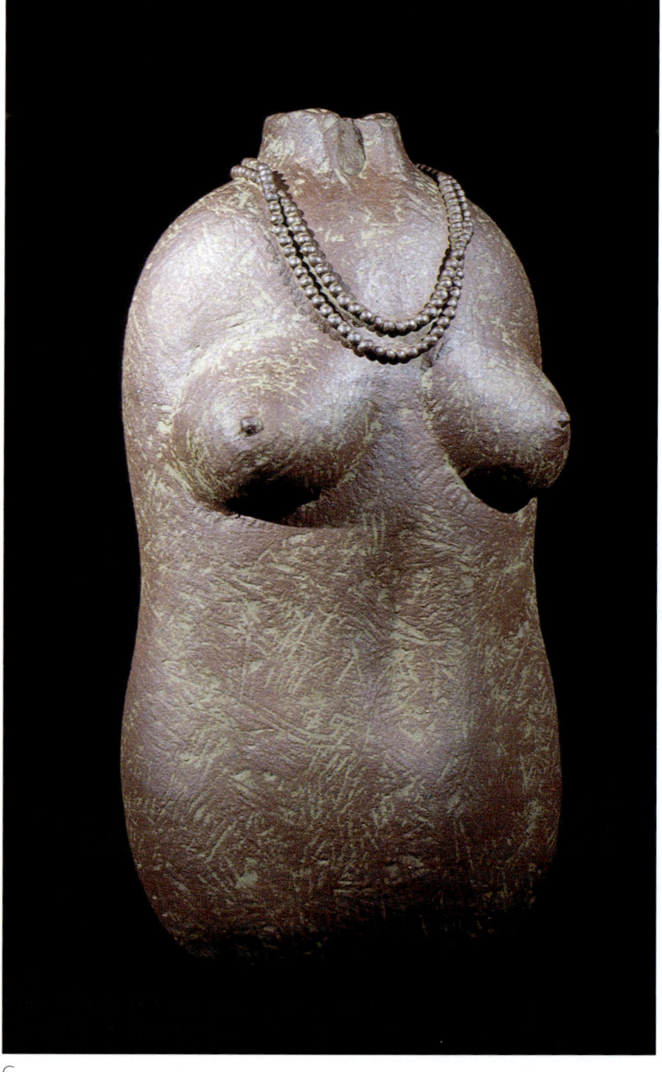

C

Tom Wolver

Influenced by the visual and spiritual nature of the African, American Indian and ancient Mexican cultures, Tom Wolver's art reflects an attempt to re-unite with the ways of the shaman, the sorcerer and the warrior, and to explore the profound possibilities of the 'inner journey' that each initiate travels to become a realized soul.

Wolver works in varied mediums of clay, bronze and wood. Commissions are welcomed for both outdoor and indoor sites. Prices will vary depending on size and complexity. Portfolio available upon request.

Also see this GUILD publication:
The Designer's Reference: 7

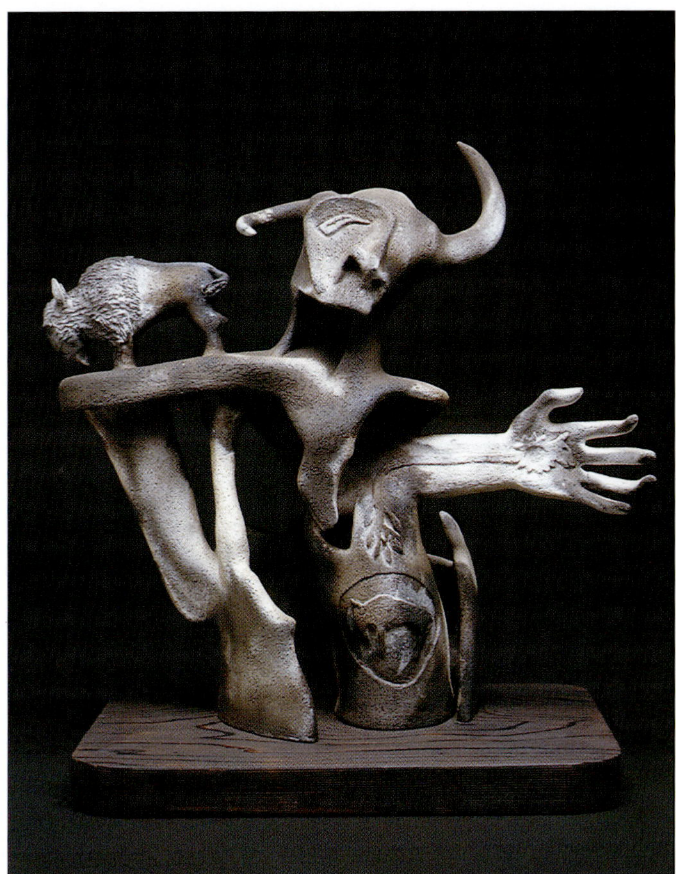

Heart of the Buffalo, 1992, clay, 20½"H

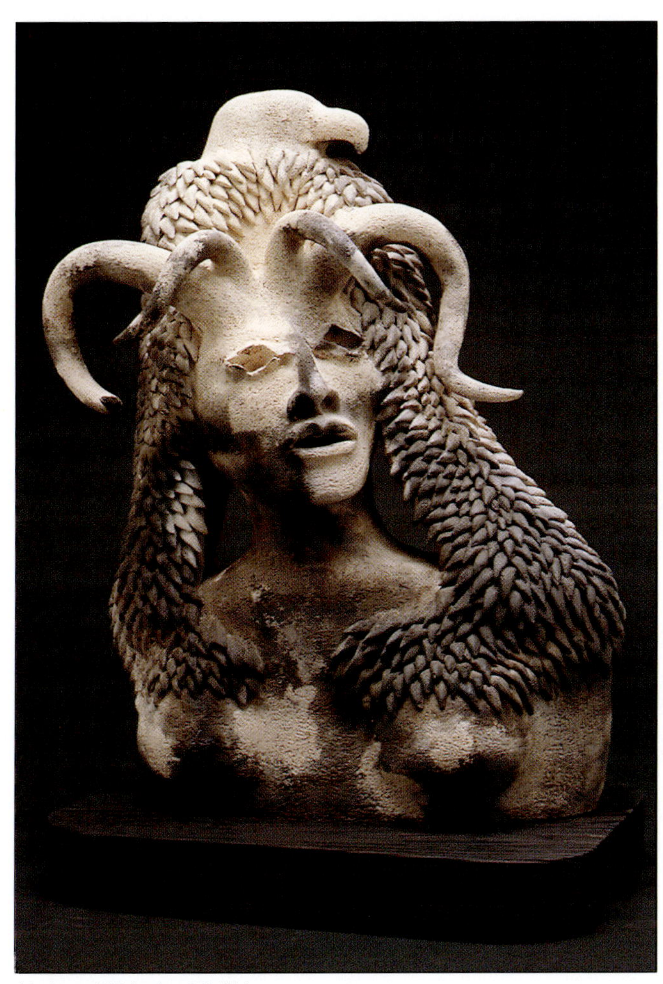

Medusa, 1994, clay, 21½"H

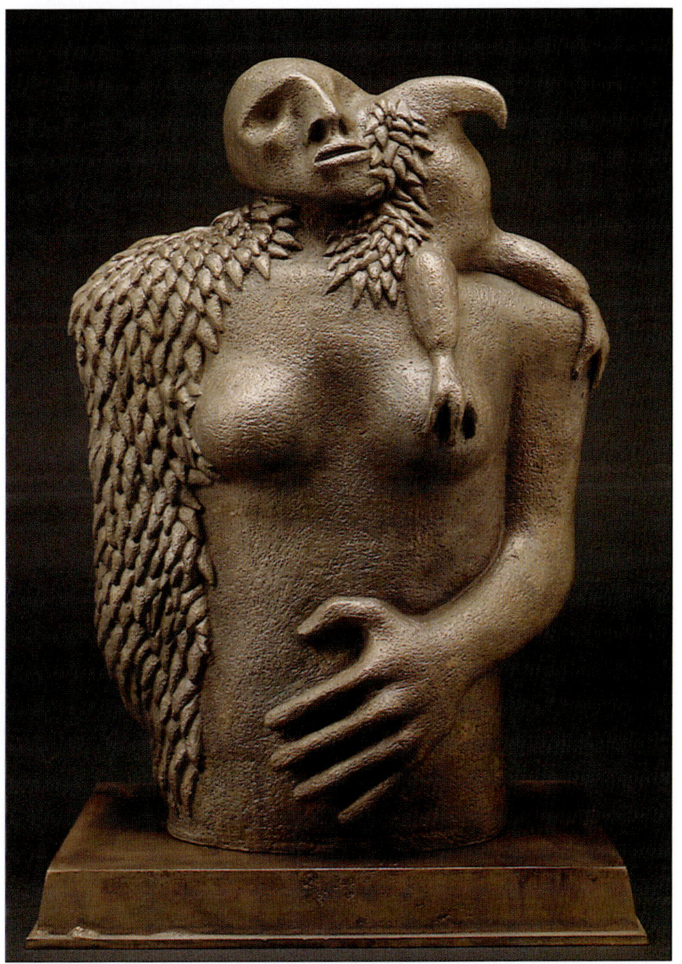

She Who Flies, 1992, bronze, 22½"H

Photos: Tony Grant

Betsy Ross

Betsy Ross' work combines wheel-thrown vessels with hand-built appendages. Her hand-painted earthenware is available in a multitude of finishes, from lustres to patinas. Each piece is signed by the artist.

Ross' new body of work features actual metallic patina surfaces (shown) representing a variety of metals. She continues to offer the *Mini-Vessel* series, miniature renditions of her larger works, with the same attention to style and form.

Commissions are welcome.

Also see these GUILD publications:
The Gallery & Retail Edition: 1
THE GUILD: 5
The Designer's Reference: 6, 7, 8

SHOWN: antique brass patina vessel, 15"H; mini-vessel, copper patina, 5½"H

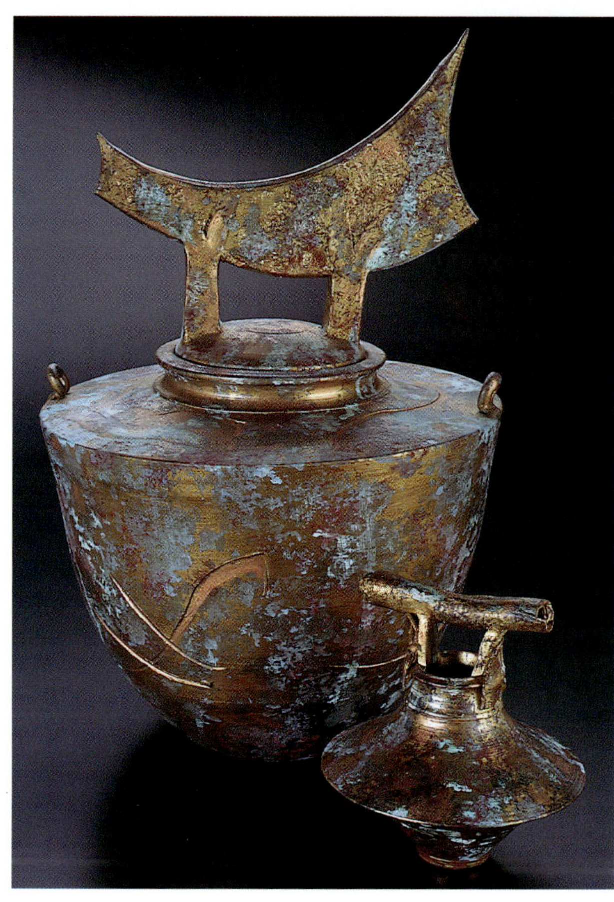

Kevin Osborn
Labor Temple Design

Kevin Osborn has produced predominately commissioned work for over 20 years. Influenced by primitive techniques and classical forms, these wheel-thrown, pit-fired porcelain vessels have a polished luster with a patina of gold or silver leaf and forged steel handles. Sizes range from 14" to 60"; work can be custom designed for private or public spaces.

SHOWN: bowl, 14"H x 25"W; tall vessel, 36"H x 14"W; round vessel, 27"H x 18"W

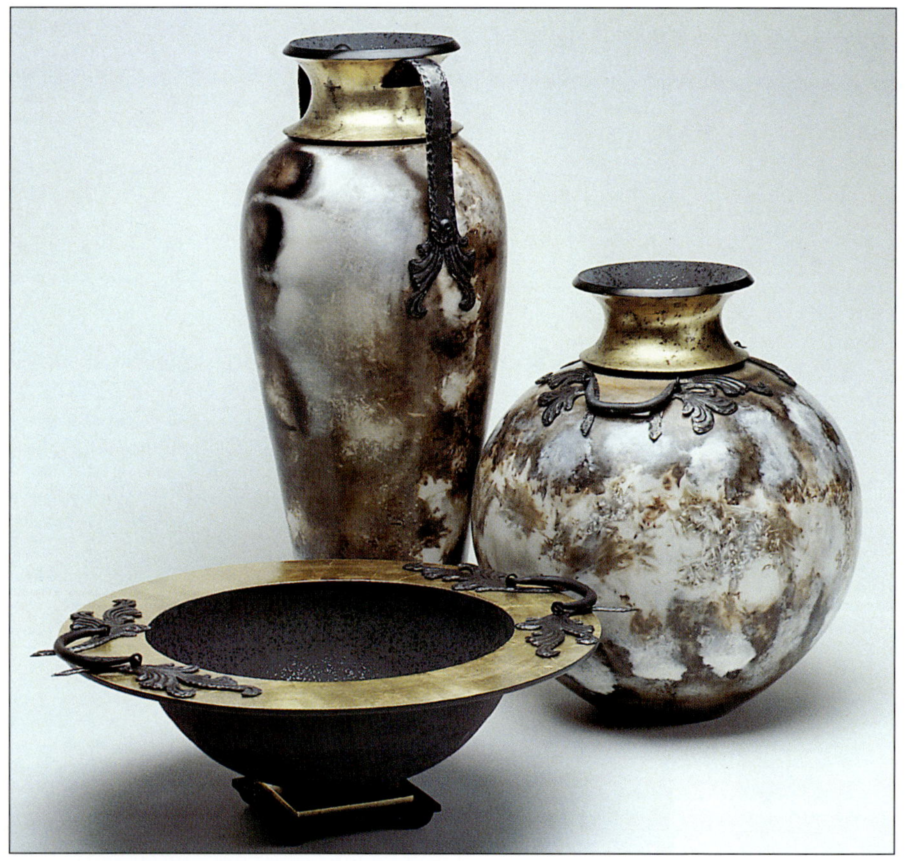

Nancee Meeker

Nancee Meeker, whose studio is in Rhinecliff, New York, has been a studio potter since 1973. Her stone-burnished and pit-fired vessels have been admired and collected by individuals, corporations and museums around the world—including the Smithsonian Institution and the Museum of FIne Arts in Boston.

After a sabbatical from clay—with travel and study in Ireland, Mexico, Turkey, Australia and Italy—Ms. Meeker's new works have a richer focus and a satisfying complexity, but still retain their timeless elegance.

These unique vessels are decorative and do not hold liquids.

A *New Leaf Bowl*, 1994, thrown, etched, stone-burnished Kiziloren terra sigillata, smoked, 12" x 12" x 9"

B *New Flow Bowl*, 1994, thrown, carved, stone-burnished Kiziloren terra sigillata, smoked, 12" x 12" x 10"

C *Alien Series*, group of three pieces, 1994, thrown, altered, stone-burnished terra sigillatas, smoked

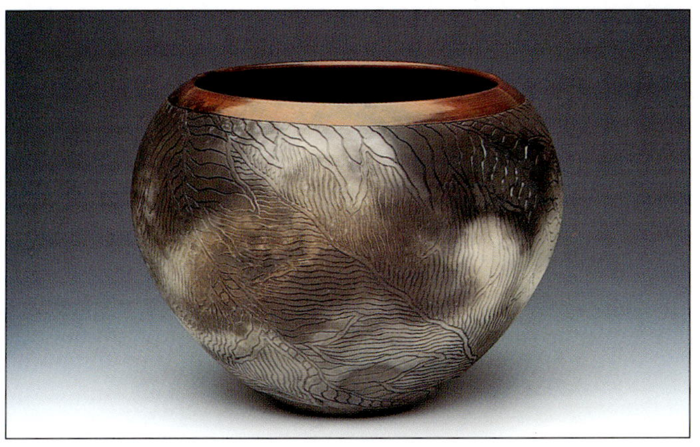

A

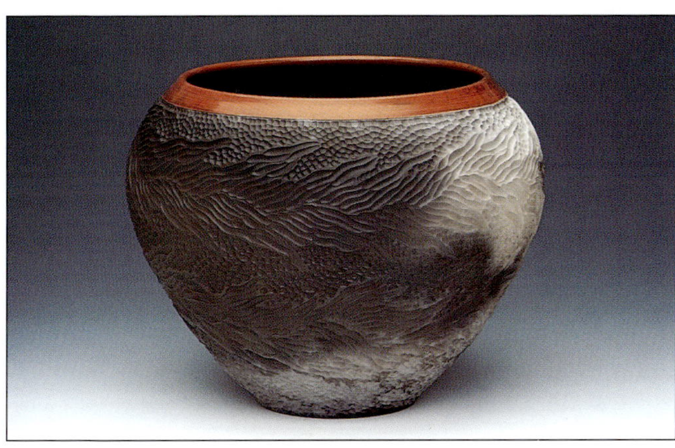

B

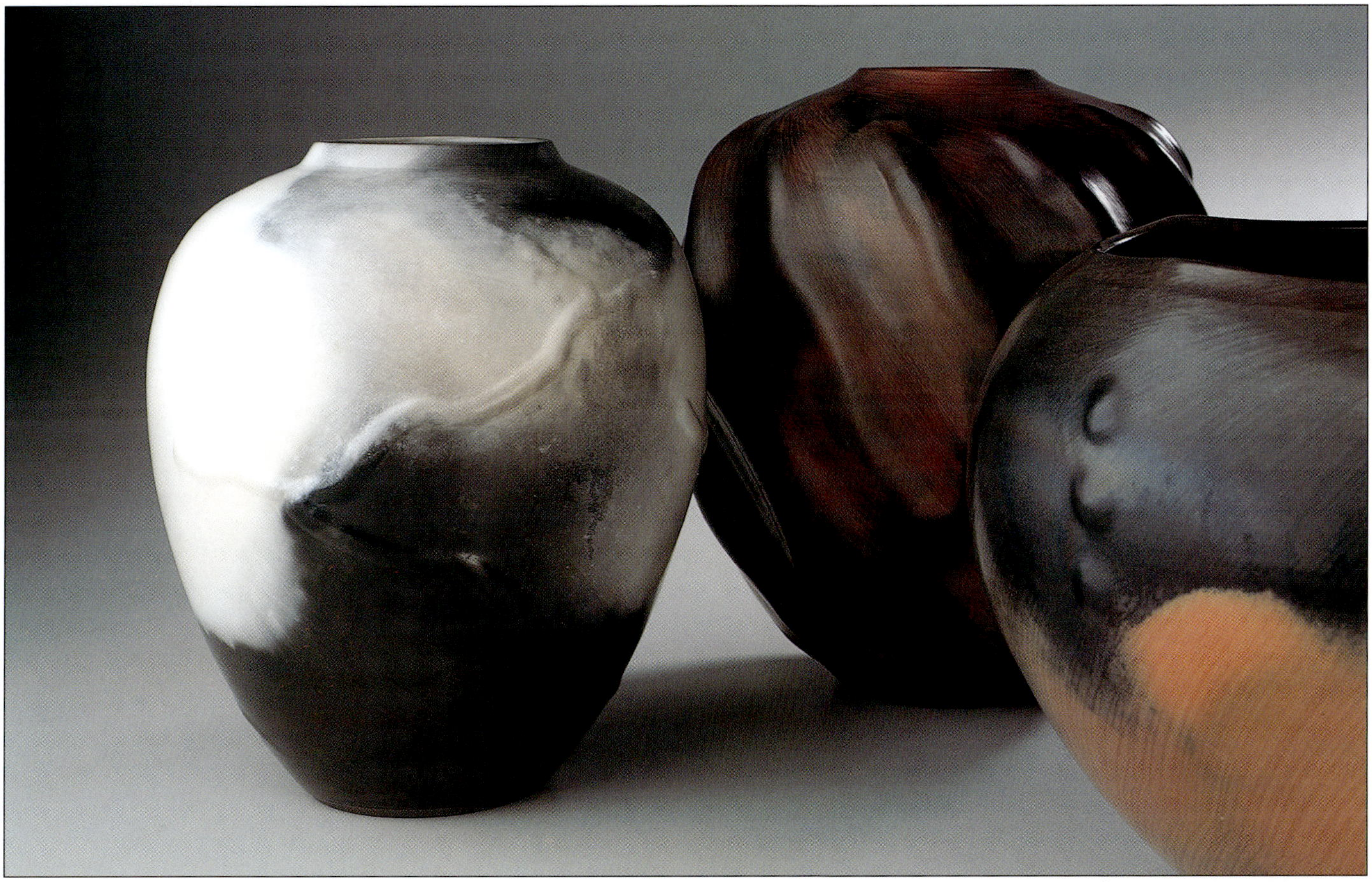

C

Joan E. Scheckel:
Ceramic Artist

Joan E. Scheckel

Joan's medium is clay, yet she still utilizes textures to create a dichotomy between what is real and what is illusion. She incorporates actual paraphernalia, along with clay apparatus, into her 'clothing line.'

Dr. U. Feelgood is a piece dedicated to today's medical doctor, prepared for any emergency.

Joan welcomes special order commission work and would be glad to discuss a ceramic piece of your favorite sport or occupation.

Joan is represented in galleries nationwide.

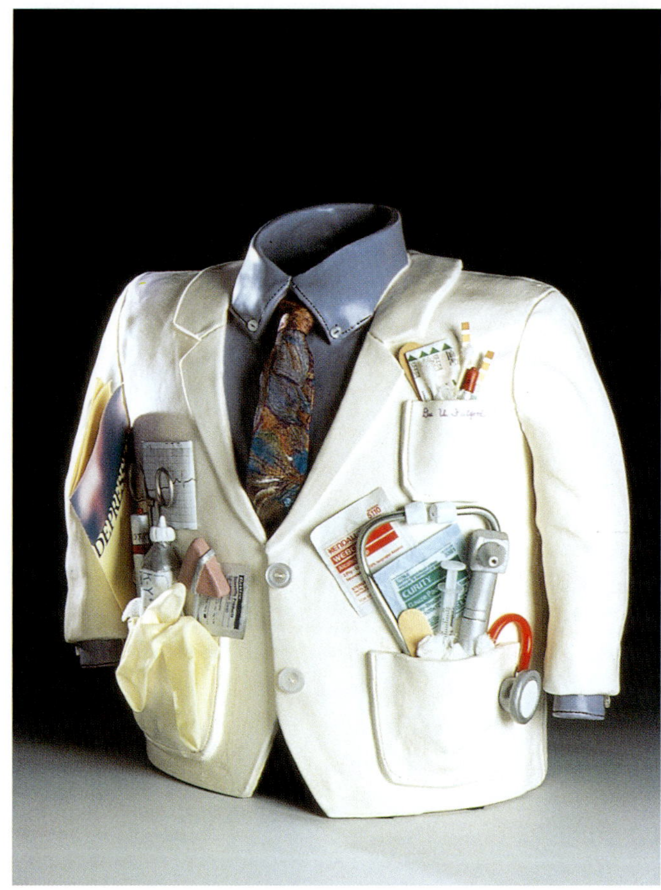

Dr. U. Feelgood, clay, other media, 16"H x 13"W x 12"D

CERAMICS MONTHLY

PROFESSIONAL PUBLICATIONS, INC.
1609 NORTHWEST BLVD
PO BOX 12788
COLUMBUS, OH 43212-0788
FAX 614-488-4561
TEL 614-488-8236
$22/year

Ceramics Monthly **offers a broad range of articles—including artist profiles, reviews of exhibitions, historical features, and business and technical information—for potters, ceramic sculptors, collectors, gallery and museum personnel, and interested observers.**

George Marlowe
The Ceramic Masques & Faces of George Marlowe

Artist George Marlowe creates a diverse and unique collection of ceramic Masques & Faces. His creations include the satirical *Silly Dali* and *Picasso Clown;* the whimsical *King, Queen, Jack* and *Poker Joker* ensemble; an array of international faces; and a haunting series on aliens.

His work has been displayed in many fine art galleries on the West Coast, including Gallery Rodeo in Beverly Hills.

SHOWN: *Poker Joker*, 1993, ceramic and acrylic, 8" × 10"

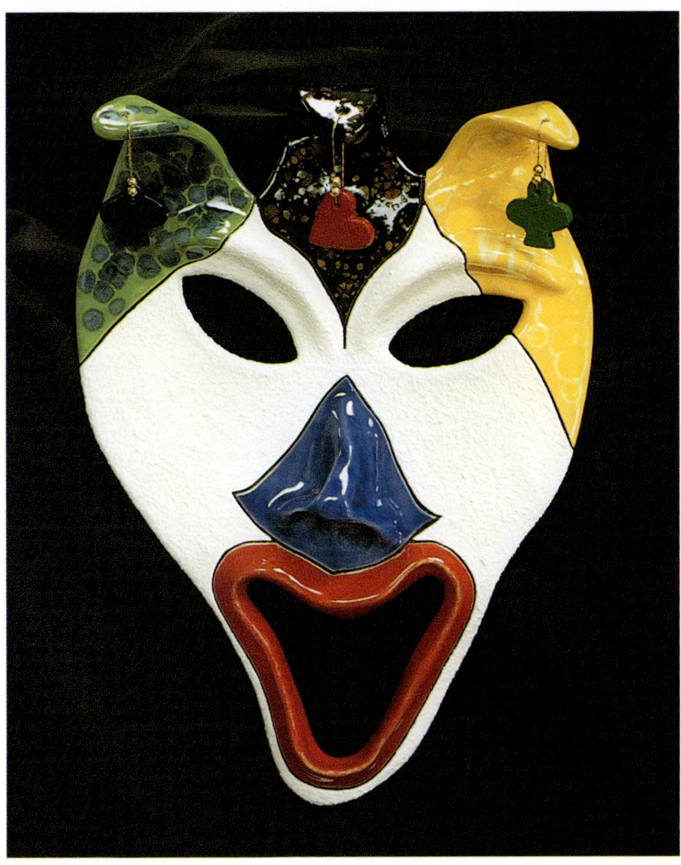

Margaret Southwell
Margaret Southwell's Fanciful Animals

The lion and the lamb, playful tigers, musical zebra, calico hippo, harlequin giraffe, and other ceramic animal whimsies reflect Southwell's rich background in antiques, art and music. They have been represented by a New York gallery for seven years. They are in many major collections, but are most often bought by people who are captured by their charm. Each piece is unique.

Father and Son, 1994, glazed ceramic sculpture, father lion 10" × 10" × 4½"; son lion 4½" × 4½" × 2"

Gavin Ashworth, New York, NY

Lois S. Sattler
Lois S. Sattler Ceramics

Lois Sattler's unique, hand-built porcelain
pieces include jewelry, platters, vases and
bowls. The collaborations with metal artist
Stephen Thompson include wall pieces,
funnels with stands, and custom works.
The piece shown, a collaboration, features
a porcelain vase on a metal stand and is
approximately 5' tall. Ms. Sattler has a
national and international reputation.

Also see these GUILD publications:
THE GUILD: 1, 2, 4
The Designer's Reference: 6, 8

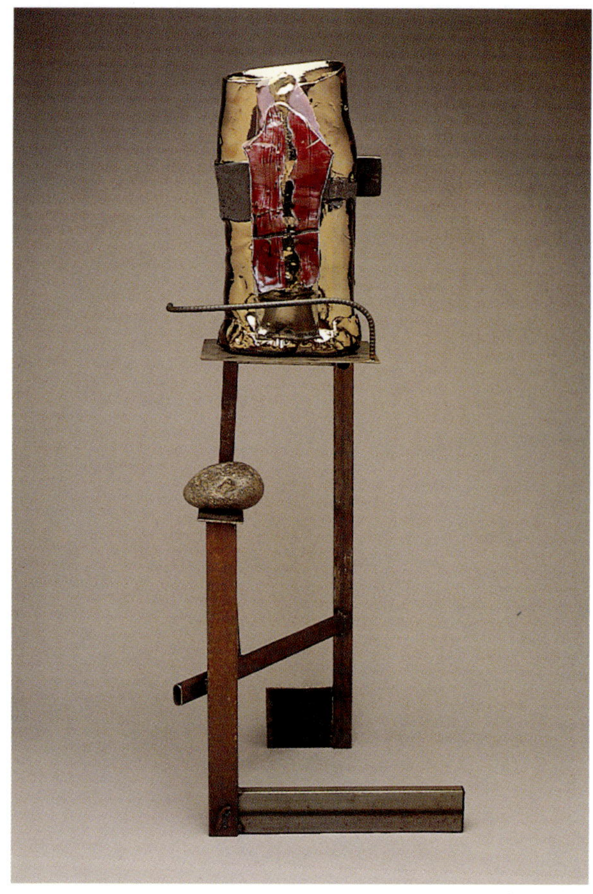

George Post

Robin Renner

While best known for her pit-fired pieces
—shown here *Arch Series* and *Spirit Pots*—
Robin Renner also works with vapor glazes
over stains and oxides, allowing the firing
process to influence final outcomes.

Examples of this work are shown: *Still
Figure—K9*, *Effigy Figures*, *Global Series*
and vases from the *Fragments* series.

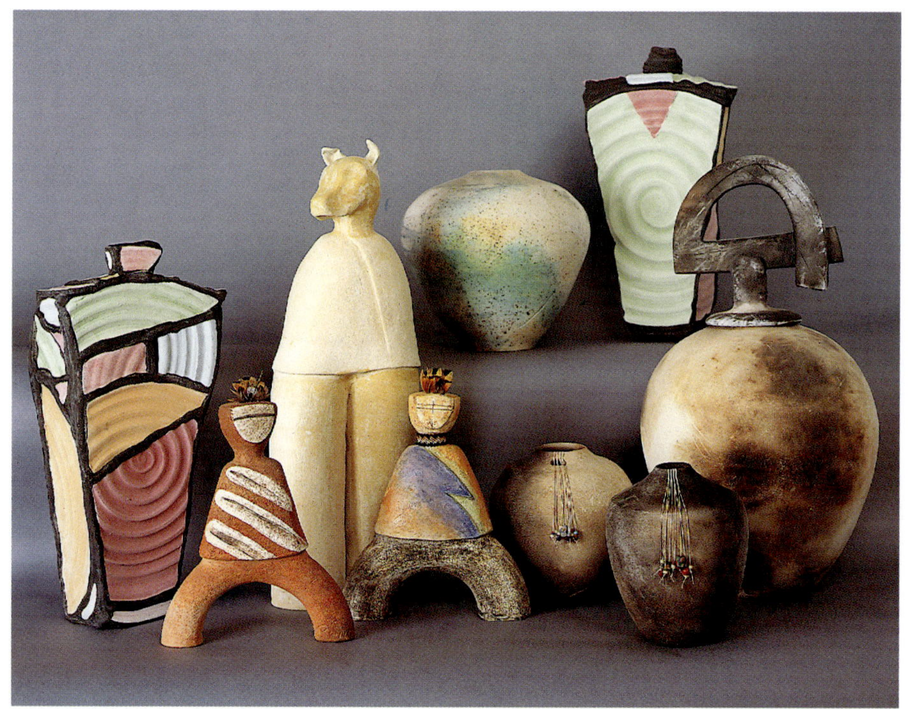

CERAMICS

Carol Green Studio
Carol Green

A studio artist for 20 years, Carol Green works in porcelain and in metals. In her most recent work, she takes advantage of the rich color and jewel-like quality of crystalline glazes by combining them with precious metals and gemstones.

Carol also produces paperweights, vases and ikebana dishes.

Corporate gift commissions welcome.

SHOWN: cobalt jar, sterling silver lid with carnelian, 2¾" × 3"; *copper* green jar, sterling silver lid with malachite, 3¼" × 3¼"

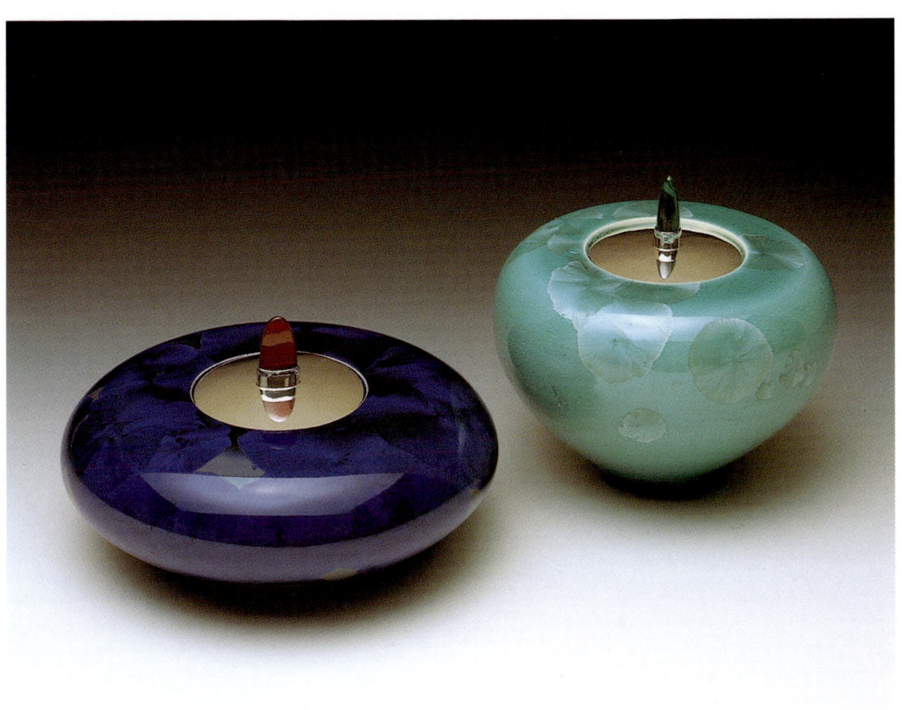

Jerry Anthony

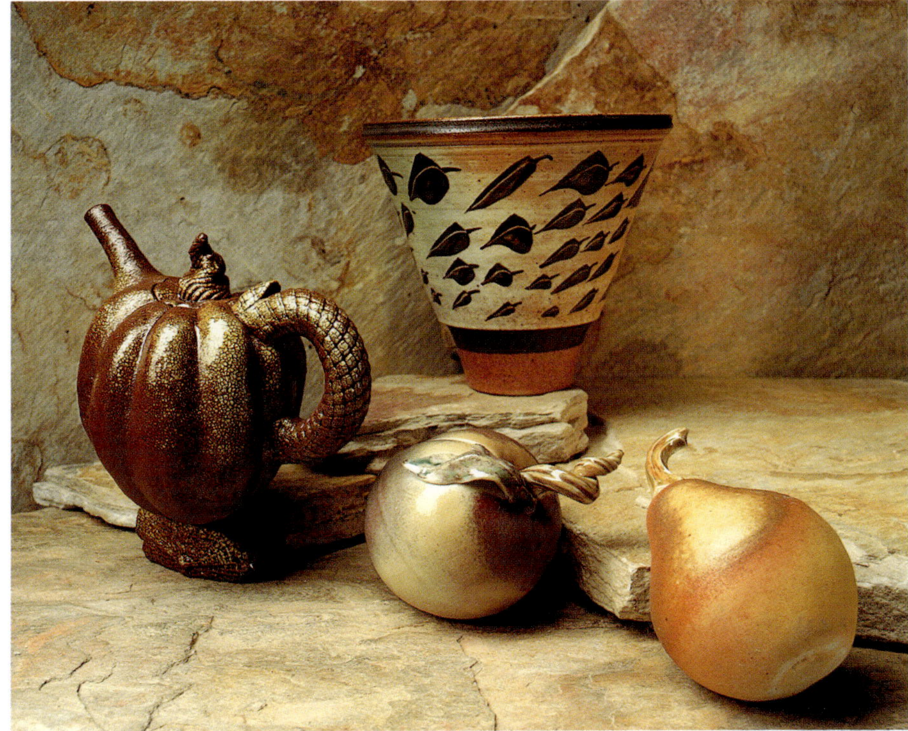

Sarah Frederick

A new look. Sarah Frederick, well known for the colorful organic forms she designs for the Sarah Frederick Studio Pottery, has created an elegant series of unique, whimsical forms in porcelain and stoneware.

Limited editions are available to galleries and designers. Photos and prices available on request.

SHOWN: *Petal Vase,* 6"H; teapot 4"H; porcelain fruit 2½"

metal metal metal metal metal

metal metal metal metal 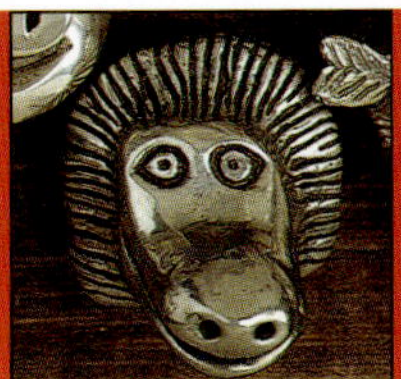

Judie Bomberger

Judie Bomberger designs and produces a variety of whimsical metal sculpture for the home and garden. She creates affordable art that makes people laugh.

Created from hand-cut or wrought steel, pieces range from duplicated to one-of-a-kind. Covered with multi layers of oil-base and acrylic coatings, they spring to life under her guidance and touch.

Brochure available upon request.

A one-of-a-kind hand-wrought and painted candleholders, approx. 2'H

B *Fairy Table*, hand-wrought, painted steel, approx. 3'H. On top of table: *Hog Mama*, two-dimensional, approx. 20"H

C *Freida*, rusted two-dimensional garden sculpture, available in 2' and 3' heights

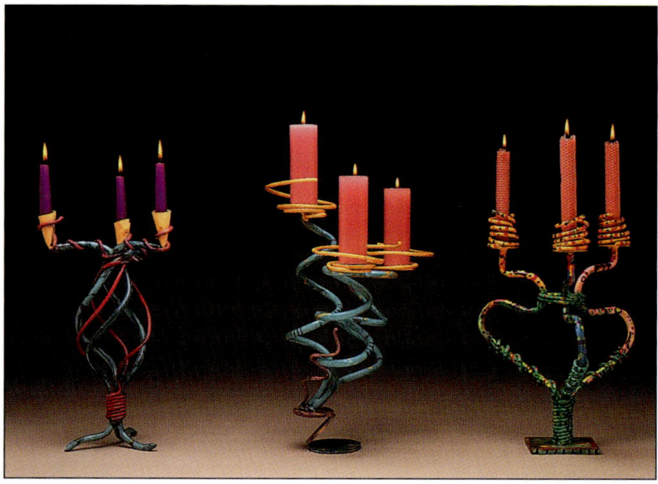

A

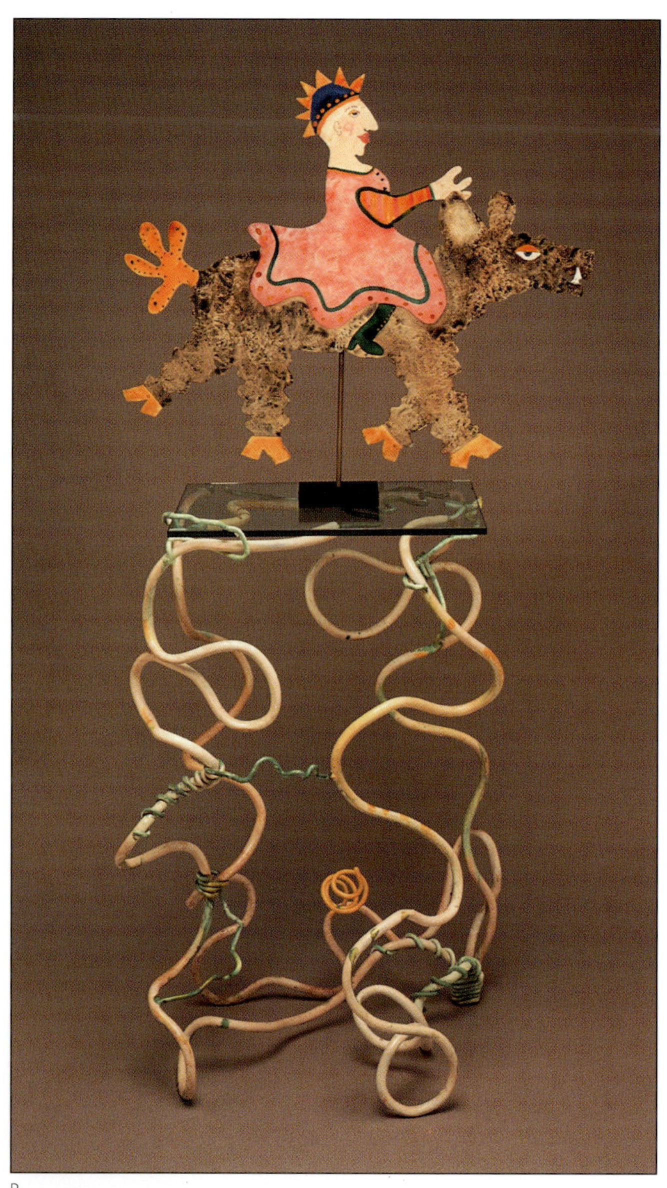

B

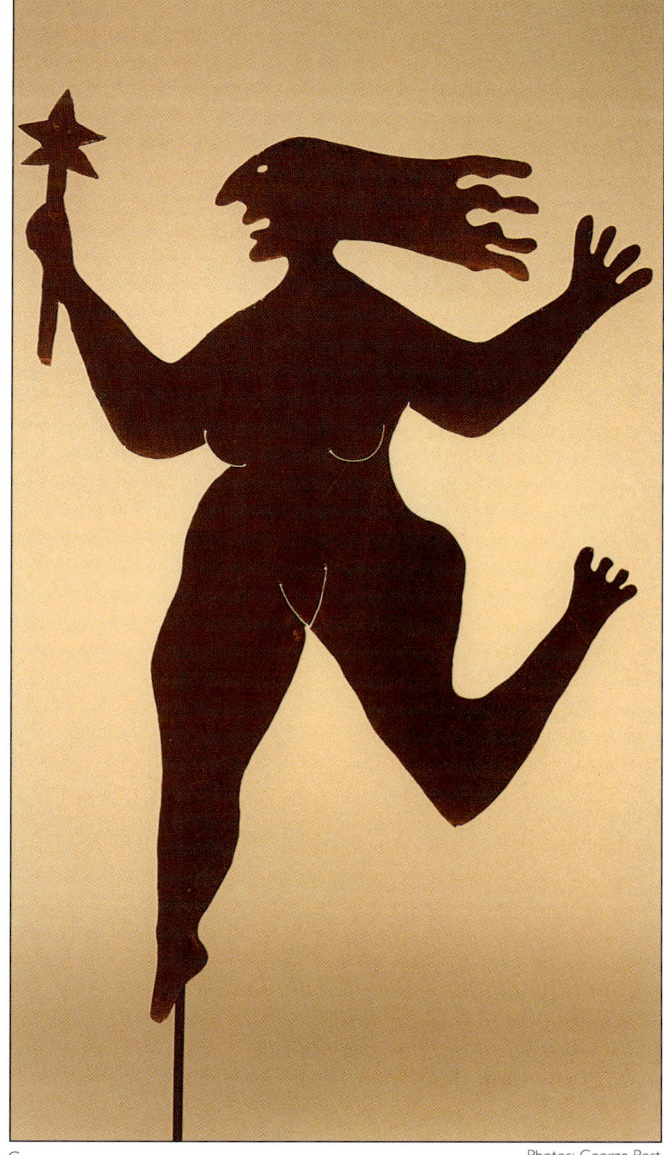

C

METAL

Axelsson Metalsmith
Viking Forge

Chris Axelsson offers individual and limited-edition works in iron, bronze and steel. Commissions include sculpture, architectural adornment and original furnishings.

The artist maintains gallery and studio representation with a showroom at The Barnyard center in Carmel. Axelsson's work has been honored and awarded by national associations. Portfolio available.

Also see this GUILD publication:
The Gallery & Retail Edition: 1

SHOWN: *Sundial*, 36"H x 36"W x 30"L, forged steel with brass numerals

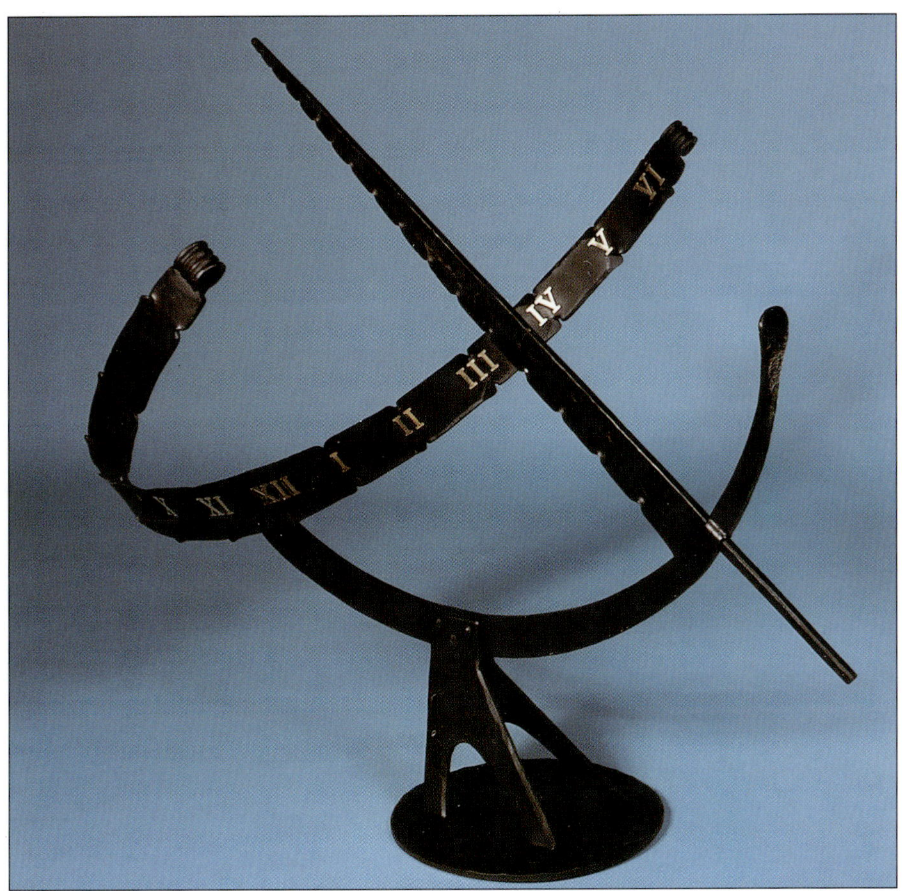

Steven Hensel
Plumage

For over 18 years, Steven Hensel's passion for rich, natural textures, colors and patinas has been applied to furniture, architectural elements and accessories. His work has won numerous national and international awards and has been published in dozens of publications. Clientele includes American Airlines, Paramount Pictures, Learjet, Chase Lincoln Bank, as well as many notable personalities and royalty. He was commissioned to create much of the furniture for a U.S. embassy completed in 1992.

SHOWN: *Firenze Verde Series*, 10"H to 22"H, steel, recycled glass, bronze and copper. Other pieces in this collection include candlesticks, mirrors, screens and tabletop accessories

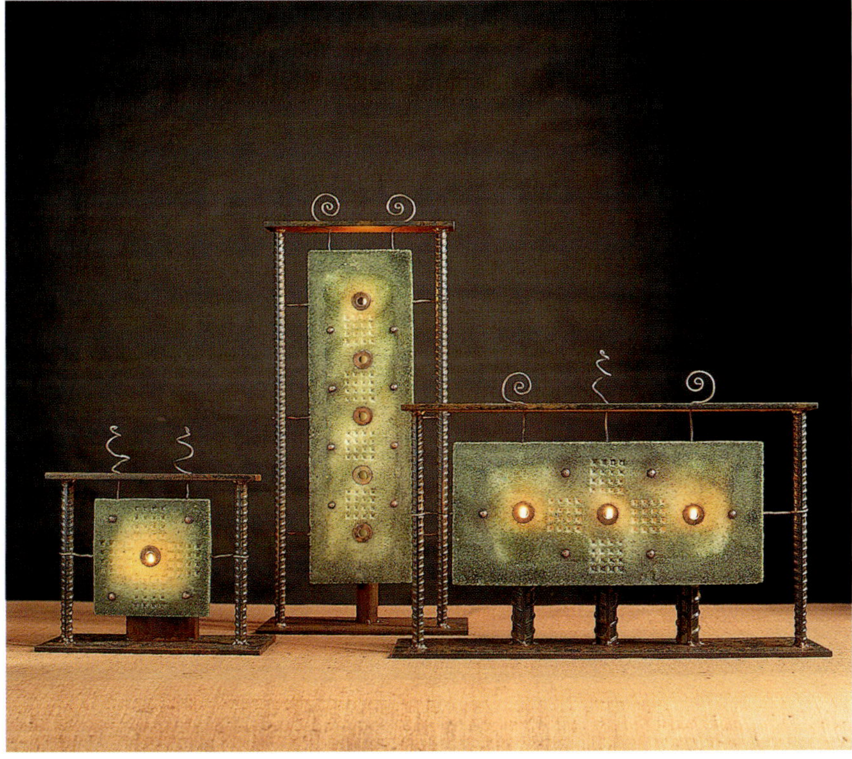

David M. Bowman Studio
David M. Bowman

David Bowman has been working with metal for more than 20 years, developing his own idiosyncratic construction method for hollowware and wall pieces. His work is fabricated from brass sheet. Some pieces are etched to provide more surface interest and all are colored using sculptural patina processes.

Also see this GUILD publication:
The Designer's Reference: 8

SHOWN: patinaed brass vase

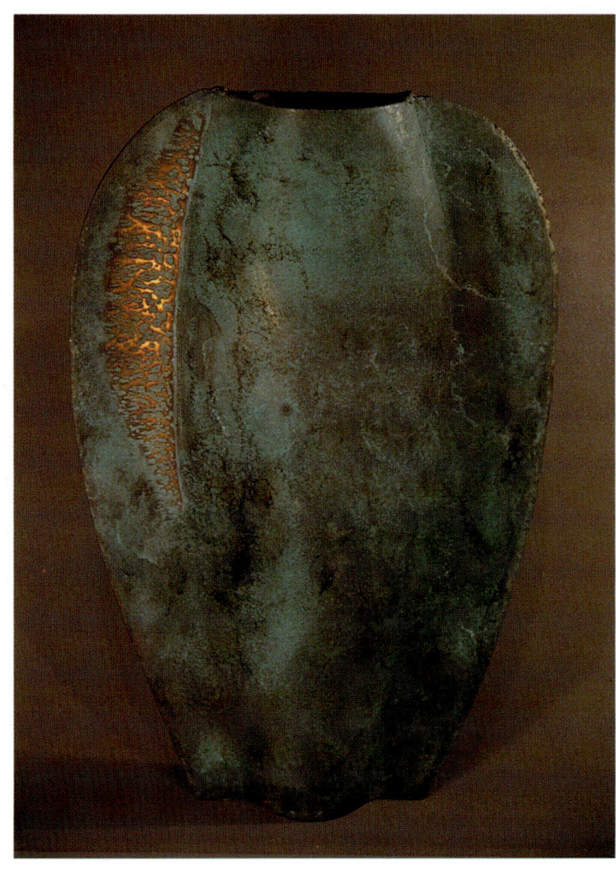

BRM Design
Bruce R. MacDonald

Bruce R. MacDonald has been creating metal artifacts from jewelry to architecture for 14 years. The studio is currently busy with tabletop functional sculpture—small furniture for the home. Our work is globally represented. Enjoy.

SHOWN: *Andromeda* spice machine, *Helios* sugar bowl, *Molly* creamer, *Orbs* salt and peppers, 1994, metal , glass, wood, powder paint, 24K gold and chrome plate

John D. Goodman

H.C. Fine Metal Work

Holly E. Churchill

Holly Churchill has created modern, yet classic, sterling silver flatware pieces with a variety of unique finial ends from which to choose. She has been a metalsmith since 1987 and has recently come up with her own innovative line of sterling flatware. She did this by marrying a background of jewelry designing and a knowledge of antique sterling silver restoration.

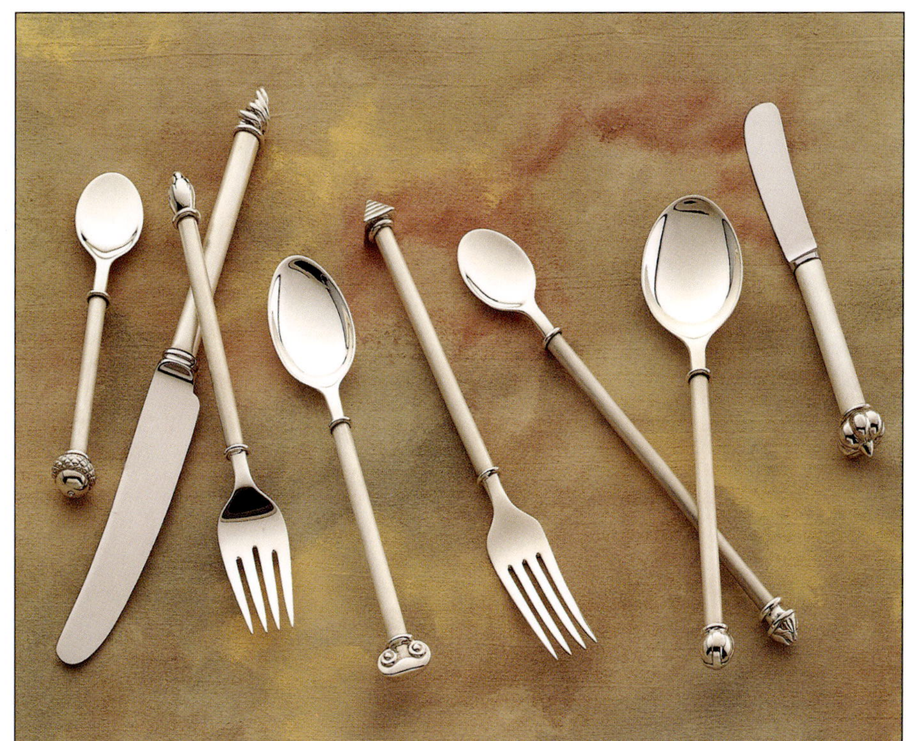

Kevin Brusie, Portland, ME

Jayne Redman

Jayne Redman Jewelry

Jayne Redman's work invites touch. Her jewelry and tabletop items are inspired by natural forms rich in surface and contour. Jayne fabricates her pieces in gold and silver, using time-honored techniques such as chasing and repoussé. She carves each stone by hand to perfectly integrate every element of her one-of-a-kind designs.

SHOWN: *Pink Knot #3*, 1994, scent bottle, sterling, rose quartz, 3¼" × 2"

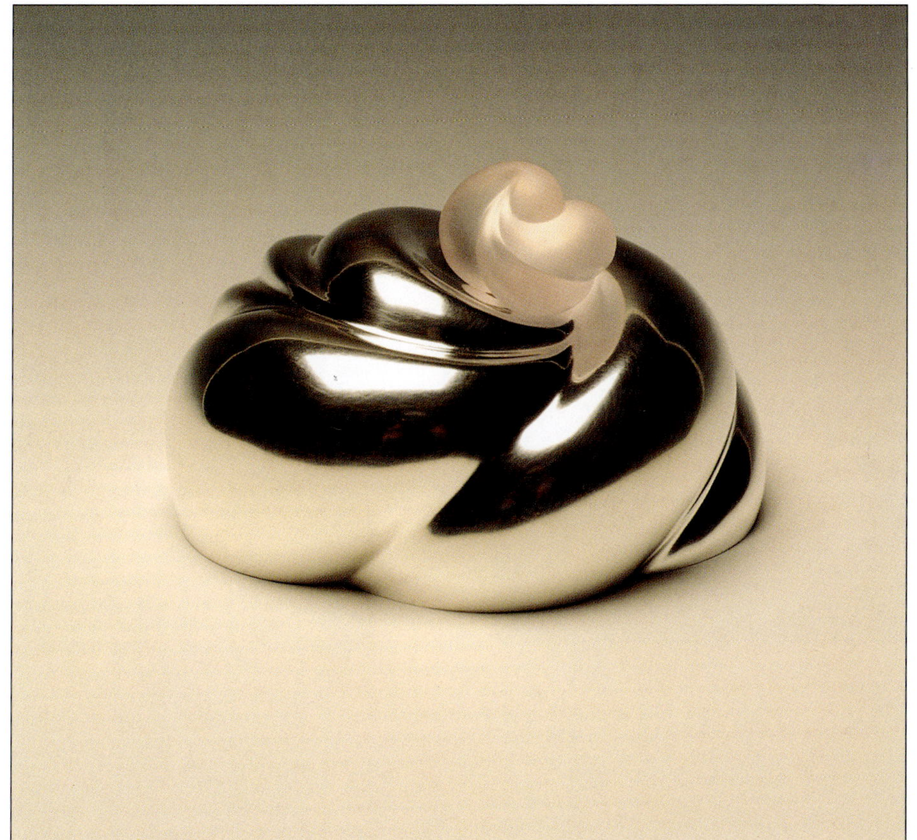

Jim Daniels

Ram's Head Forge
Lance Cloutier

Forged iron candleholders, fireplace equipment, tables, garden accessories and custom work.

Design influences range from clean Shaker images to strong Asian forms.

"The challenge has always been to take a raw piece of iron and shape it into something warm and appealing. After 25 years, I still forge simply because I enjoy it."

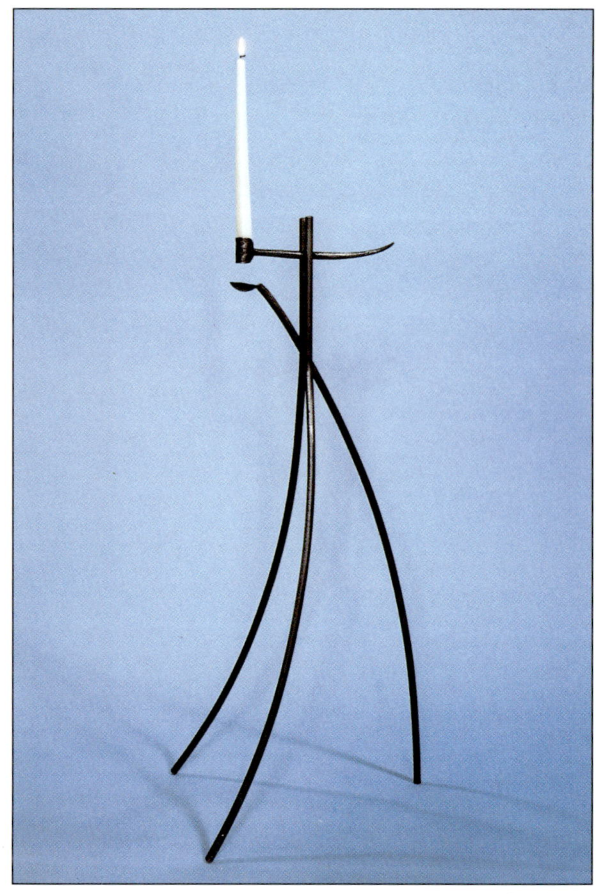

Dan Buikema

Jack Brubaker
Jack Brubaker Designs

Jack is best known for his production series of forged candleholders. He also designs sculpture and sundials for the garden, and furniture and door hardware for the home. Brubaker frequently lectures and demonstrates in both the U.S. and Europe. His work continues to be a proven best seller.

Also see these GUILD publications:
The Gallery & Retail Edition: 1
THE GUILD: 1, 2

SHOWN: pair of small classic singles, approx. 11"H, black steel, other sizes and styles available

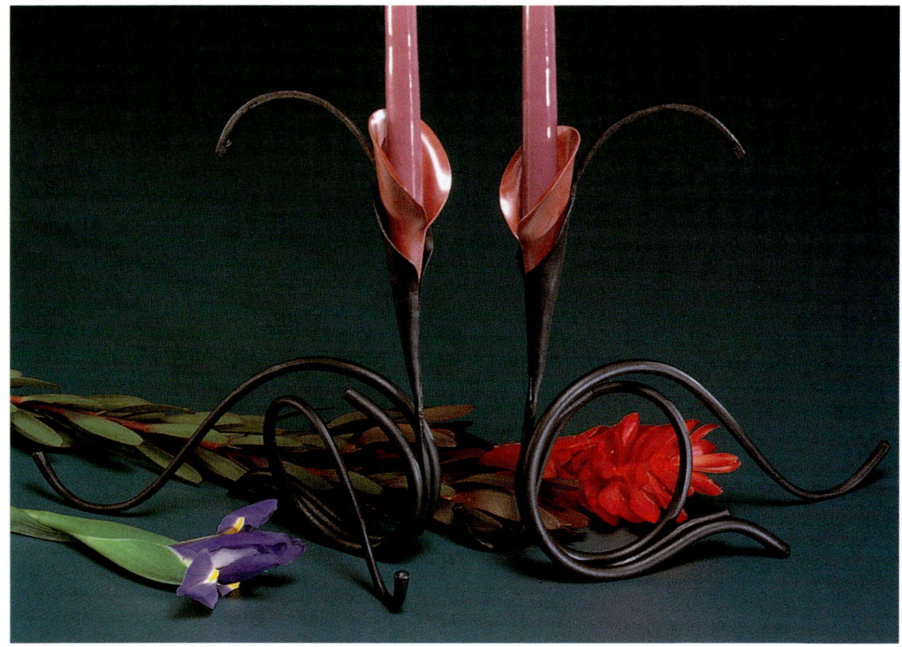

Christopher Thomson
Christopher Thomson Ironworks

Christopher Thomson designs and hand forges accessories and furniture in his unique style for residential and commercial interiors. Many famous athletes, movie stars, producers, writers, and national and international corporations have chosen his ironworks for their custom homes and corporate offices. His enduring designs, executed with ultra-high-quality craftsmanship during building and finishing, ensure a client's investment.

Also see these GUILD publications:
The Designer's Reference: 8, 9

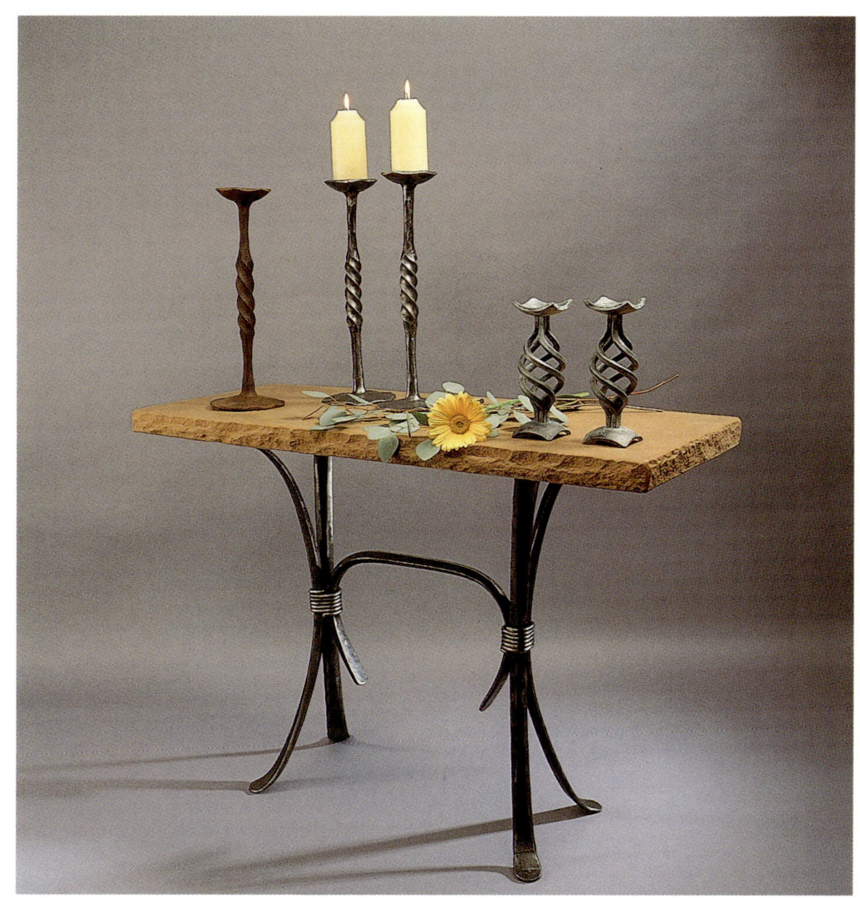

Herb Lotz

AMERICAN CRAFT

**AMERICAN CRAFT COUNCIL
72 SPRING ST
NEW YORK, NY 10012-4019
FAX 212-274-0650
TEL 212-274-0630
$40/year**

American Craft, a bimonthly magazine, focuses on contemporary craft through artist profiles, reviews of major shows, a portfolio of emerging artists, a national calendar and news section, book reviews, as well as illustrated columns reporting on commissions, acquisitions and exhibitions.

Roux Roux

Steve and Anita Vaubel, jewelry designers, have created Roux Roux, a line of products including drawer pulls, corkscrews, bottle stoppers, coat racks, mirror frames and metal containers. All figures have threaded brass sleeves for a secure fit.

Figures are offered in a variety of sizes with 80 different designs available. Will create custom work based on client's theme.

Catalog available.

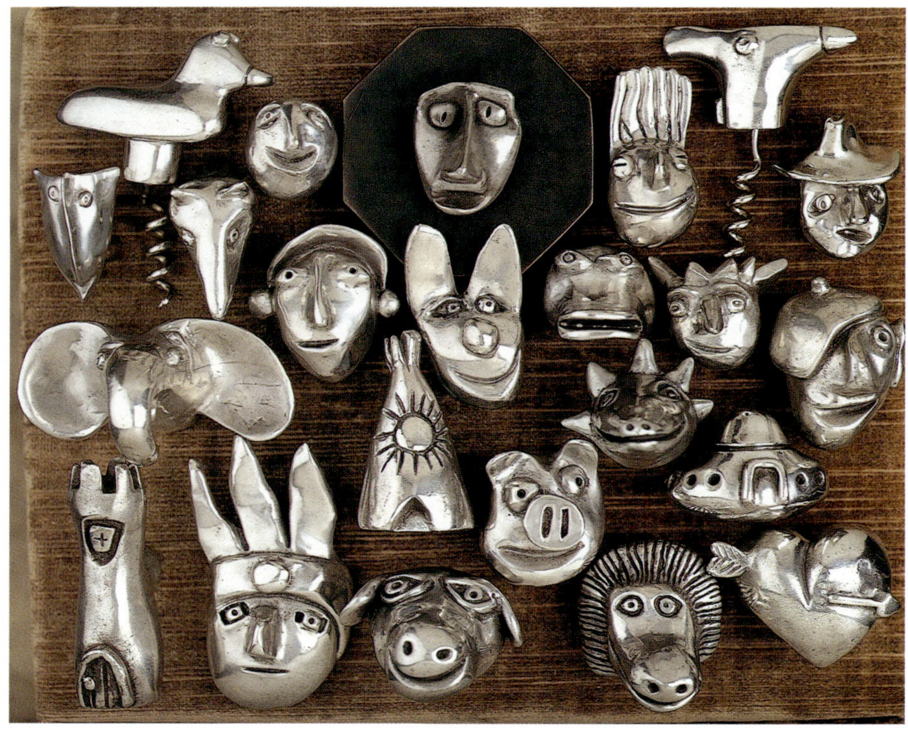

Shatsby Bronze
Chris and Pat Shatsby

Chris and Pat Shatsby have been producing cast bronze sculptural vessels for the past 12 years. Their beautifully crafted and patinated bronzes are in numerous major corporate collections and in private collections worldwide. Shatsby Bronze accepts commissions for both large and small sculpture.

The door knockers shown are a sample of designs available for your special location.

Also see these GUILD publications:
THE GUILD: 2, 3

Jerry Anthony

Don Drumm
Don Drumm Studios, Inc.

Internationally known as a pioneer in the use of cast aluminum as an artistic medium, Don Drumm has created a collection so extensive that it includes everything from jewelry and cookware to one-of-a-kind sculpture and furniture.

Drumm has also begun to explore the contemporary artistic potential of pewter. The pewter collection now includes jewelry, mirrors, boxes, candleholders, and sculpture, as well as Christian and Judaica art.

Aluminum and pewter catalogs available.

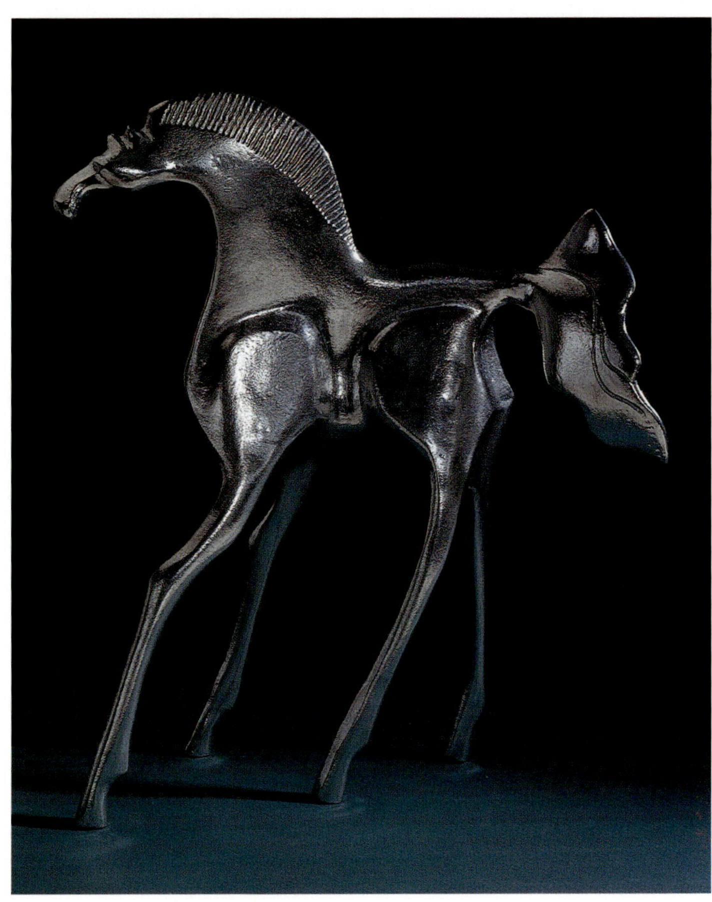

Gene Olson
The Mettle Works

Gene Olson works with cast, fabricated and woven metal, and carved stone. His works may be found from Florida to Japan. Some are wall mounted, while others are free standing or hung draped through space.

In over 25 years as an artist, Olson has created building facades, fountains, light fixtures, and stage sets, often working closely with designers, architects, and public agencies. He currently works from his studio just northwest of the Twin Cities.

Also see these GUILD publications:
THE GUILD: 1, 2, 3, 4, 5
The Architect's Source: 6, 7

SHOWN: metal assemblage, wall mounted, 72" x 46" x 5"

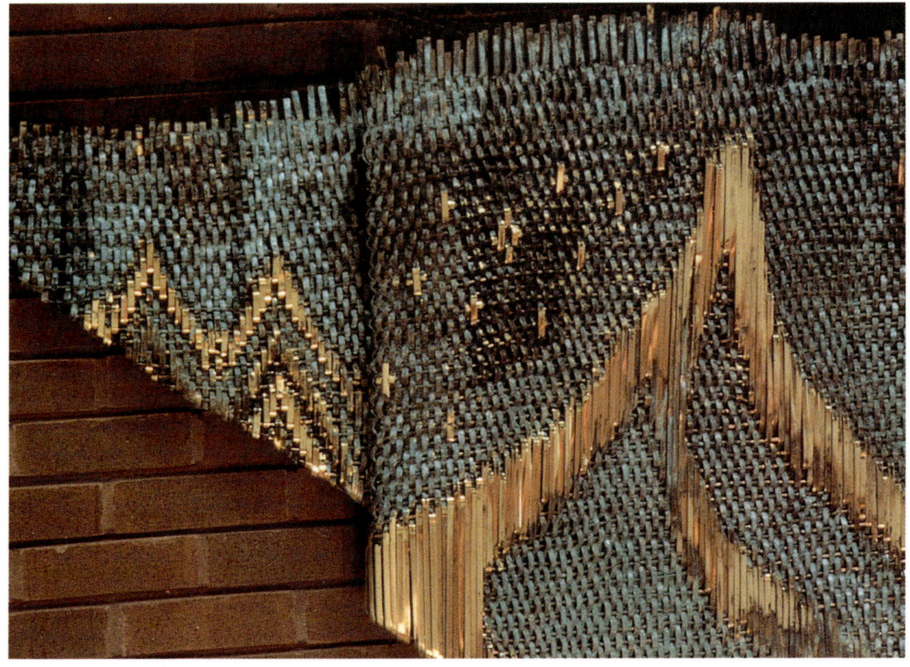

wood wood wood wood wood wo

d wood wood wood w*o*od w*o*od 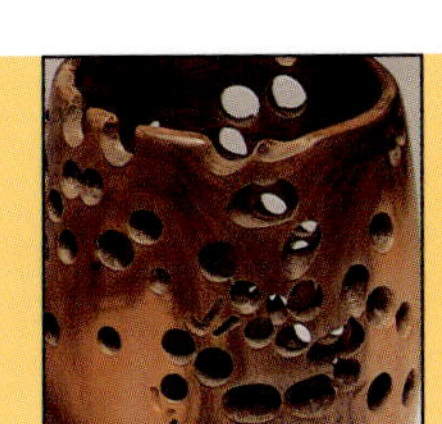

Karl Sacksteder
Kris Sacksteder
Weird Woods

The Sacksteder brothers have sculpted wood for 14 years, perfecting the art of bandsaw boxes. They have incorporated compound curves into highly figured wood to create unique river rock shapes. The fine sanding and hand-rubbed oil and wax finish make you want to caress them. Each object is carved from a single piece of wood. Karl and Kris' work has been shown and won awards in art shows nationally.

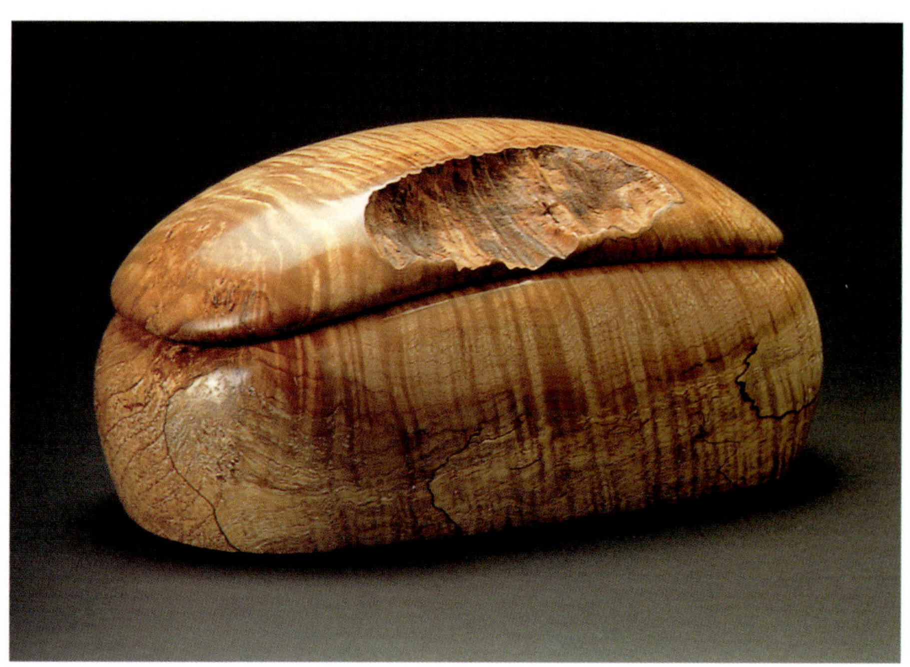

FINE WOODWORKING

TAUNTON PRESS INC.
PO BOX 5506
NEWTOWN, CT 06470-5506
FAX 203-426-3434
TEL 203-426-8171
$29/year

Fine Woodworking is a bimonthly magazine for all those who strive for and appreciate excellence in woodworking—veteran professional and weekend hobbyist alike. Articles by skilled woodworkers focus on basics of tool use, stock preparation and joinery, as well as specialized techniques and finishing.

Judy Ditmer

Judy Ditmer has been turning wood full-time for eight years. Her handsome salad bowls express her concern with function, form and detail. They have a food-safe finish and are meant to be used.

Ditmer's sculptural bowls are part of a continuing exploration of the idea of a bowl and of the turning process. They are sprayed with clear lacquer for a durable finish.

Ditmer's work is sold in galleries across the U.S., in Europe and in Japan. It is included in many private collections. Her book, *Basic Bowl Turning*, has just been published by Schiffer Publishing, Ltd.

A   salad bowl, 1993, lathe-turned cherry, 6½"H x 9"Dia

B   sculptural bowl, 1994, lathe-turned jarrah burl, 6"H x 9"W x 10"D

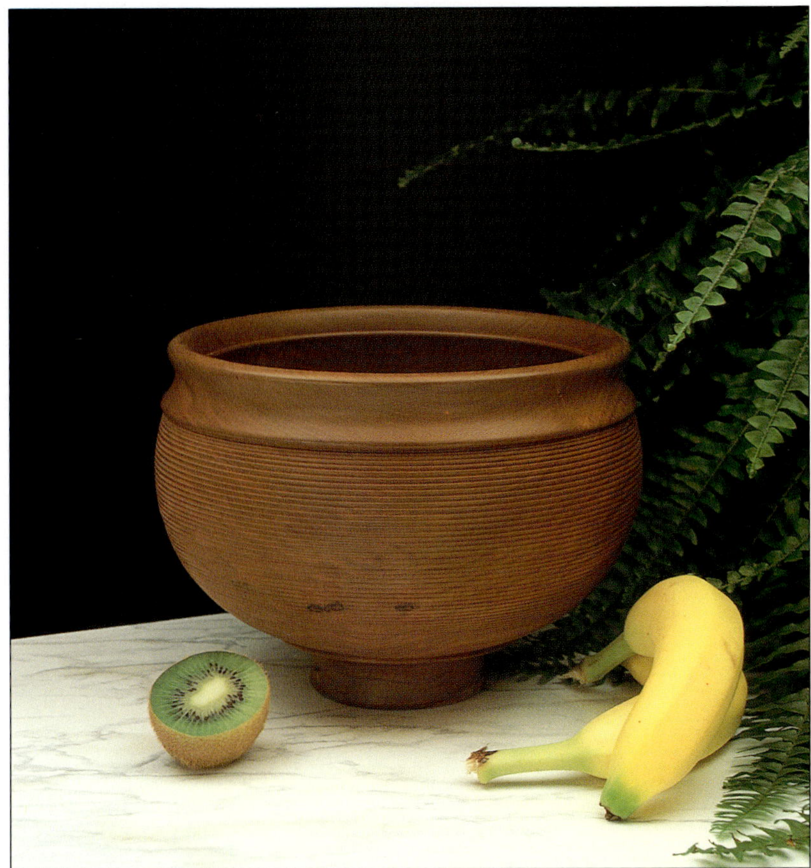

A

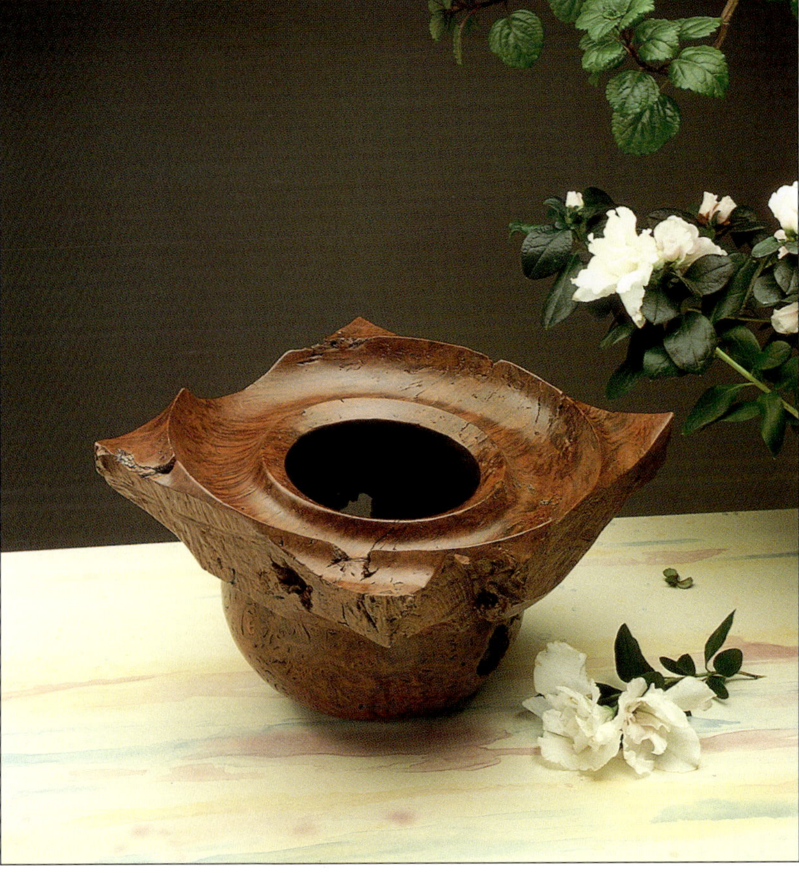

B

Bruce Hoskins

Bruce Hoskins uses many species of beautifully figured wood to lathe turn unique and aesthetically pleasing one-of-a-kind art forms.

Bruce has worked with wood for most of his life and has been turning since 1985. He is a charter member of the American Association of Wood Turners, the International Wood Collectors Society and other related organizations.

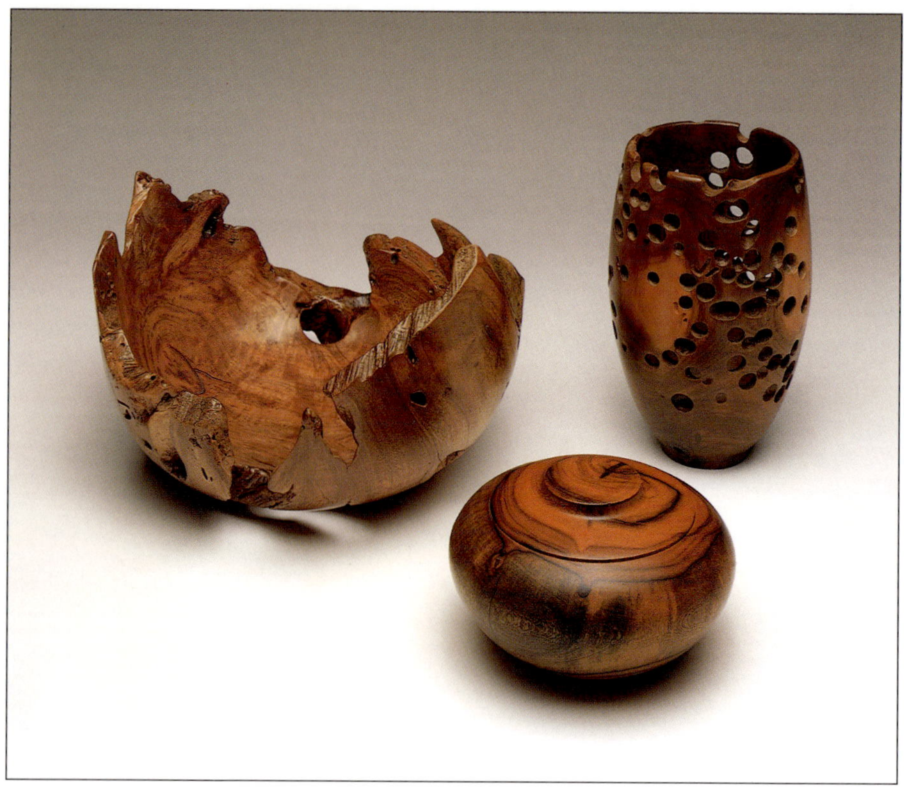

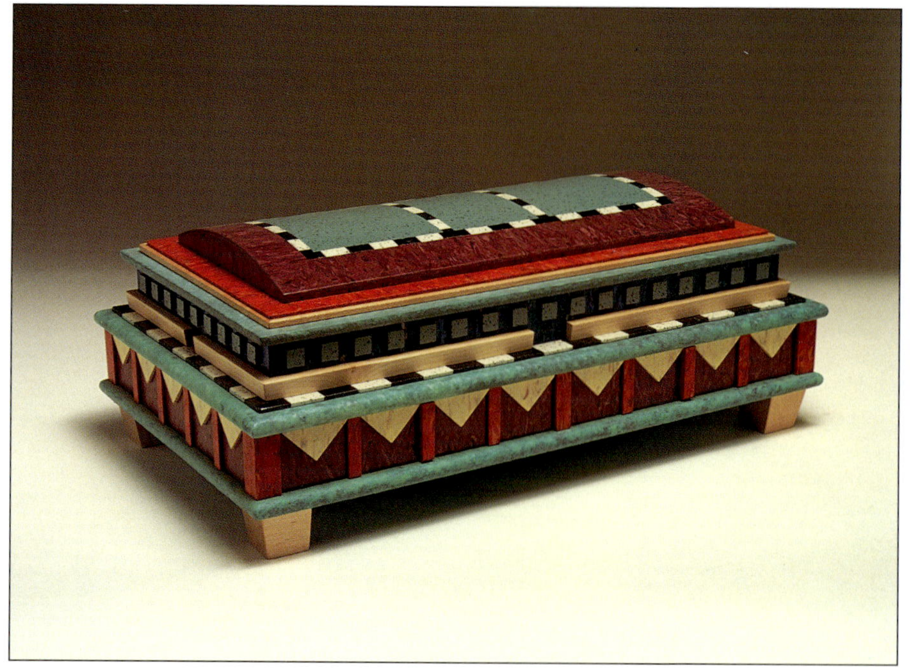

Marc Coan
Marc Coan Designs

Marc's *Temple Boxes* developed from a long-term fascination with architecture. His unusual use of natural and painted woods decorated with vinyl composition tile has allowed him to create colorful, dramatic pieces. The jewelry box shown is available in a variety of sizes and designs. It has a hinged lid with divided compartments and two concealed drawers in the base, and measures 12" x 20" x 8".

Artistry in Wood
John W. Clem

Wanting to create more than fancy wood turnings, the artist has collected colorful woods, many rare and exotic, used in various designs, some taken from Native American blankets, baskets and pottery.

No colored stains or dyes are used, only woods in their natural colors.

Many pieces are enhanced by the addition of native soapstones.

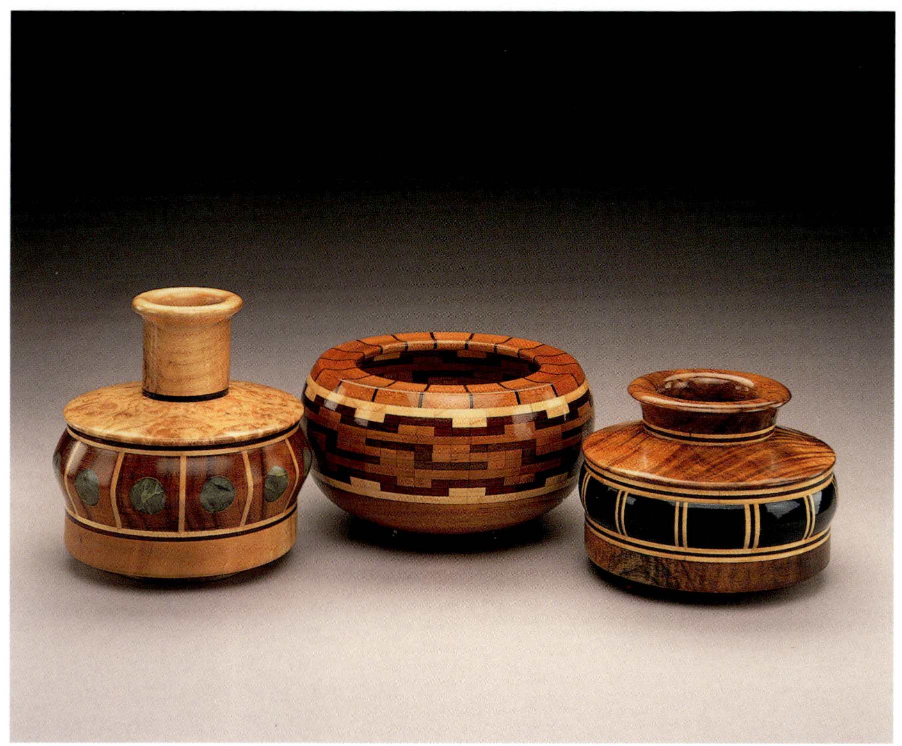

©1994 Wally Hampton

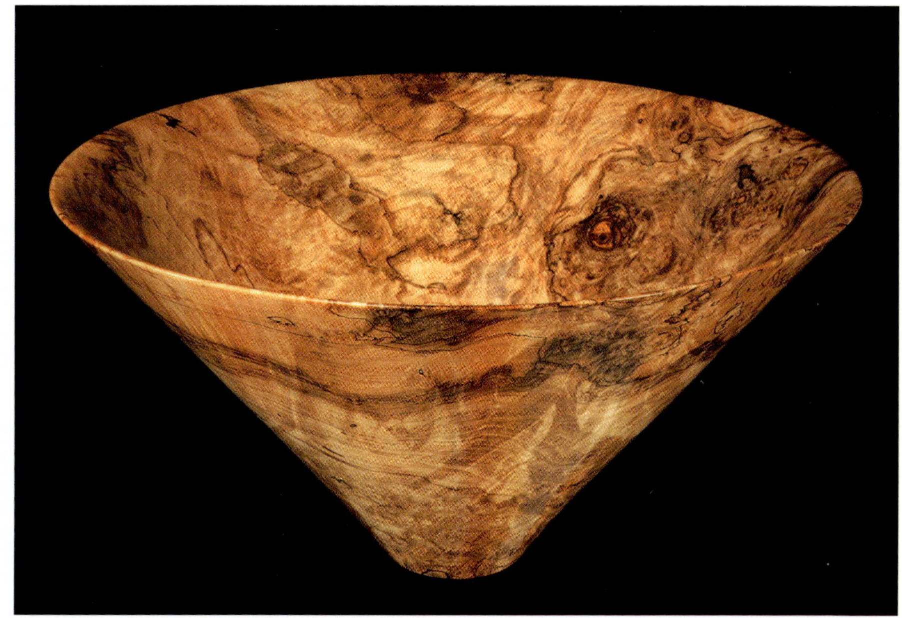

Phil F. Brown
Fine Turned Wood

Phil creates accessory vessels and durable bowls from burls and solid wood. He turns big leaf maple burl, koa, maples, apple, cherry and other eastern U.S. woods and burls.

A sensuous vessel reveals the inner beauty of a once-majestic living tree.

Also see this GUILD publication:
The Gallery & Retail Edition: 1

SHOWN: spalted maple burl vessel, 6¾" × 12⅛", base: 2⅜"

Ginny's Ear•Nest™
Ginny Bass

In 1986, frustrated by the jumbled mess on her dresser, Ginny Bass created a wall-hanging earring holder. That holder has evolved into Ginny's Ear•Nest™.

These unique, patented wooden earring holders, allow you to turn your earrings into a beautiful wall-mounted or dresser-top personal art piece.

Racks are beautifully handcrafted in golden oak or other woods and come in a wide variety of sizes.

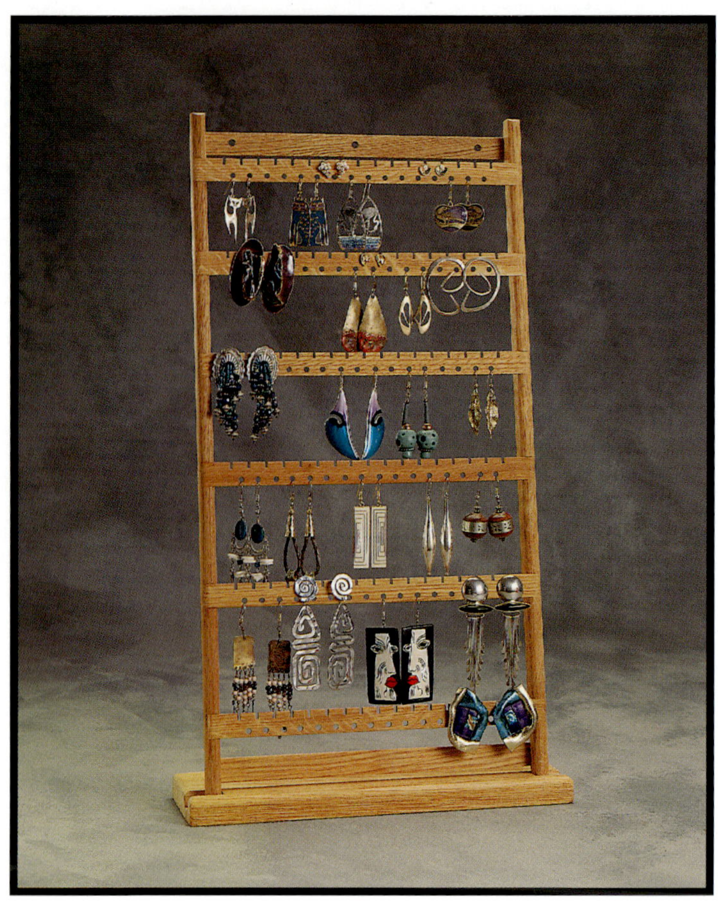

WOODSHOP NEWS

SOUNDINGS PUBLICATIONS, INC.
PRATT ST
ESSEX, CT 06426
FAX 203-767-1048
TEL 203-767-8227
$14.97/year

Woodshop News**, published monthly, includes features and descriptions about new technology, artists and their techniques, trade news and source information.**

Jeffrey Cooper

To stay enthused as a woodworker, Jeffrey
Cooper makes things that are more than
commodities, that are exciting and unique.
His children's chairs, as shown, are popular
in private homes and especially in children's
healthcare facilities. Not only that, Jeffrey
Cooper will create commissioned work for
all sorts of projects calling for wood sculpture, not too literal, somewhat naif.

Also see these GUILD publications:
THE GUILD: 5
The Designer's Reference: 6, 7, 8, 9

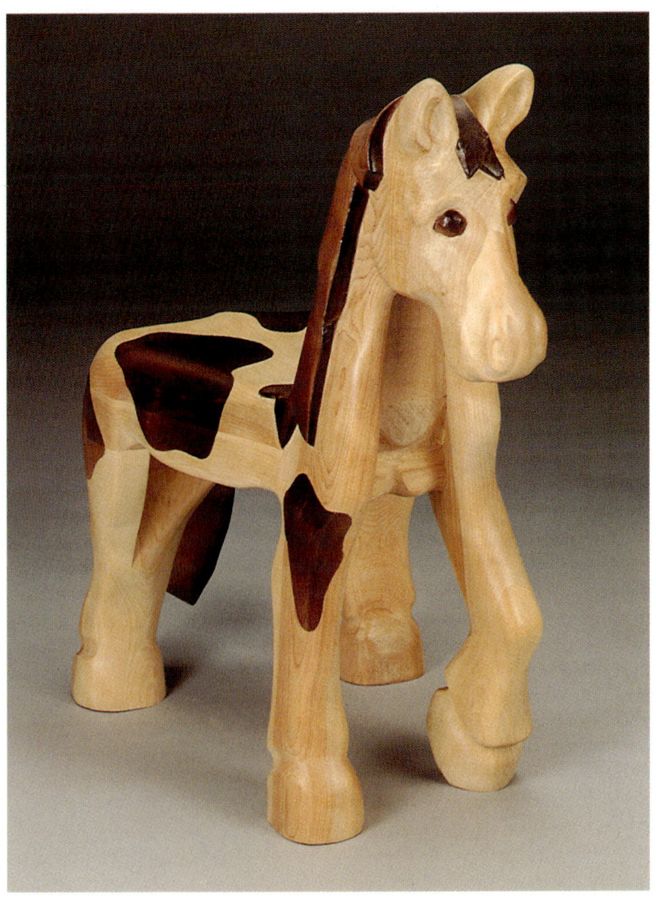

Michael Bauermeister

Trained as a sculptor, Michael Bauermeister
has been designing and building original
furniture and cabinetry for over 15 years.
The carved bowl series, which began three
years ago, allows freedom of form, texture
and scale. The bowls are surprisingly light.
No tropical hardwoods are used.

SHOWN: #26, 1994, carved, laminated cherry
with patina, 12"H x 14"W

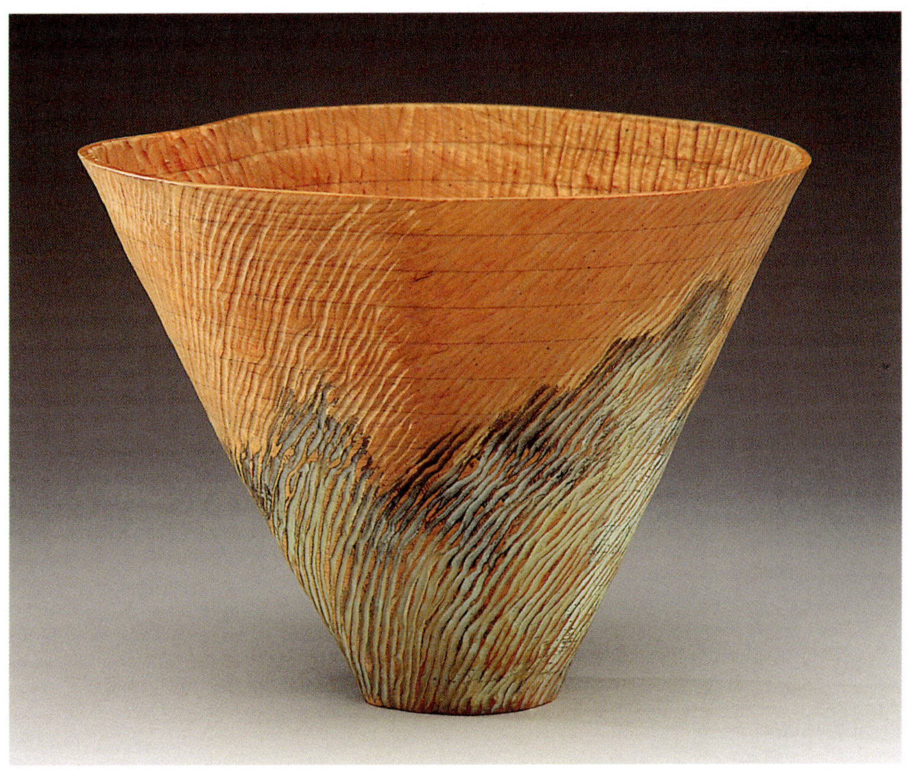

John Phelan, St. Louis, MO

furniture & lighting furniture &

furniture & lighting

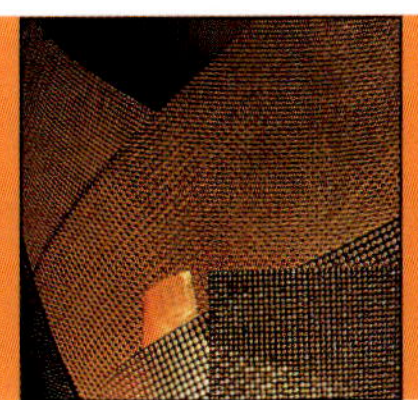

Cole Studios
Jeff Cole/Lauren Cole

Trompe l'oeil (fool the eye) furniture and accessories by Jeff and Lauren Cole reflect their fascination with fine detail and illusion of reality. Heirloom-quality boxes, tables, cabinets and clock towers (as shown) are handcrafted with domestic woods, painted, and protected with durable, easily cleaned polyurethane.

The Cole's work is represented by more than 80 galleries and featured in catalogs such as Neiman Marcus, Plummer McCutcheon, and Levenger.

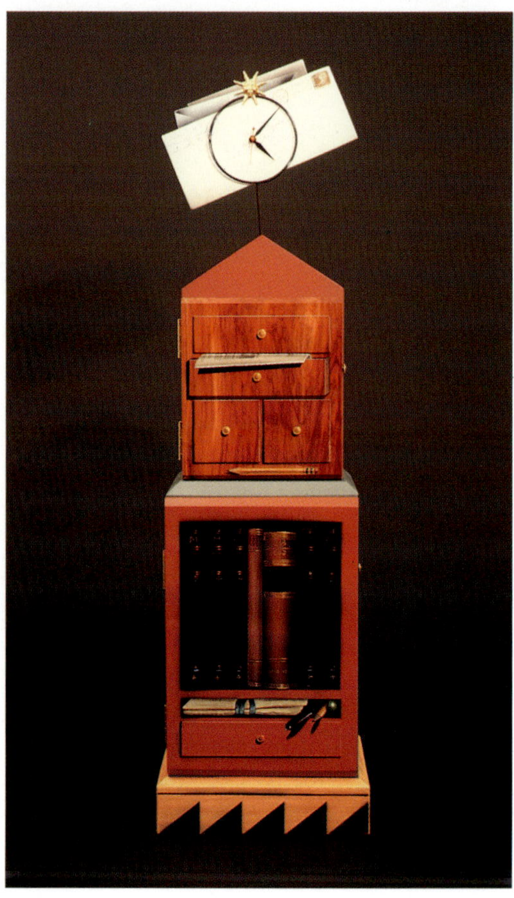

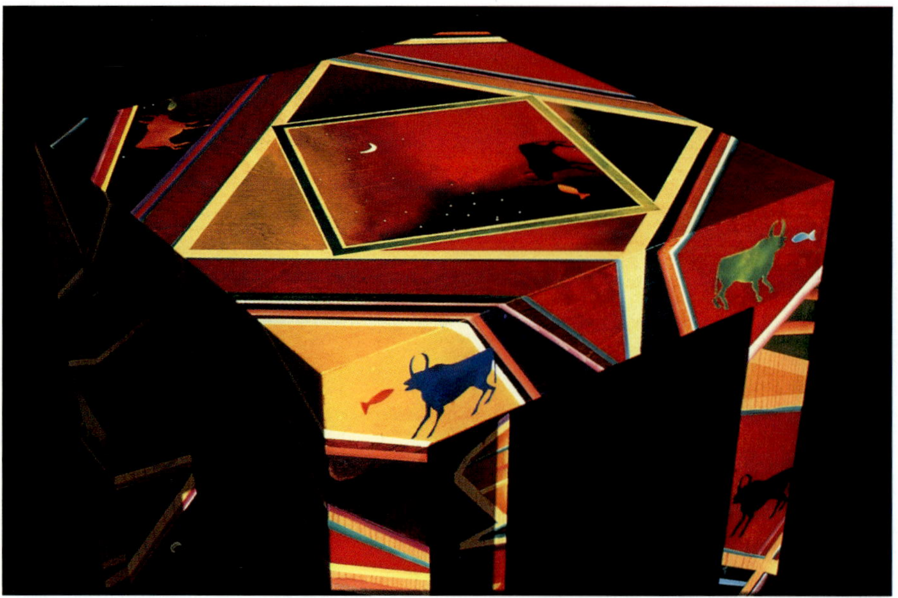

Shirley Novella Post Cox

The vibrant tables by surface designer Shirley Cox are covered with cultural patterns and symbols. Bright stains maintain the wood grain and opaque paints add contrasting accents. The tables, which are designed and constructed by the artist, are functional, protected with multilayers of durable finish. Cox has exhibited in galleries and regional and national shows for over 15 years.

SHOWN: *The Bull and the Fish* (top detail), 1993, 18" x 18" x 40"H

Charlie H. Thompson
Functional Sculpture

Charlie Thompson's 19 years of design and craftsmanship skills are obviously reflected by his sensuous designs and exquisite finish. Successful designs must create an emotional impact on the observer and an almost uncontrollable urge to touch.

Permanent exhibits include South Carolina Arts Commission and South Carolina's Governor's Office. Thompson is an exhibiting member of the American Craft Council.

Commissions accepted.

A *George*, dresser, MDF, birch, urethane, 42"H x 81"W x 16"D

B *Collection Amantes: I, II, III*, boxes, MDF, lacquer, 16" x 7" x 3", collection is the life story of two lovers, consisting of 15 poses with 25 originals of each pose

C *Tillie*, chest of drawers, MDF, maple, urethane, 82"H x 27"W x 16"D, edition of 11

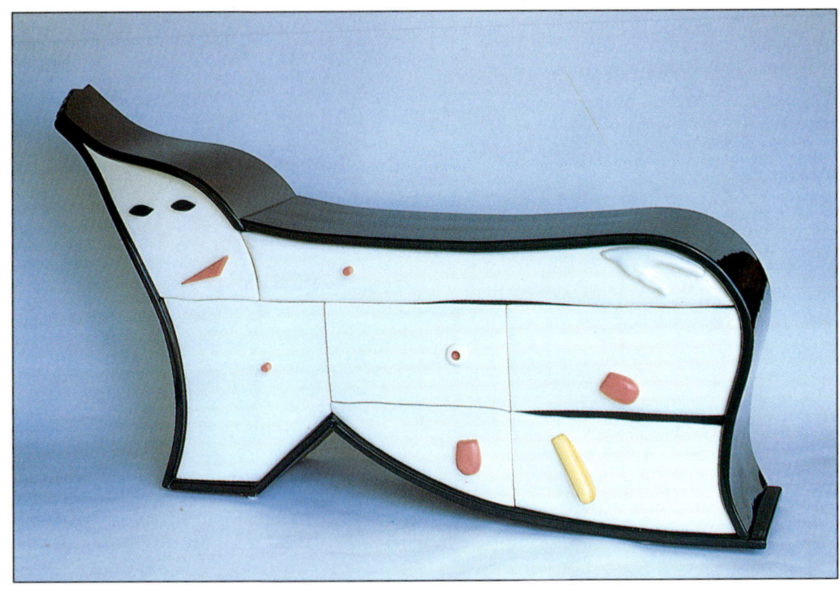

A

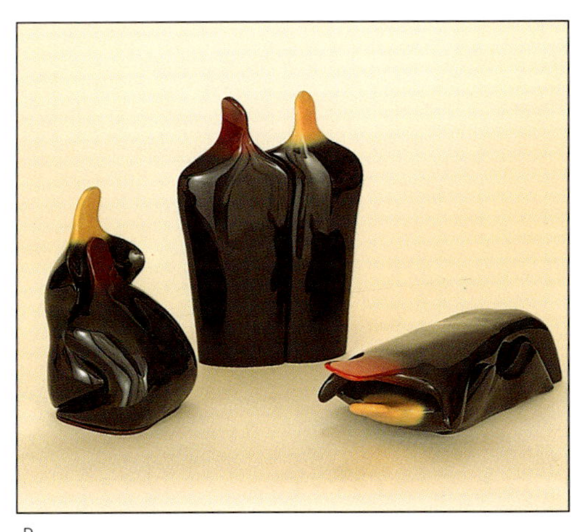

B

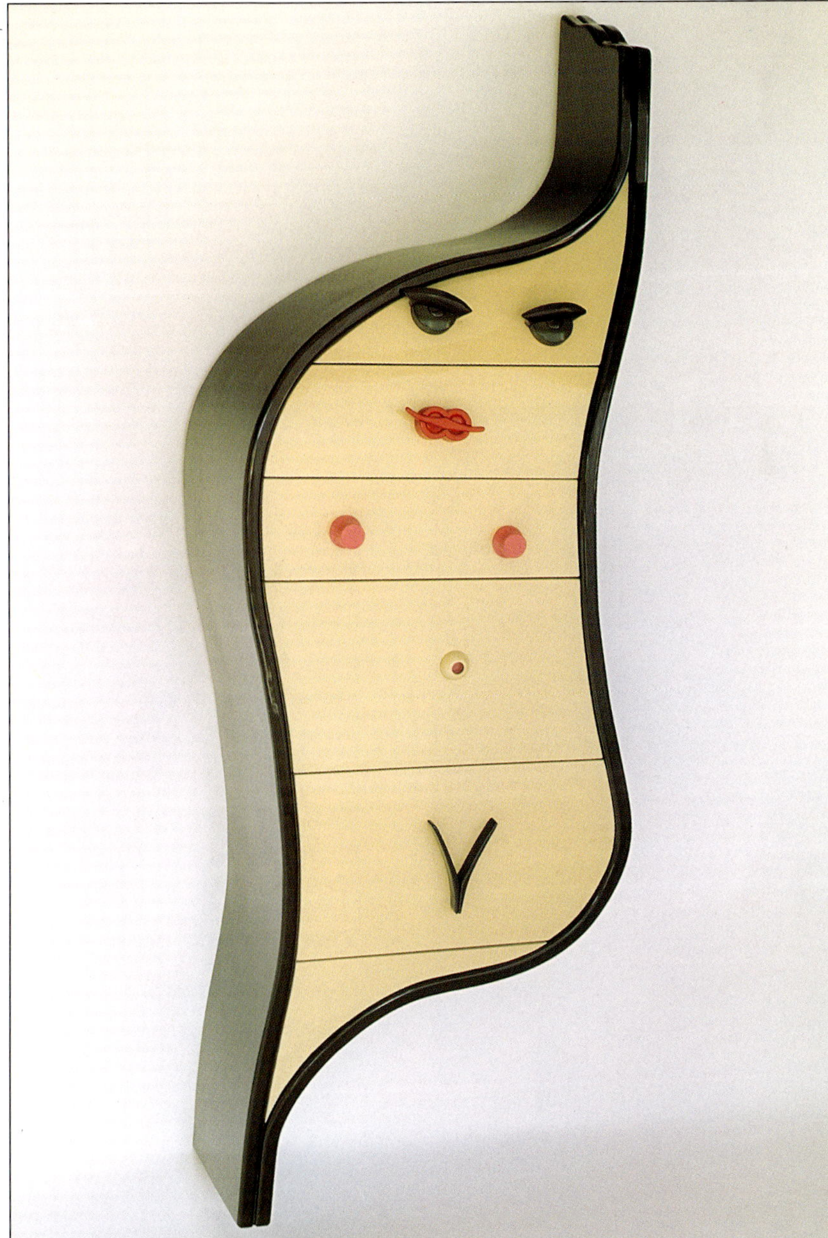

C

Warren Carther
Carther Studio Inc.

Mr. Carther has shown his work on three continents and is best known for his 20 × 22 foot sculptural glass wall located in the Canadian Embassy, Tokyo.

He pushes the material to the edge sculpturally, creating form and taking full advantage of the unique visual properties of glass. He is able to do so without compromising its functionality.

Also see these GUILD publications:
The Designer's Reference: 6
The Architect's Source: 7, 9, 10

SHOWN: *Pyramid and Sphere* table, 1991, glass, laminated with optically clear adhesives and abrasive blast carved, 96" × 40" × 30"

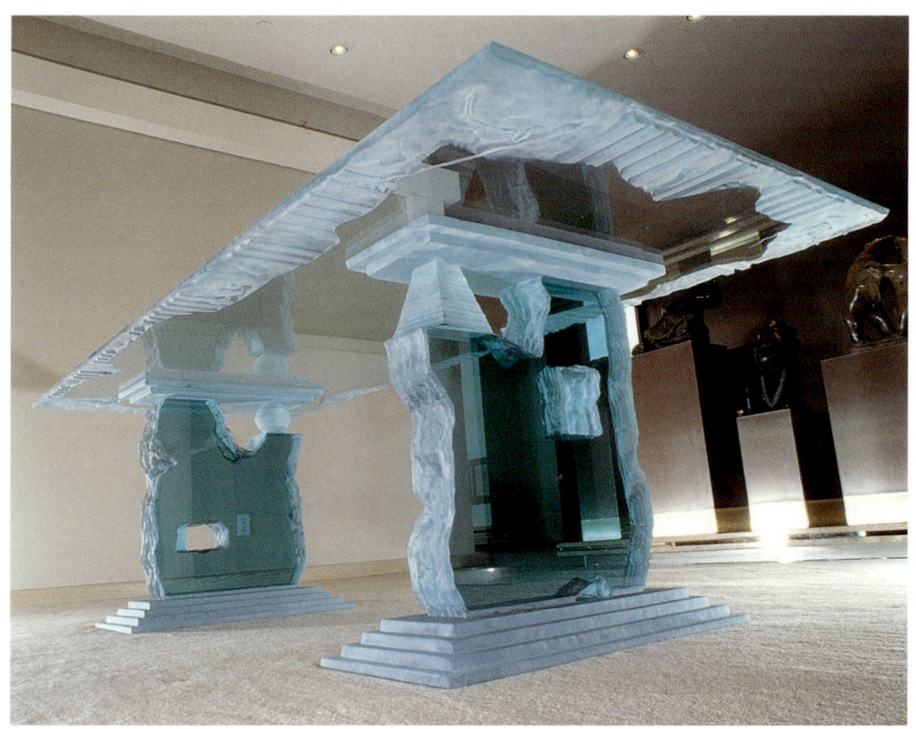

HOME FURNITURE
THE TAUNTON PRESS, INC.
63 S. MAIN ST
NEWTOWN, CT 06470-5506
FAX 203-426-3434
TEL 203-426-8171
TEL 800-888-8286
$20/year

This new, full-color quarterly is both a 'how-to' and a portfolio of top contemporary furniture-makers. Articles include illustrated design features and artist profiles.

Abby Morrison
Ace Woodwork

Unique burlwood vessels and furniture that accentuate the natural beauty of these organic forms have been Morrison's speciality for over 14 years. The sensuous curves are designed for comfort, with contoured seats and supportive backs.

With a strong background in traditional joinery, Morrison welcomes commissions and collaborations of a wide variety, particularly those that incorporate unusual and burled wood.

Also see these GUILD publications:
THE GUILD: 5
The Designer's Reference: 6, 9
The Architect's Source: 6

SHOWN: *Venus' Chair*, 1990, box elder burl, 39"H x 43"W

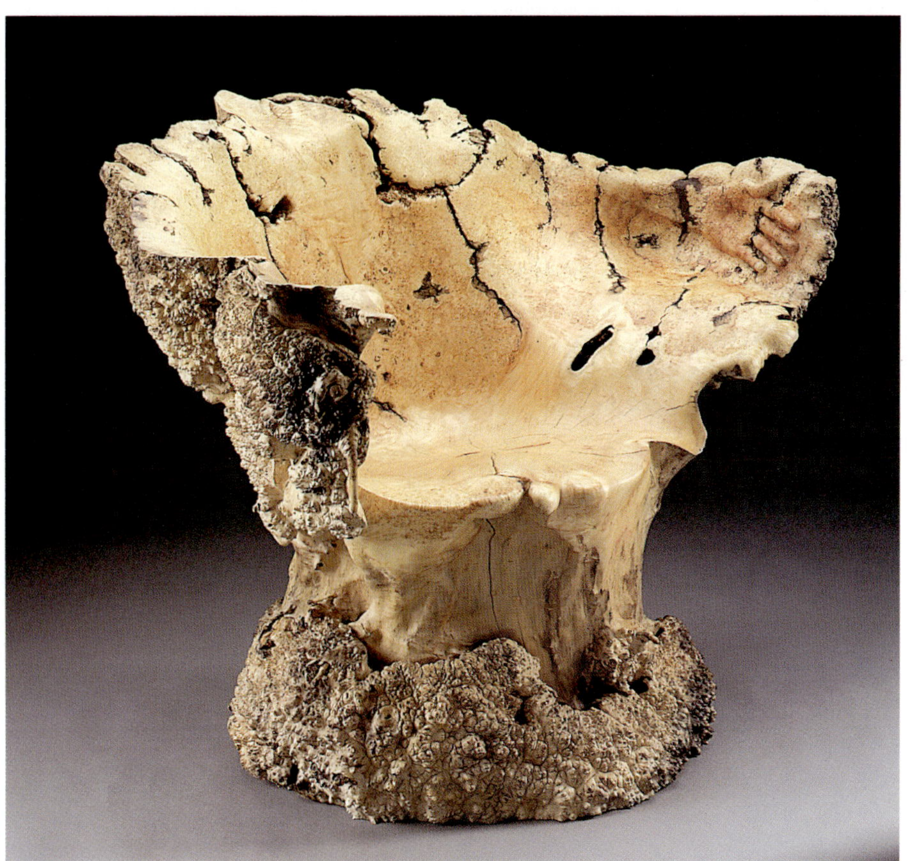

William Thuss

Craig Nutt

Well-known for his imaginative furniture and sculpture, which often employ vegetable motifs, Craig Nutt blends innovative design with impeccable craftsmanship.

Craig Nutt's work has appeared in many publications, including *American Craft*, *Fine Woodworking* and *Craft in America*. Public collections include the Birmingham Museum of Art, the High Museum of Art, and the Fine Arts Museum of the South.

Also see these GUILD publications:
THE GUILD: 1, 2, 3
The Architect's Source: 10

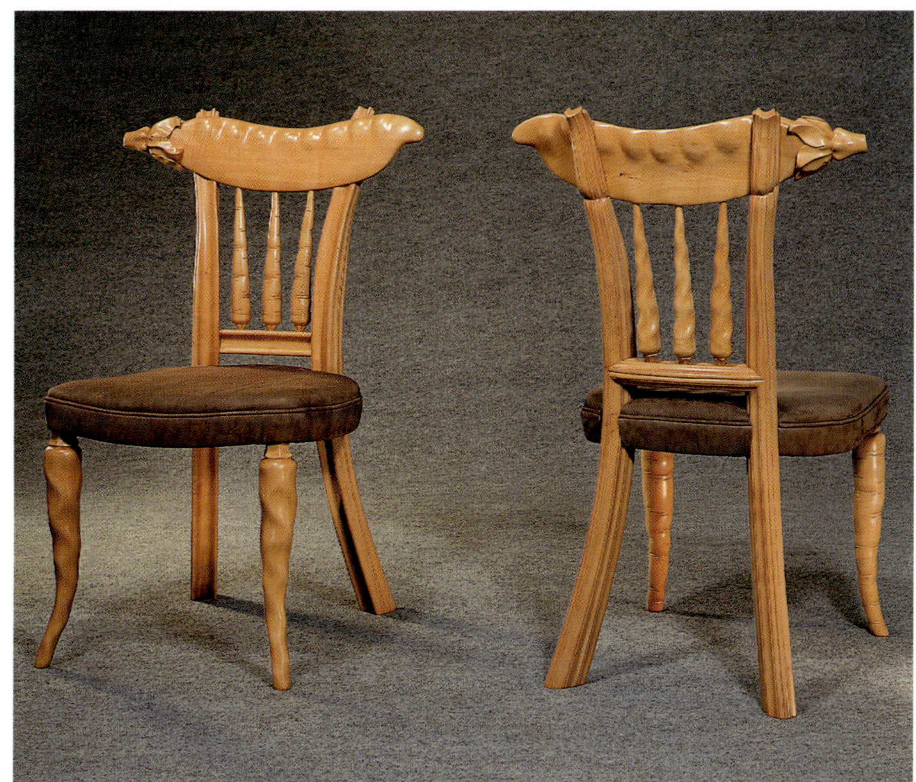

Celery Chairs With Peppers, Carrots, and Sno Peas, 1993, Swiss pear, leather, each 19" x 22" x 37"

Ron Diefenbacher
Ron Diefenbacher Designs

Diefenbacher's unique designs stress the individuality of each project and are displayed in private collections, executive offices, and galleries nationwide.

A designer and craftsman for over 15 years, Ron has a graduate degree in Furniture Design and teaches at Washington University.

Also see these GUILD publications:
THE GUILD: 5
The Designer's Reference: 6, 8

SHOWN: padauk dining/conference table, 84" × 42" × 29"

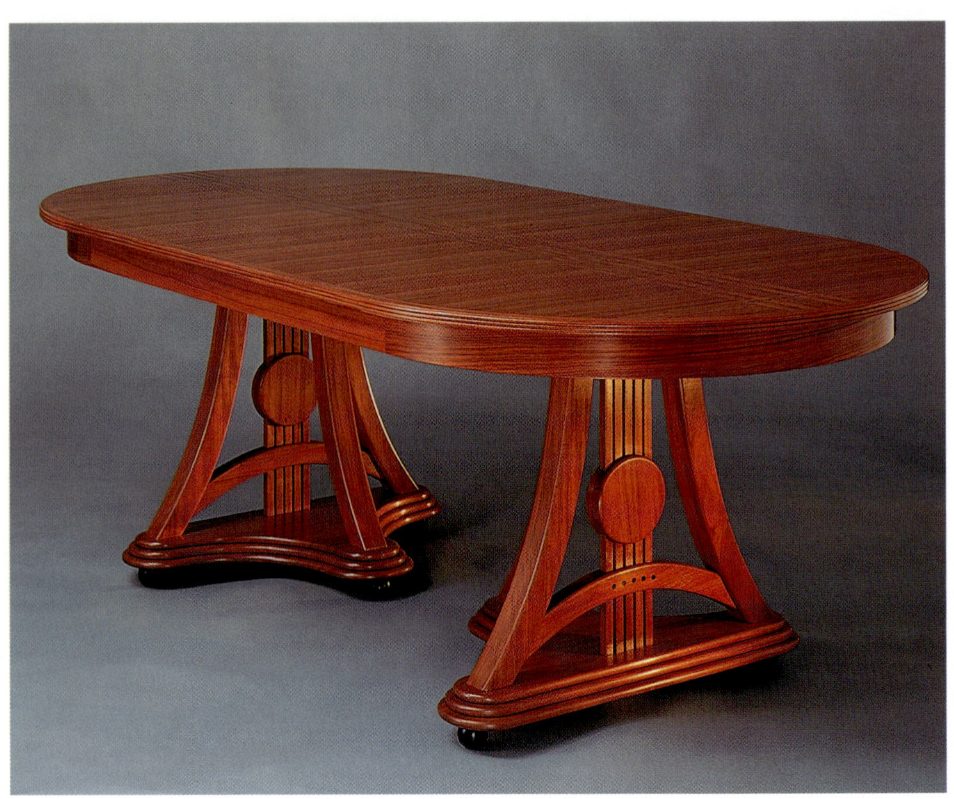

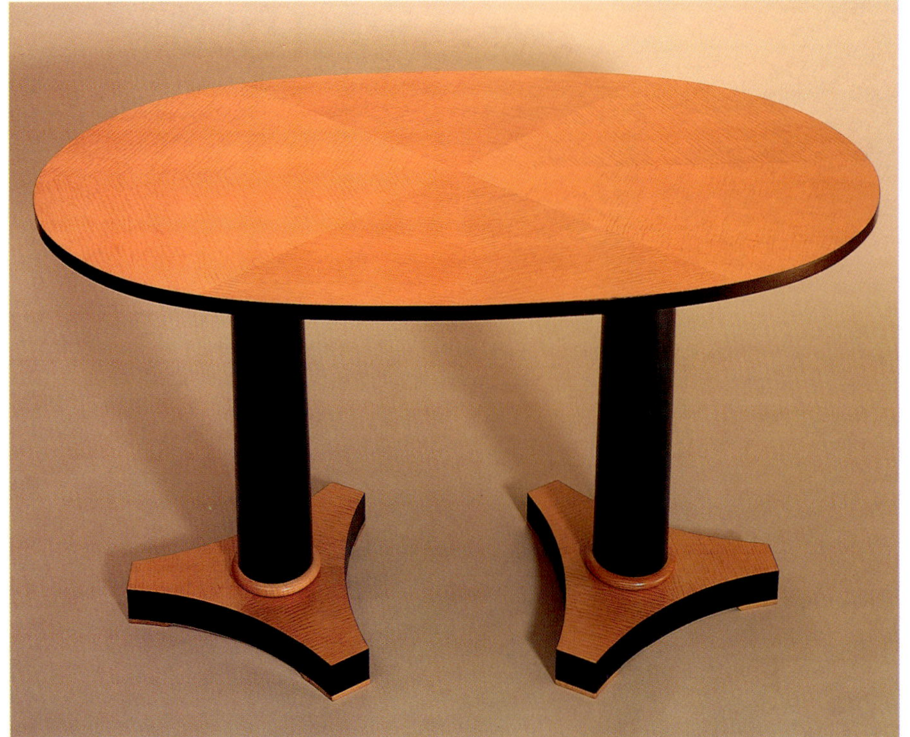

Occasional table in curly and ebonized maple

Richard Faughn

The Century Guild
Nick Strange

Since 1982, The Century Guild has specialized in making and designing one-of-a-kind or limited-edition furniture for residential, corporate and ecclesiastical settings. This extensive experience produces traditional and contemporary pieces distinguished by well-proportioned design, special materials and time-tested construction techniques. Additional information is available upon request.

Also see these GUILD publications:
THE GUILD: 5
The Designer's Reference: 6, 8

Peter Maynard
Maynard & Maynard Furnituremakers

For more than 20 years, Peter Maynard has designed and built classic fine furniture in both traditional and contemporary interpretations.

His work has been shown in *Architectural Digest* and *Interior Design* magazines. *Traditional Home* magazine featured Peter in an article titled "20th Century Masters: Five of the Country's Best Furnituremakers."

Also see these GUILD publications:
THE GUILD: 5
The Designer's Reference: 6, 8

SHOWN: Pembroke table in butternut and English dining chair in mahogany

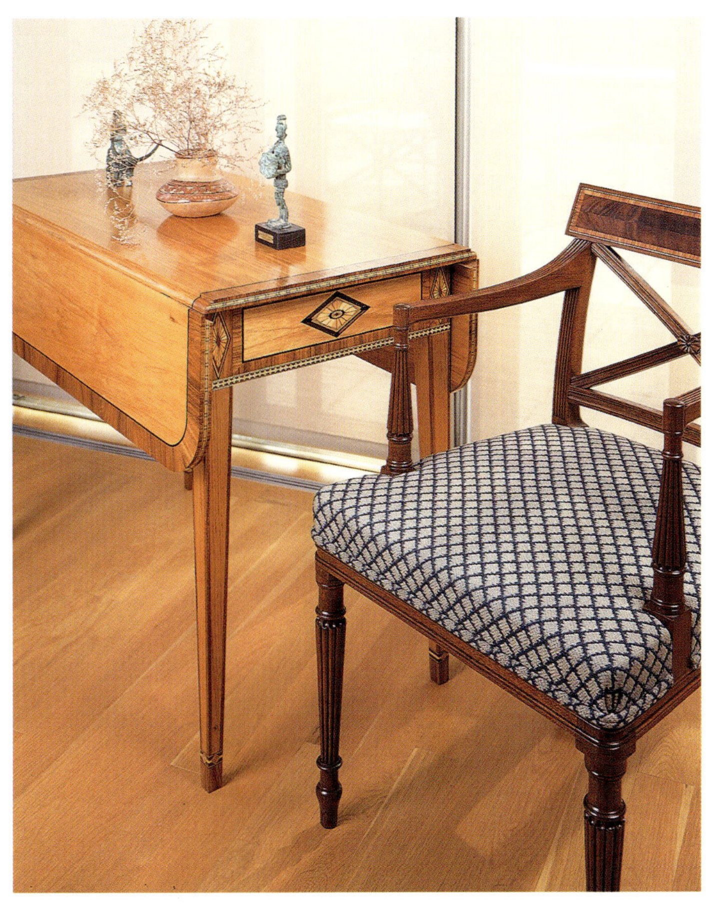

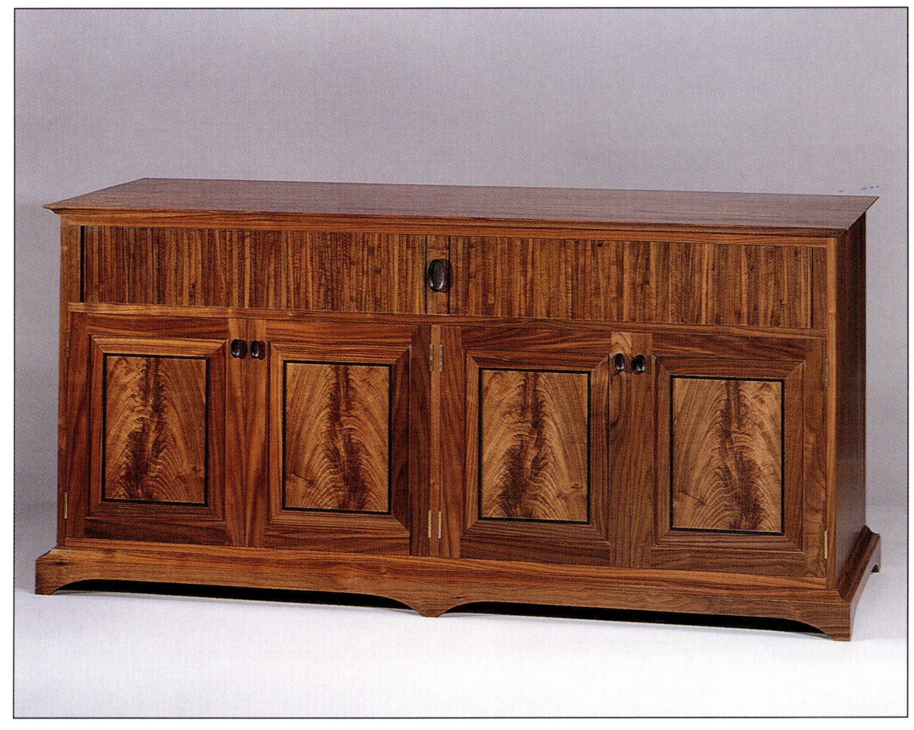

Wm. B. Sayre, Inc.
William Sayre

Fine commissioned furniture executed to the designs of specifying architect, interior designer, or residential customer.

Working in the finest hardwoods available, collaborating in a wide range of other media to produce heirlooms of distinction and innovation.

Full design services available. Complete production facilities.

Brochure available upon request.

Also see these GUILD publications:
THE GUILD: 5
The Designer's Reference: 6, 7

SHOWN: stereo cabinet, 1994, black walnut, 64¼" × 21½" × 30½"

John Dodd Studio

John Dodd has maintained a professional furniture design studio for the past 14 years. A graduate of the School for American Crafts, his work has been exhibited nationally in numerous museums and galleries.

Also see these GUILD publications:
THE GUILD: 1, 2, 5

SHOWN: table niche, a backdrop for a precious object, curved cherry panels with laminated curly ash slat, 84"H x 26"W x 19"D

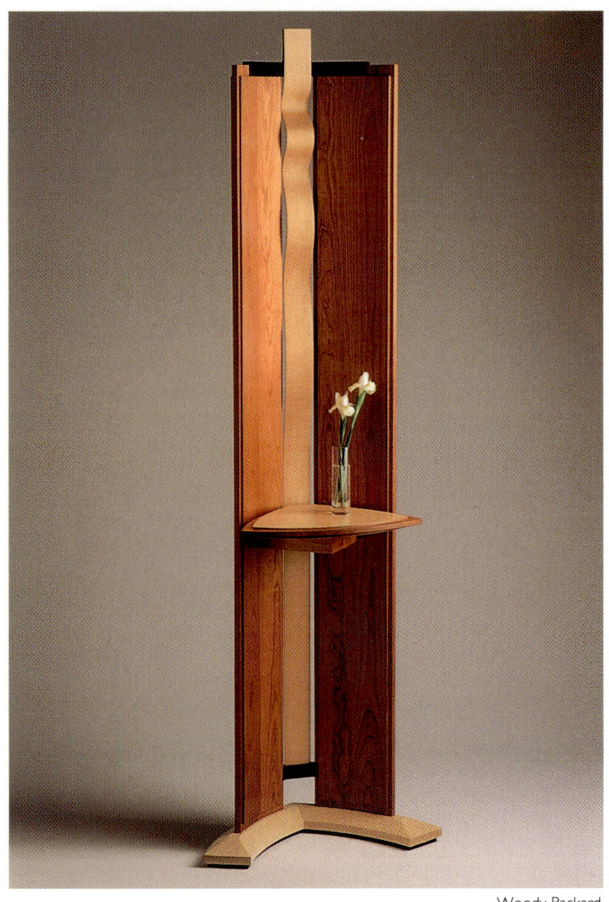

Woody Packard

John Hein

John Hein has received fellowships from both the NEA and the NJ State Council on the Arts. He has participated in over 50 museum and gallery exhibitions since he began making furniture in 1986.

John designs and builds furniture with a traditional respect for nature; a purity of craftsmanship combined with a contemporary structure are the aesthetic principles influencing the design and construction of his pieces.

Also see these GUILD publications:
THE GUILD: 5
The Designer's Reference: 6, 9

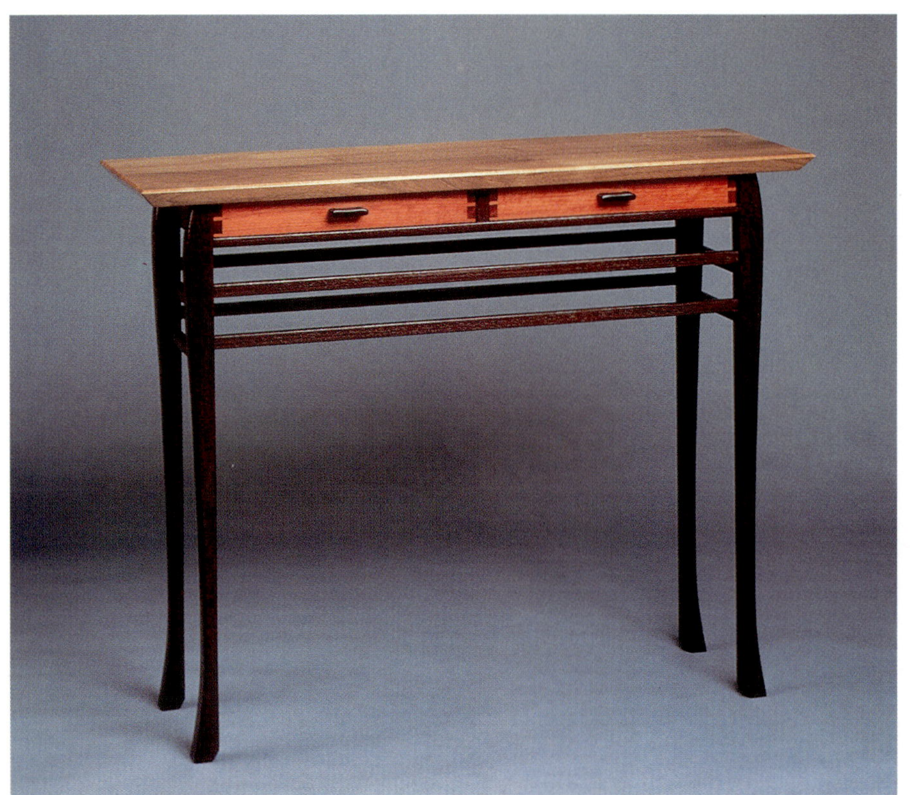

Hall table, 1994, English walnut, wenge and chakte kok, 32" x 40" x 14"

Michael Slack

Christian Thee
Christian Thee & Associates

Using his background as a theatrical designer, Christian Thee has focused his talents towards residential trompe l'oeil, hotel and restaurant murals, and fine art for galleries.

Shown here is *Space Bridge No. 11*..This name refers to the combining of a two-dimensional painting with three-dimensional painted table, bridging the gap to create functional trompe l'oeil. The painted linen napkin, flower pot, shadows and jeweled box all combine to create the illusion.

A portfolio is available upon request and project discussion is invited.

Also see these GUILD publications:
THE GUILD: 3, 5
The Designer's Reference: 8, 9
The Architect's Source: 7, 10

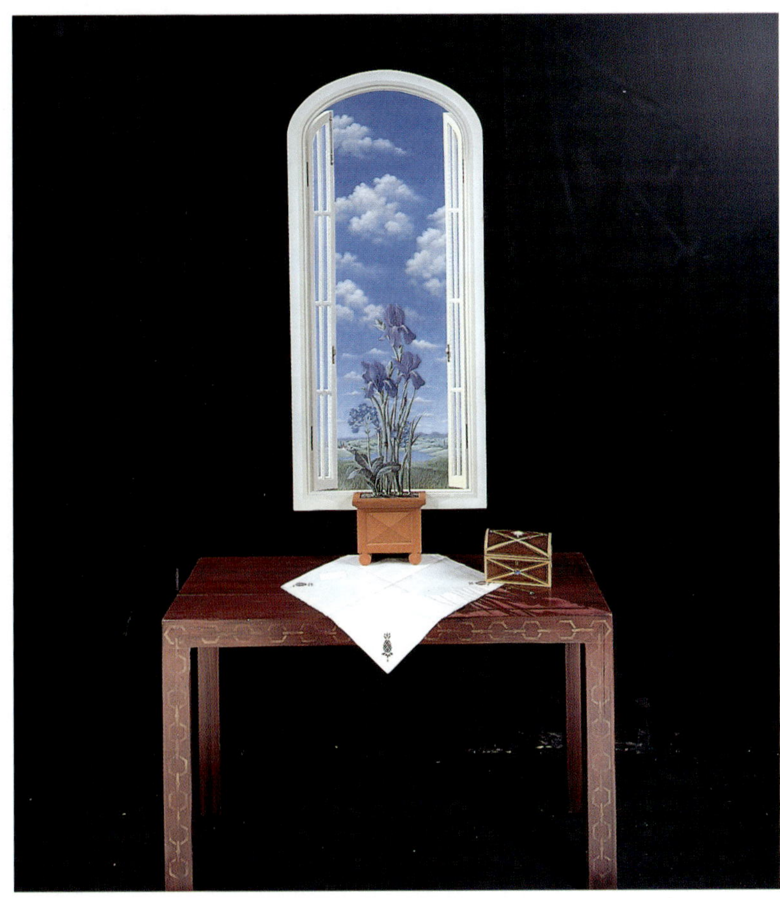

Michael Jon Flores
Michaeljon, Woodworker

Michael Jon has been designing and building heirloom-quality furniture for more than 25 years.

His unique style, combined with traditional mortise-and-tenon joinery, has led him to create a complete line of garden furnishings. Numerous awards include Best of Show at Beckman's. His work, which is shown in museums, galleries and private collections, also includes Craftsman-style furniture.

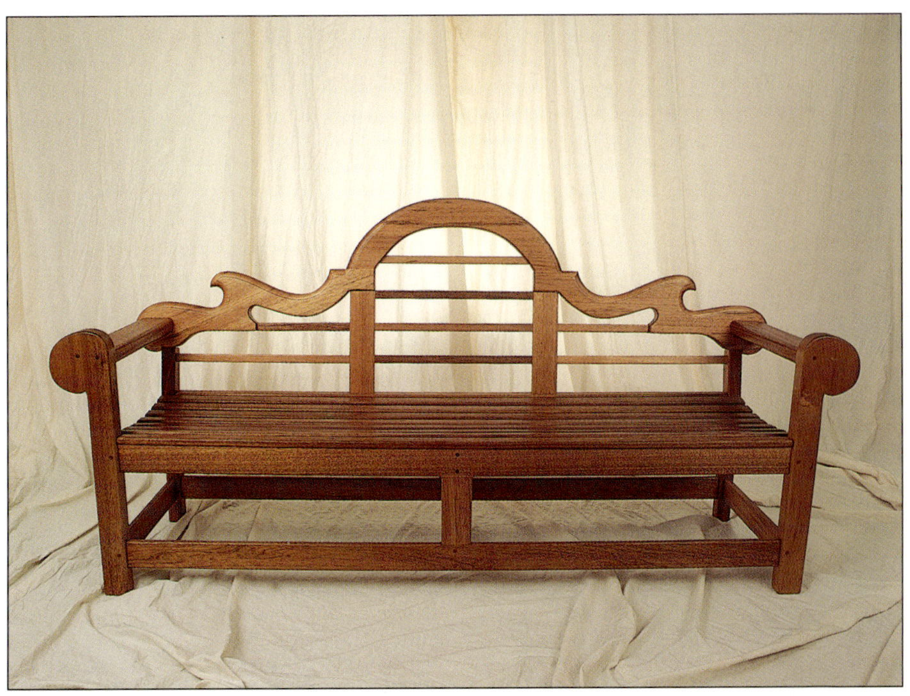

English garden bench, mahogany, 6½'

Covello Photography, Stockton, CA

Marilyn MacGregor

Marilyn MacGregor, a painter for 20 years, creates richly colored screens, tables and mirror frames. The elegant, whimsical pieces draw the eye and mind to rest and consider the jewel-like beauty of the earth's creatures.

The work is shown and collected in the U.S. and Europe.

Also see this GUILD publication:
The Gallery & Retail Edition: 1

SHOWN: table-top screen, 25" x 17"

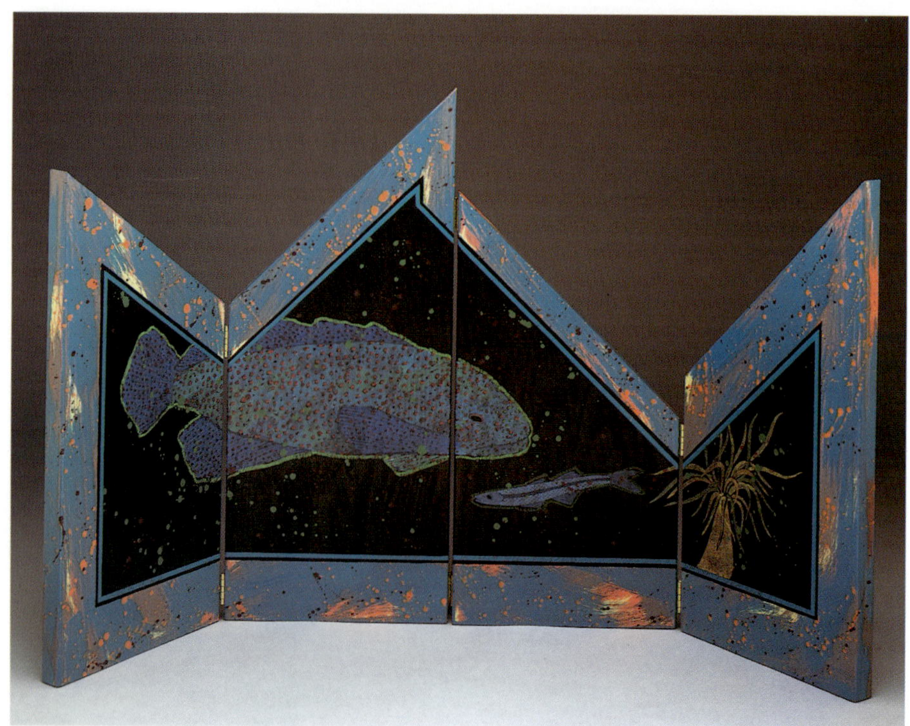

George Post

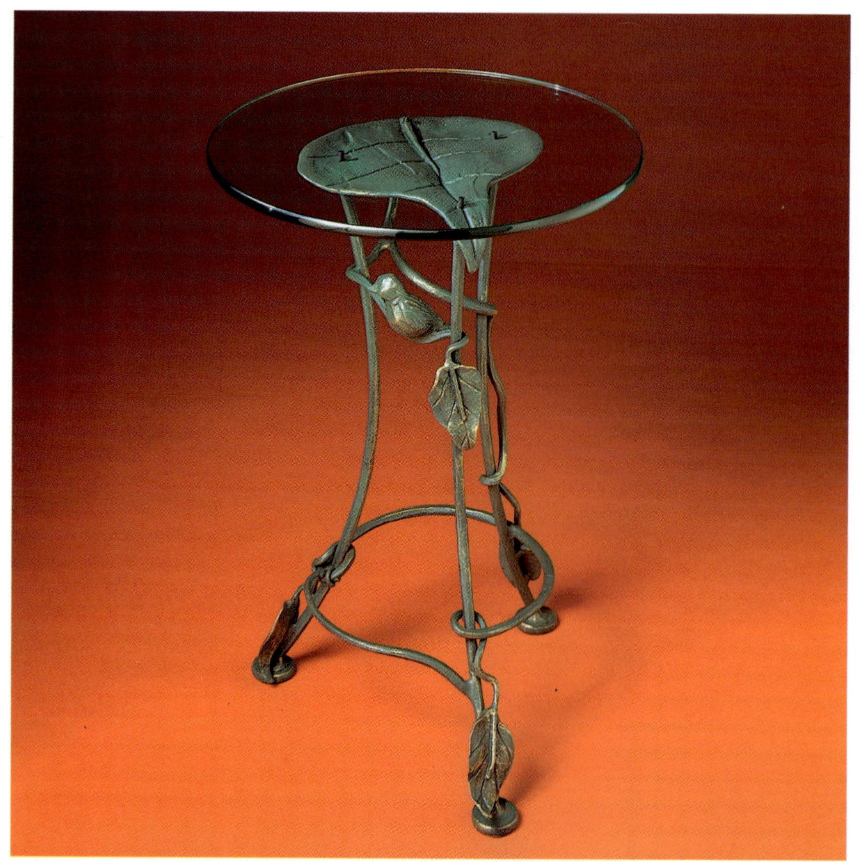

Kinetic Corporation

Craig Kaviar
Kaviar Forge

Kaviar Forge is a sculpture studio that specializes in hand-forged metal work. The work is distinguished by a natural ambiance, with extreme attention to fine craftsmanship and, in the case of furniture, comfort and utility. Craig Kaviar really enjoys working with designers and is able to customize projects, not only through his design and forging skills, but also by providing a large assortment of metals and finishes.

Work is delivered on time and within budget.

SHOWN: *Forge Iron End Table #510-D*, with glass top, 24"H x 20"Dia

Phoenix Studios
Carl Radke

Carl Radke, owner, designer, glass blower, has been working with glass for 25 years. In the early 1970s he became focused on recapturing the luster and color of glass produced in the United States around the turn of the century. Carl is one of the few glass artists who continues this expensive and difficult medium. Working with Carl is Chris Funk, glass blower for 17 years, Kua Turner and Dave Mills, apprentices.

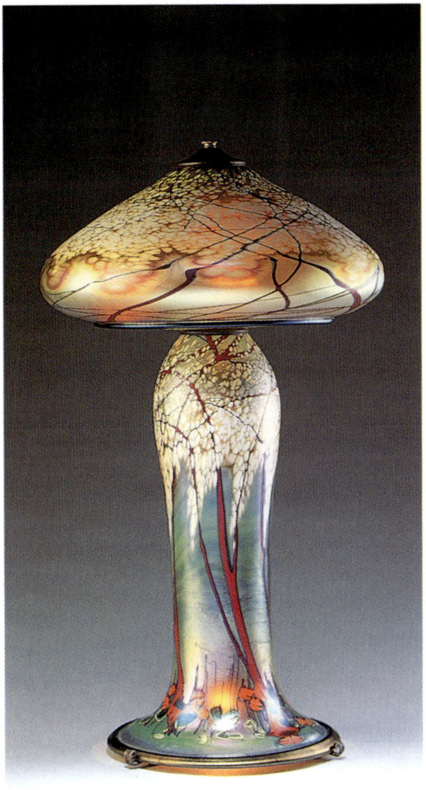

Table lamp, 27" x 14"

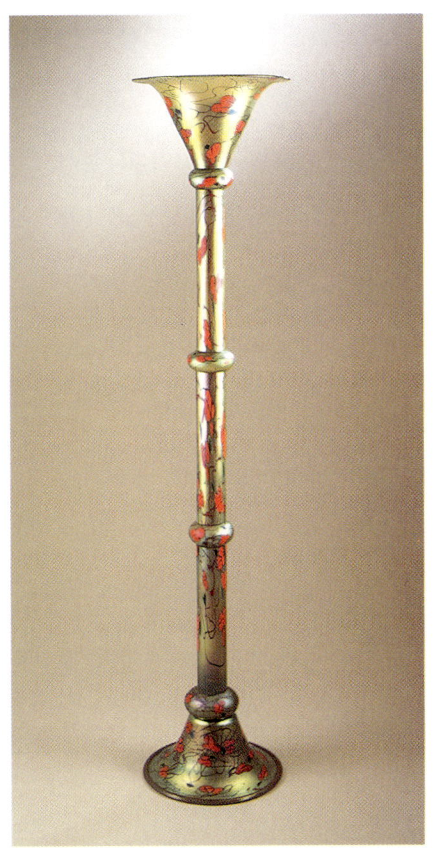

Floor lamp, 62" x 14"

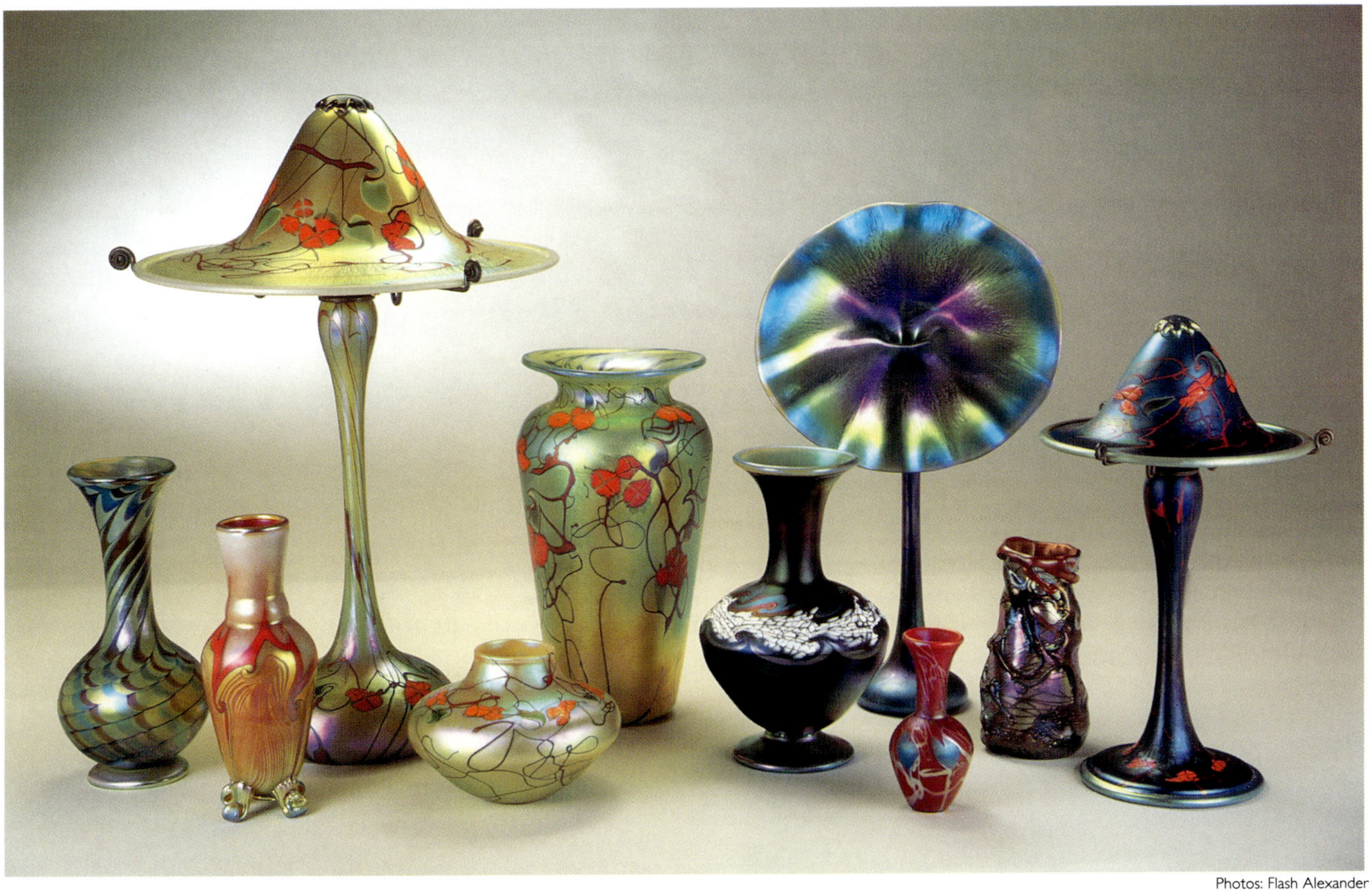

Photos: Flash Alexander

Kevin Ragaller Studios
Kevin Ragaller

Kevin Ragaller Studios has created elegant blown glass objects for 15 years. Catering to private collectors, his emphasis is on quality, design and execution. You will find his work to be unique, innovative and functionally sophisticated. New for 1995 is a series of glass and bronze sculptures shown at Ausi Gallery.

SHOWN: *Light and Elegant*, blown glass, 30"

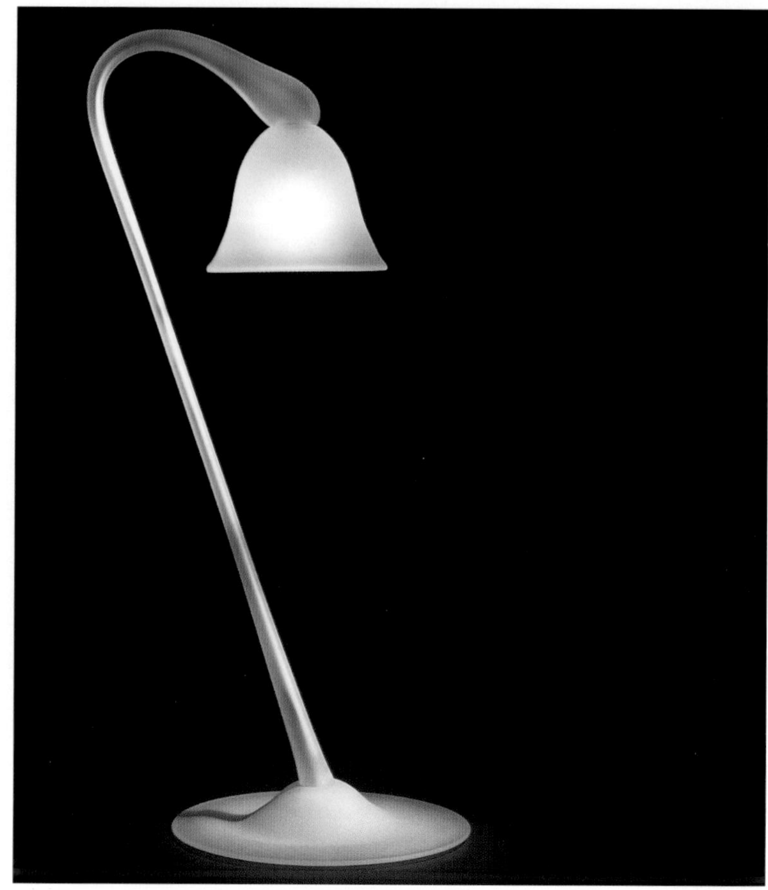
Peter L. Bloomer

GLASS MAGAZINE
THE GLASS WORKSHOP
647 FULTON ST
BROOKLYN, NY 11217
TEL 718-625-3685
$28/year

Glass Magazine, a full-color quarterly for design professionals, artists and collectors, features profiles of contemporary artists, an educational directory, and critical reviews of national and international exhibitions.

Angelika Traylor

Traylor's one-of-a-kind lamps and autonomous panels are well known among collectors of fine art glass, and her award-winning work can be recognized by its intricate, jewel-like compositions and meticulous attention to fine craftsmanship.

Traylor's work can be found in many publications and she is listed in *Who's Who in American Art*, *Who's Who in American Crafts* and *Who's Who in America*.

Also see these GUILD publications:
THE GUILD: 2, 3, 4, 5
The Designer's Reference: 7, 8, 9
The Architect's Source: 6

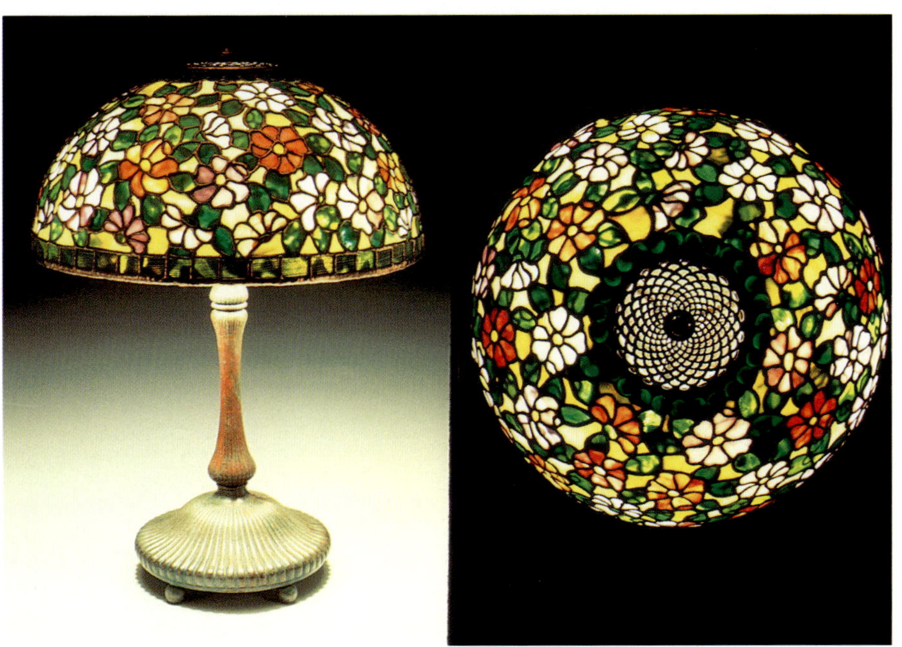

Randall Smith

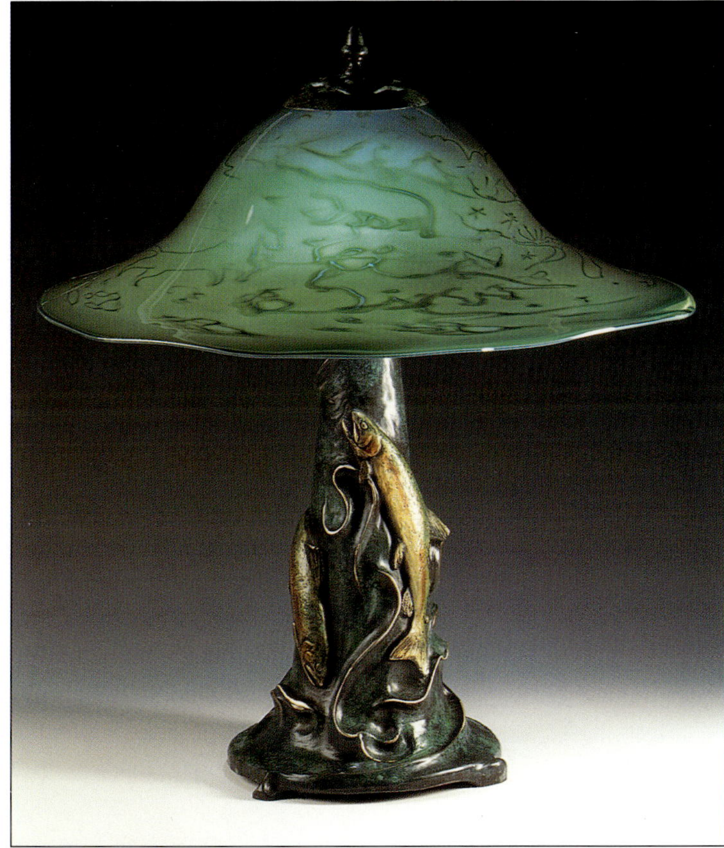

K Dahl Glass Studios
Kathy Dahlberg/Rick Steckel

Having been influenced by Swedish glass early in their careers, this husband and wife team work together as glassblower and designer to create a unique line of lighting, glass bowls and platters.

Shown here is the Rocky Mountain lamp, in which rattlesnakes, cougars, rabbits and cactus are imprinted into the hot glass with a special technique developed by the couple. The leaping rainbow trout base is an original bronze by Kathy, finished in a verdigris patina. All work is signed, numbered and dated.

"

Gary Upton
Gary Upton Woodworking Inc.

Gary Upton has been creating collectible furniture since 1976. His sculpted lighting series represents an interest in three-legged forms which he finds attractive. His designs create a distinct impact through fine joinery, sculptural detail, and the sensitive use of materials.

Gary's work has been featured in *American Craft* and *Woodwork* magazines, the book *Creative Designs in Furniture*, and the television show *Women On Wall Street*.

Also see these GUILD publications:
The Architect's Source: 6
The Designer's Reference: 6, 7

SHOWN: *Tower Lamp*, 22" × 24" × 72"

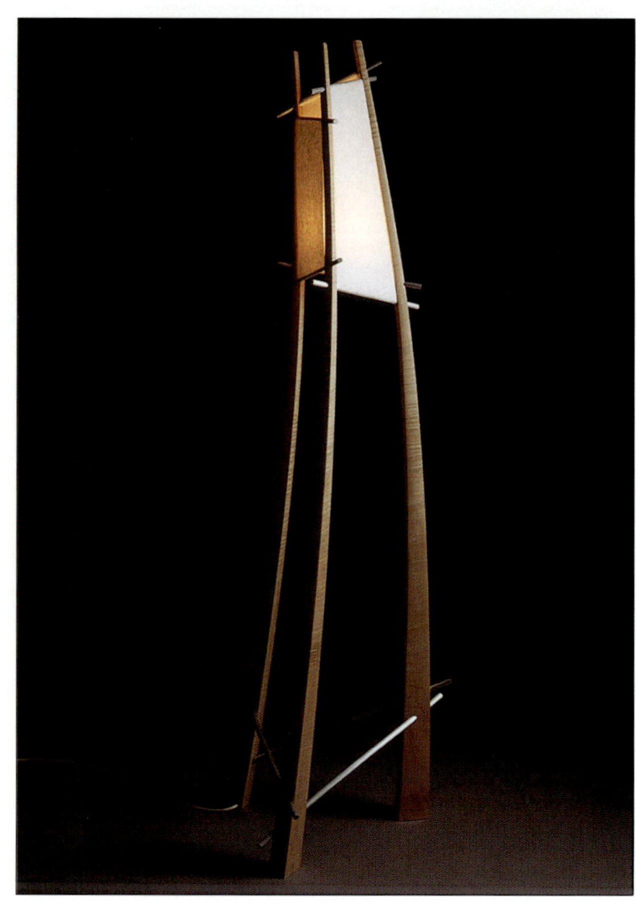

Bob Brown
Judy Dykstra-Brown
Brown Studio

Willow, bamboo, rattan, our own hand-made paper, and stone are some of the components of these one-of-a-kind light sculptures. Many styles and sizes. Custom orders accepted for floor, table or wall.

Also see these GUILD publications:
The Designer's Reference: 8, 9

SHOWN: *Spirit House*, 1994, stone, kozo paper, willow, rattan, bamboo, and other natural elements, 36"H

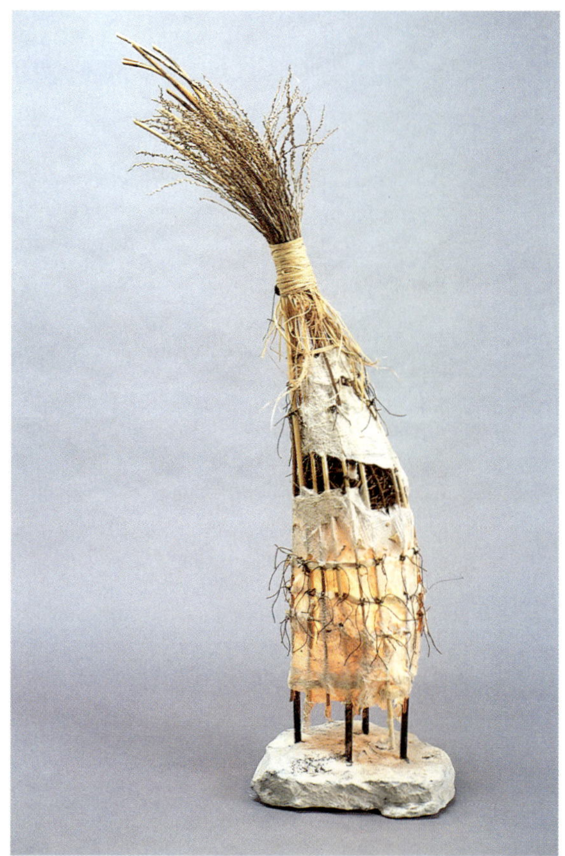

Bob Barrett

Rick Melby
Architectural Arts

Rick Melby's current focus is the design and fabrication of decorative and functional lighting and sculpture. Collected and shown internationally, his work emphasizes quality in conception and construction. A variety of hot and cold glass processes are used, with materials including metal, wood, stone and recycled objects. Limited editions, one-of-a-kind pieces, and accessories are available.

Also see these GUILD publications:
THE GUILD: 2, 3

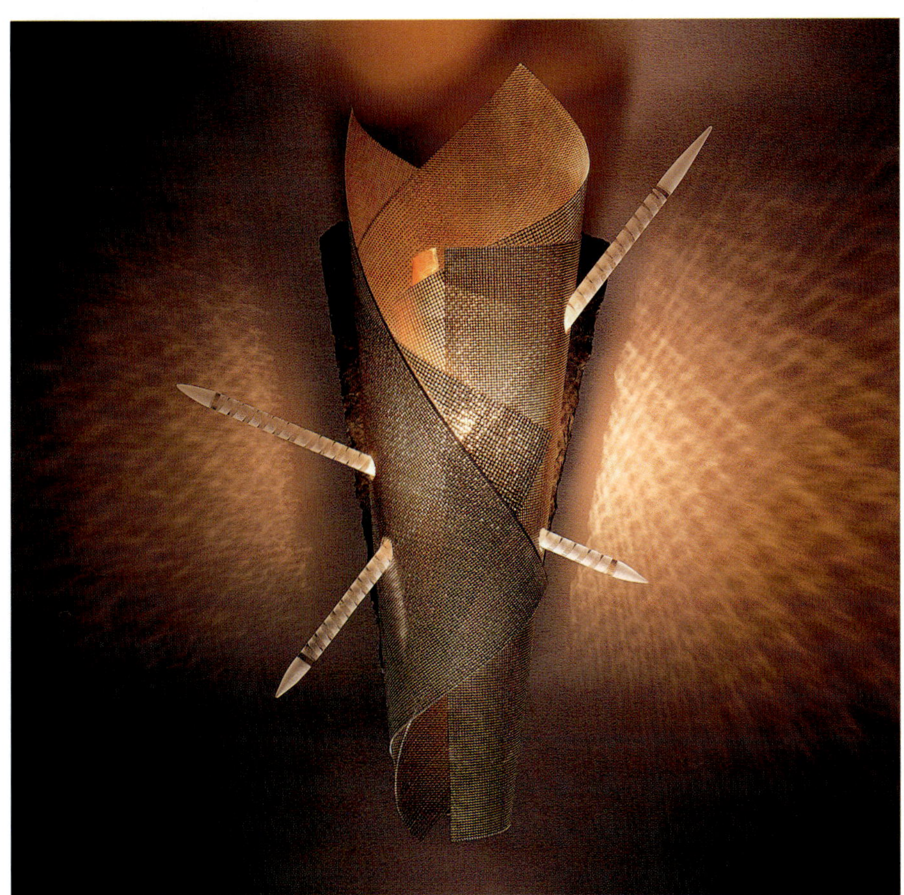

Chris Coxwell, Tampa, FL

Lenn Neff

Lenn Neff has been designing architectural leaded glass installations for 20 years. He now introduces a line of architecturally based lighted objects that represent his unique sense of elegant simplicity.

Materials for bases and pediments of Neff's 'footlight' series include hardwoods with copper leaf and patina, gold leaf, brass, and imported fossil stone.

SHOWN (left to right): *Taos* footlight, glass, brass, and cut stone, 5½" x 5½" x 17"H; *Classic* footlight, glass, brass, and copper leaf, 5½" x 5½" x 17"H; candle posts, brass and stone, 3" x 3" x 9"H

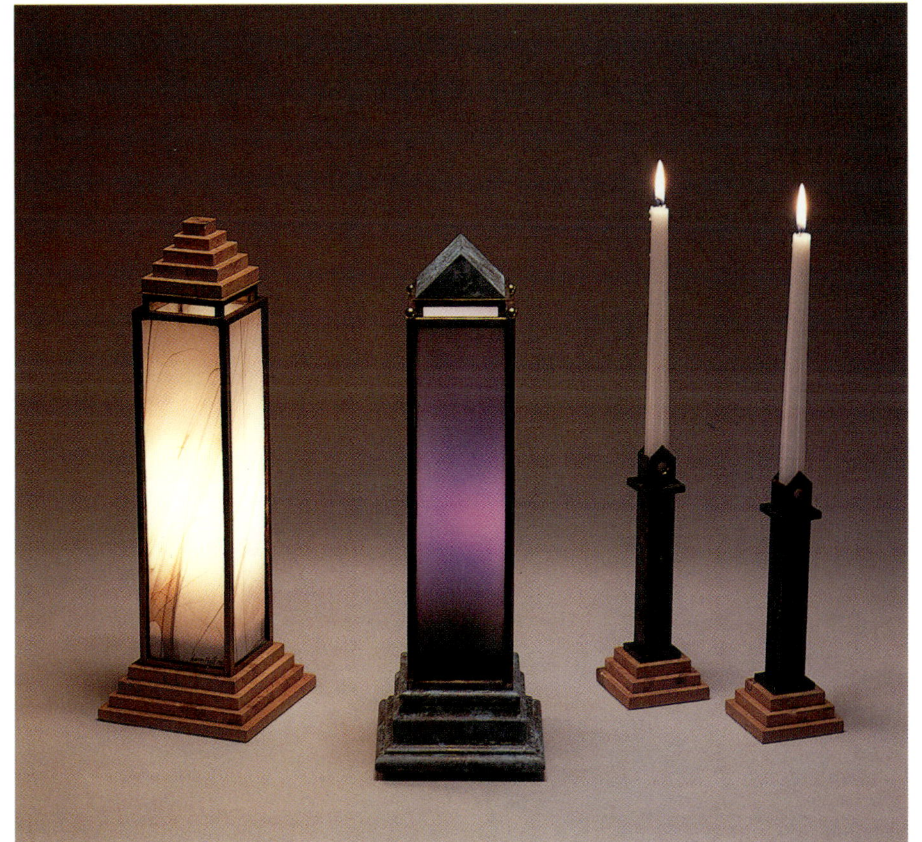

Frank Baptie, St. Petersburg, FL

other media other media ot

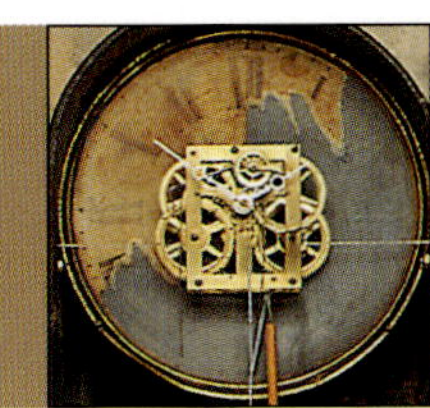

Cheryl Battaglia

Inspired by the classical, Cheryl Battaglia designs and constructs one-of-a-kind and limited-edition architectural boxes, some opening in as many as eight places. Boxes are painted and gilded in 23K gold.

Ms. Battaglia's boxes and dinosaurs are in private collections throughout the United States and have been exhibited in the windows of Tiffany & Company.

The pieces, though functional, are frequently used as strictly decorative objects and enjoyed for their elegant simplicity and the feeling of tranquility they evoke.

They are also used as special hideaways for personal treasures, cherished objects and collections.

A three-opening monuments, 12½" × 6½" × 6½"; three-opening monuments with gold ball finial, 7" × 2½" × 2½"

B boxes and trays, 2" × 2" to 6" × 6"; one opening obelisks, ¾" × 1¾" × 1¾"

C two-opening pyramids with gold ball, 9½" × 8½" × 8½"; one-opening obelisks, ¾" × 1⅛" × 1⅛"

D five-opening obelisk, 22½" × 9" × 9"; two-opening obelisk, 4" × 1⅛" × 1⅛"; one-opening obelisk, 7" × 2½" × 2½"

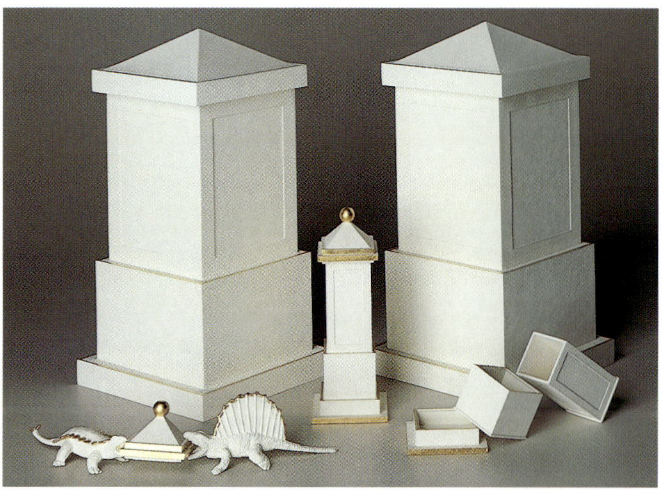

A

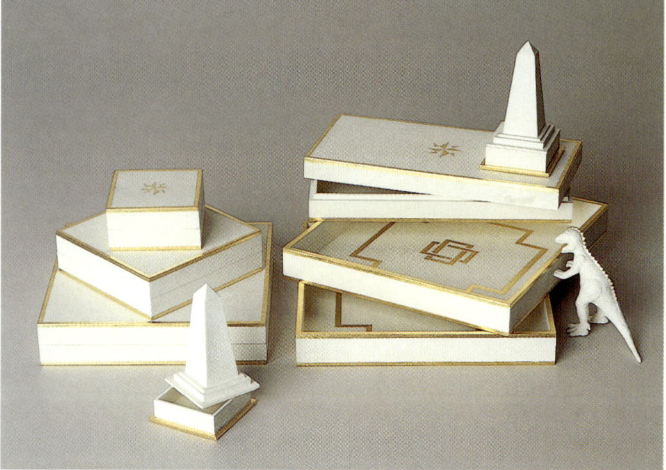

B

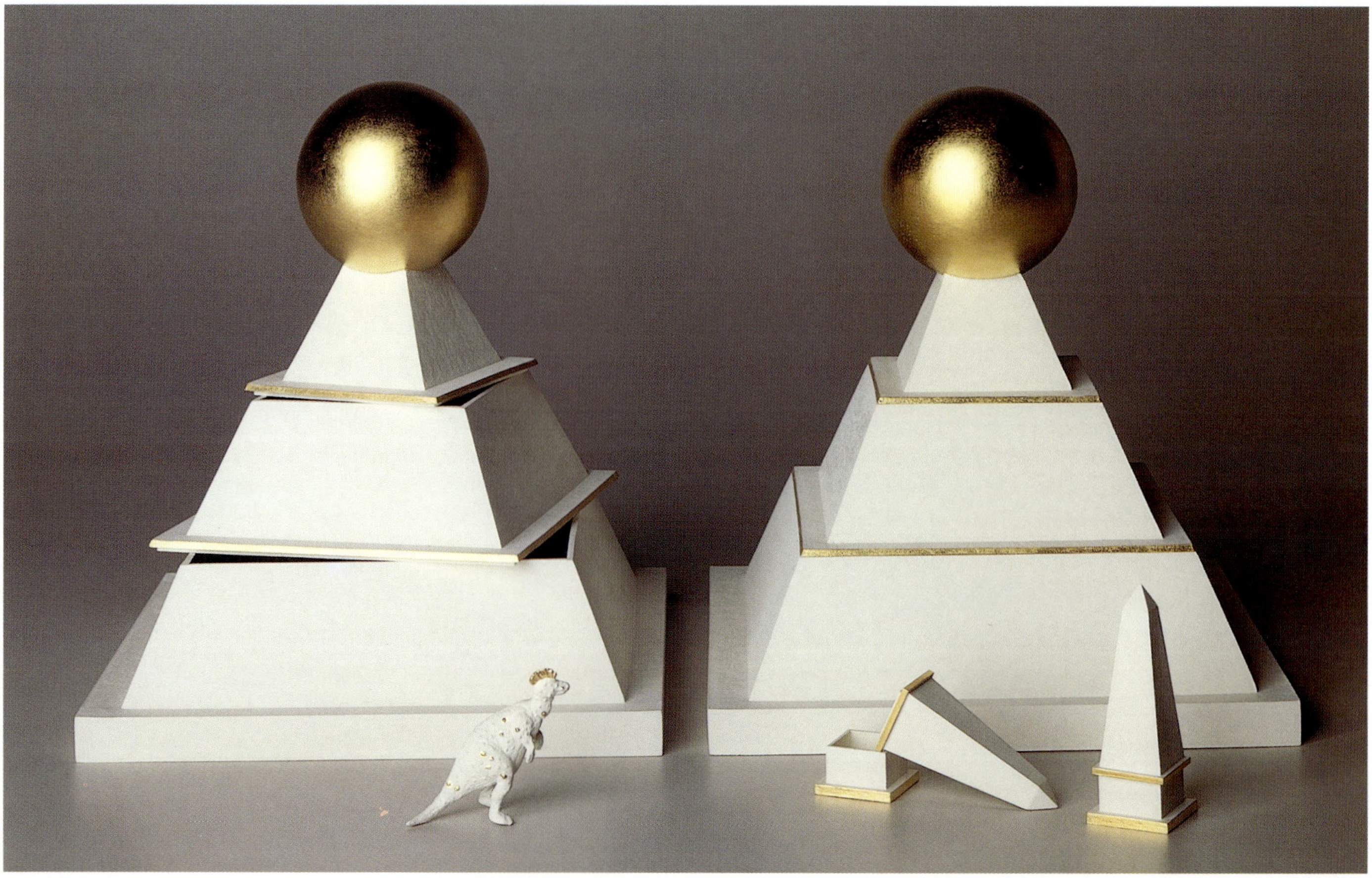

C

Photos: Alan Oransky, Boston, MA

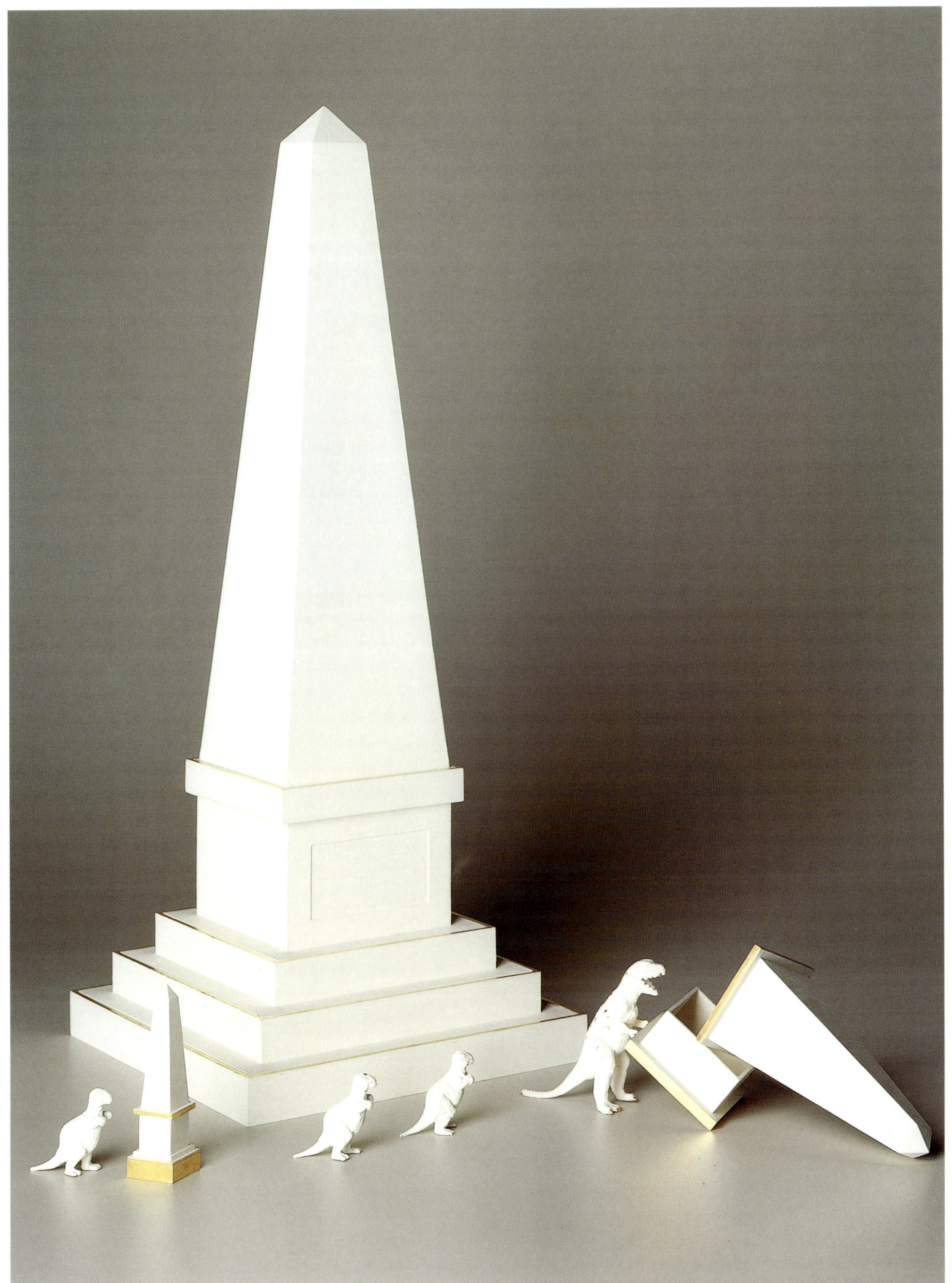

D Obelisks and dinosaurs by Cheryl Battaglia

Creative Connections
David and Joan Marshall

Creators of elegant home and office decor.

UNISPHERE™, a kaleidoscope collector's prize with extra-special qualities: richly grained lacquered woods; interchangeable marbles and wheels on the same body; strikingly designed accessory base; gold-plated triangular 'wheels'; user-friendly wide-viewing screen revealing a 3D spherical image.

This color fantasy-in-motion is both a treasure to keep and a unique gift.

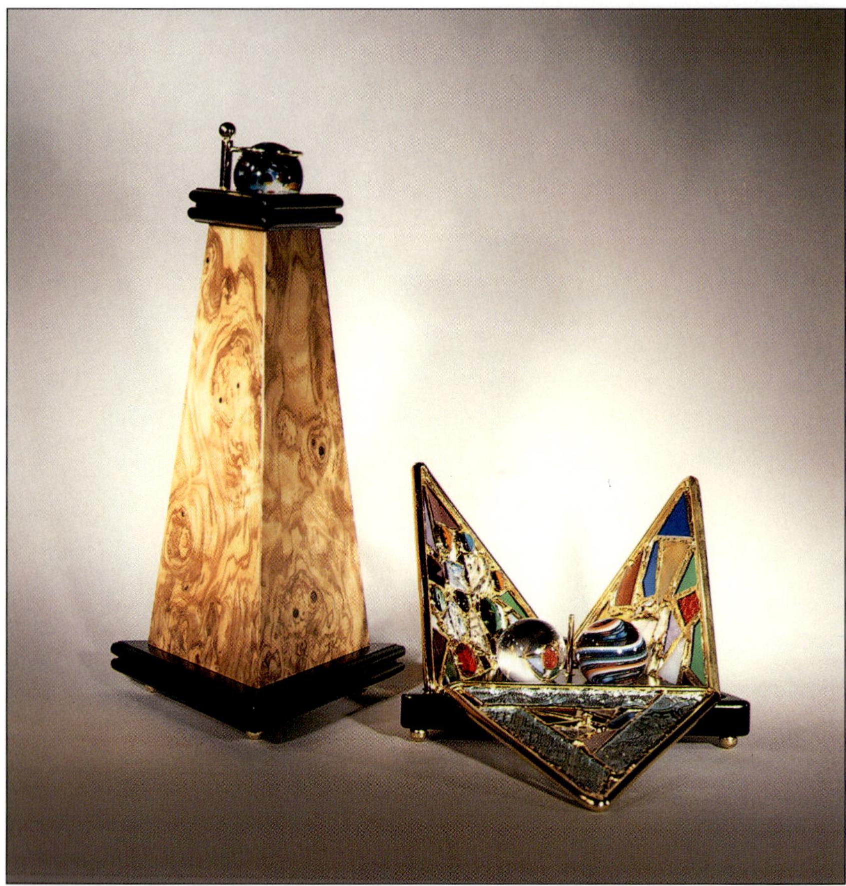

UNISPHERE™ kaleidoscope in olive ash burl

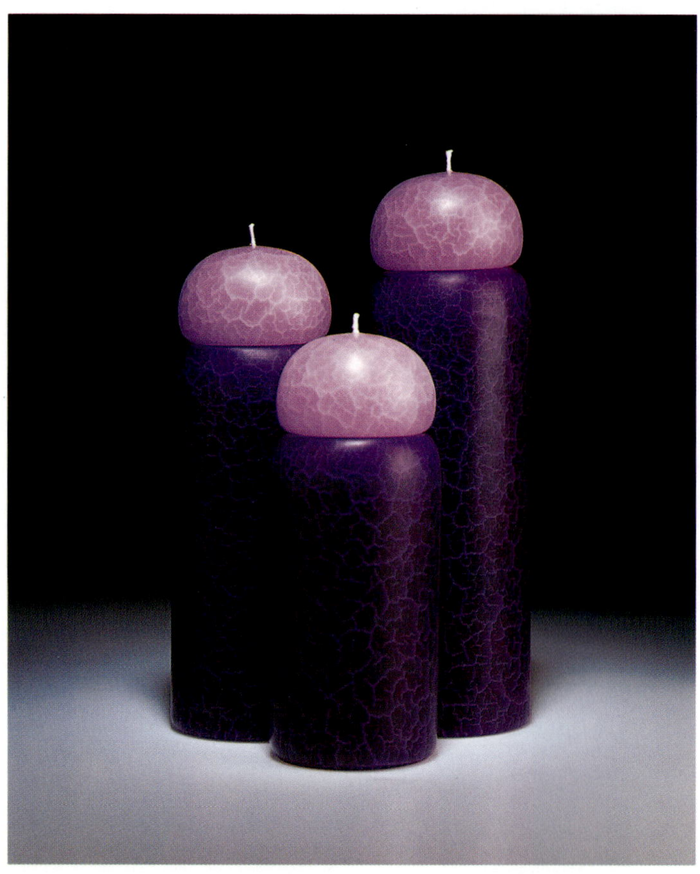

Barrick Design
Rick Faulkner

Barrick Design, Rick Faulkner's studio, creates candles designed in clustered groups of elegant contemporary forms. With a wide range of vivid colors and a unique crackle finish, his candles are beautiful and functional objects for the home. For 25 years, Faulkner's candles have been lighting up parties and brightening homes.

SHOWN: *ST#1*, base with replaceable top candle, in grape crackle wax

Linda Sue Eastman

Linda Sue Eastman intends her work to go beyond the visual—to tempt the fingertip, the hand and the senses. The pieces are functional objects created in rich, contemporary colors, incorporating leather, silk, horsehair, pigment and hardwood.

SHOWN: blanket chest, from her series of one-of-a-kind furniture and accessories, which include tables, chests, desks, mirrors and vessels

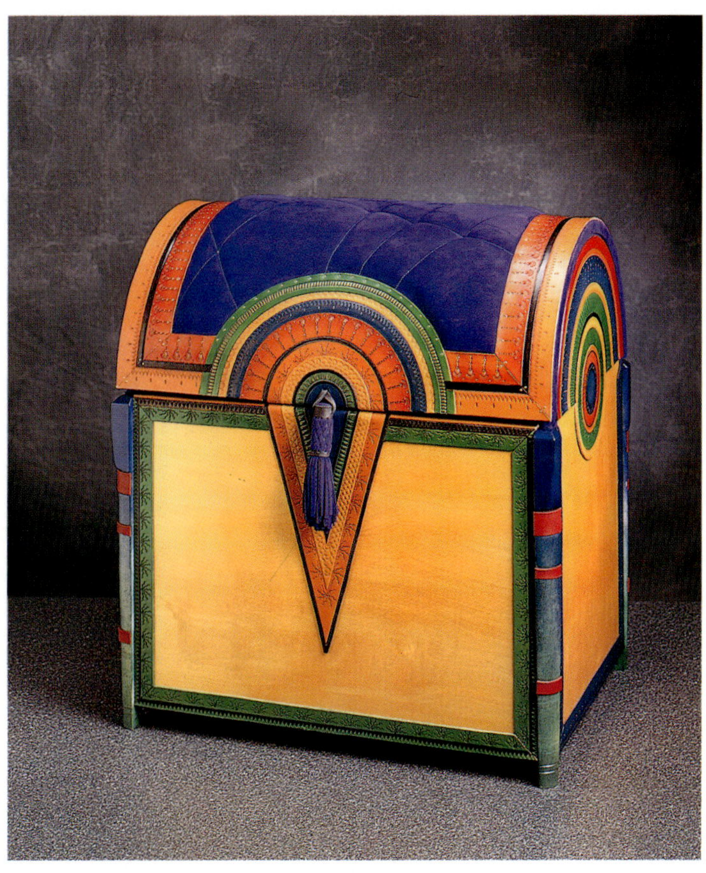

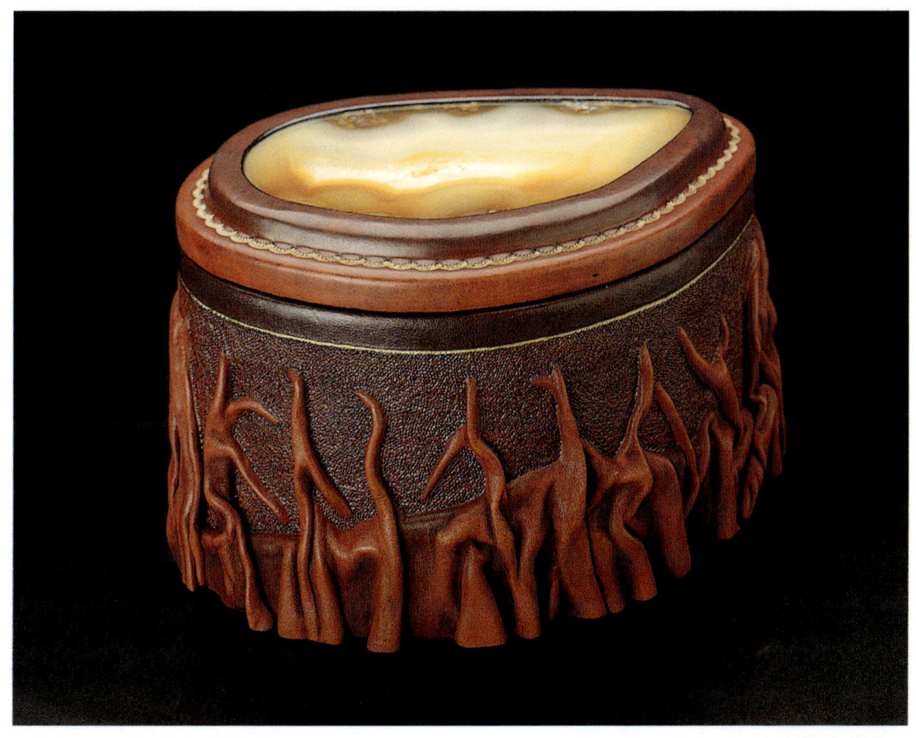

Charley Freiberg

J. Todd Barber
The Toadstool Leatherworks

During the past 25 years, Todd Barber has devoted a considerable amount of time to refining, researching and developing the contemporary, as well as primitive, techniques used in his leather art. Barber's award-winning unique and limited-edition boxes are his speciality. They are ornamented with semi-precious stones and cultural artifacts, and may be finely carved and tooled. Wallpieces, sculpture, and jewelry are other avenues he pursues in this ancient medium.

SHOWN: *Dancing Roots*, 1994, sculpted leather box, 4¾"H x 7½"L x 5"W

Jerome R. Durr
The Just Glass Studio

Jerome Durr began designing and fabricating architectural glass artworks in 1973, along with various pieces for art exhibits and gallery presentations. Jerome's work can be found throughout the United States and in France, Italy, Germany, Kuwait and Sri Lanka.

Jerome's contemporary style, using the techniques of carved and cast glass in union with stone, is distinguished by his understanding of line, color, texture and light. The melding of these elements results in a relationship with those persons interacting with the pieces.

Also see these GUILD publications:
THE GUILD: 4, 5
The Architect's Source: 6, 7, 8, 9, 10

A *O.R.G.*, leaded glass, wood, 54" × 76"

B *Descent*, a pedestal gallery piece, stone and glass, 24" × 24"

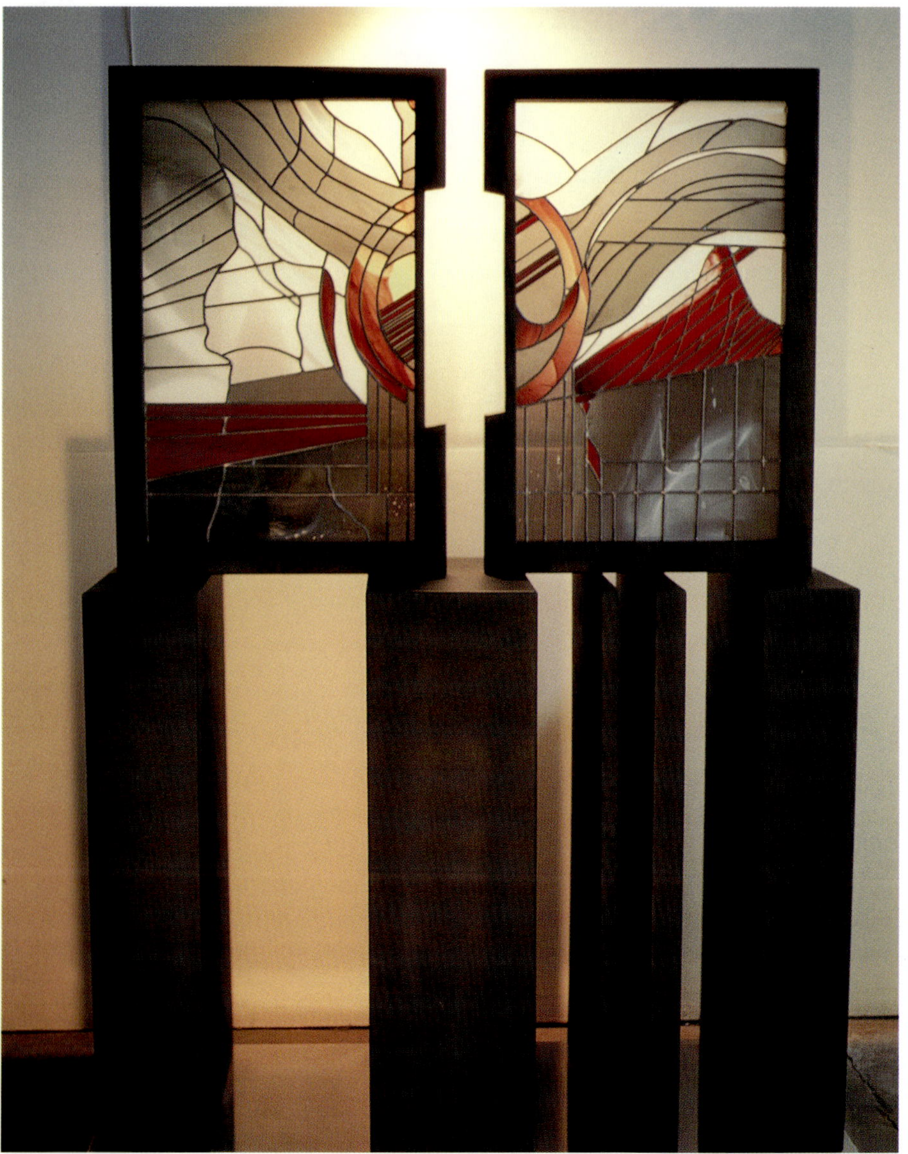

A

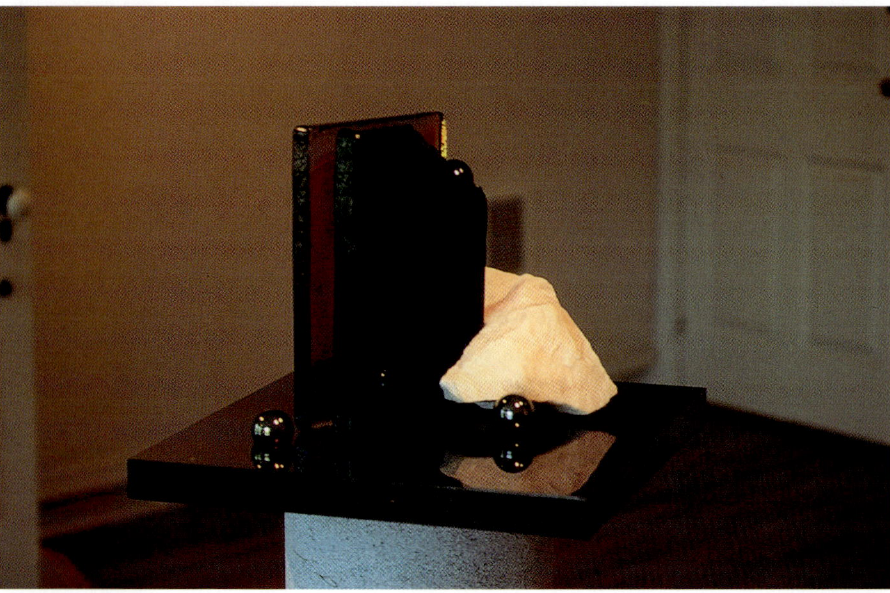

B

Gwen Weinberg
Grace Crowley
Page Twenty-Nine

The Page Twenty-Nine studio in Seattle, Washington, combines the arts of book-binding and metalsmithing. Copper, the twenty-ninth element, complements exotic cover papers and ancient tarot illustrations; a hand-torched hinge and edge open to a hand-bound journal or photo album. Other styles include day planners, checkbook covers and notepads.

Hand-torched copper bookmarks clip onto a page.

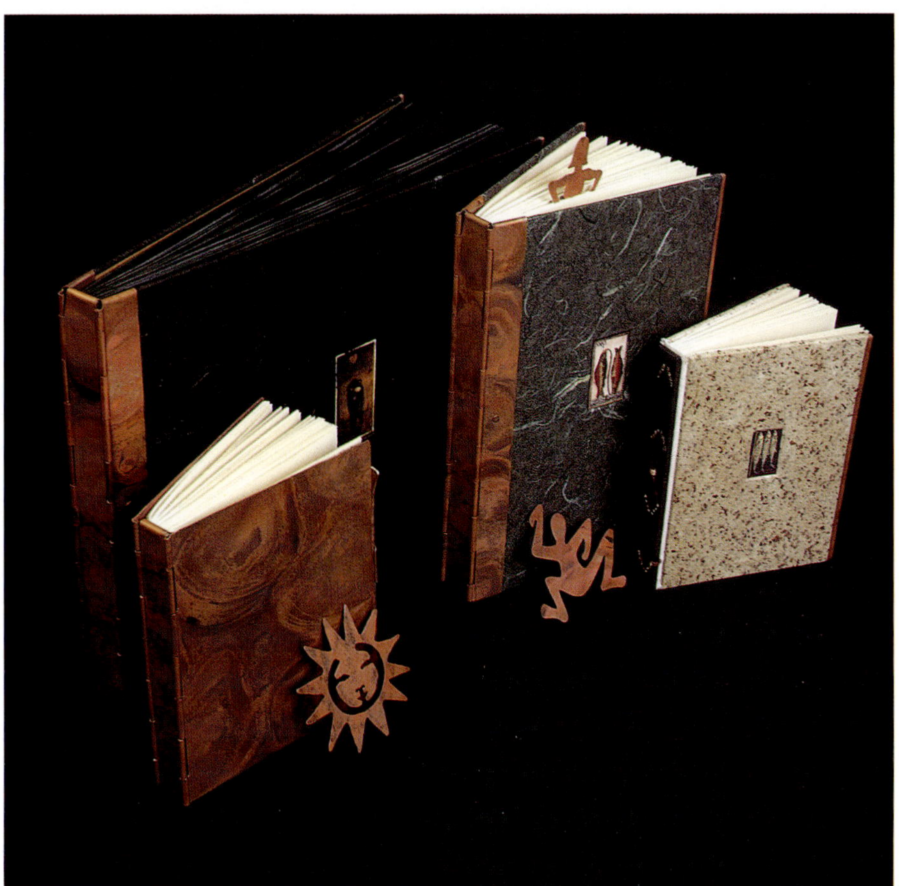

Becky Rhoades

SURFACE DESIGN JOURNAL
**SURFACE DESIGN ASSOCIATION
PO BOX 20799
OAKLAND, CA 94620
TEL 510-841-2008
$45/year**

Surface Design Journal, **a full-color quarterly magazine, is published by the Surface Design Association (SDA), a nonprofit educational organization of artists, educators, designers, and lovers of beautiful textiles and quality design. Subscription to the *Surface Design Journal* is provided as a benefit of membership in the SDA.**

THE CRAFTS REPORT

**300 WATER ST
PO BOX 1992
WILMINGTON, DE 19899
FAX 302-656-4894
TEL 800-777-7098
TEL 302-656-2209
$29/year**

Published monthly, *The Crafts Report* seeks to inform, instruct and inspire both the beginning and the established professional craftsperson, as well as the crafts retailer, by providing them with business articles, industry news and a forum for exchanging ideas and concerns.

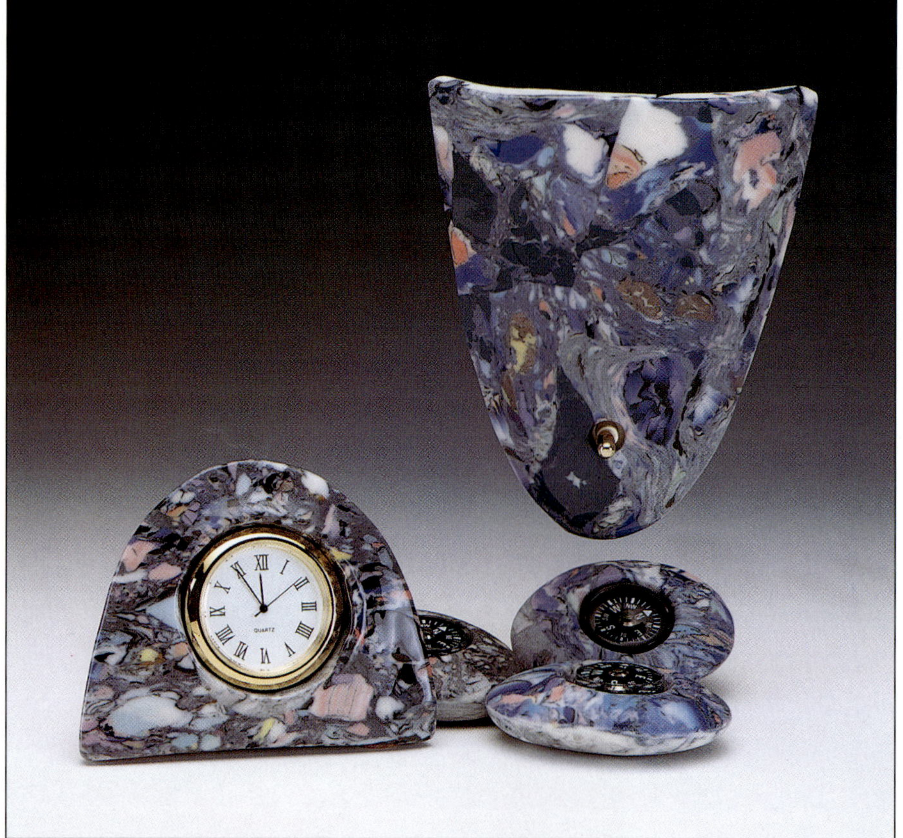

Jerry Anthony

Curtis Benzle
Benzle Applied Arts

Curtis Benzle and Benzle Applied Arts are respected for innovative and affordable porcelain decorative accessories.

Each piece carries the same design integrity and craftsmanship that has earned Mr. Benzle's creations a place in major museums, including the Smithsonian, the Cleveland Museum of Art and the White House Contemporary Craft Collection.

This acknowledged standard of excellence is your best guarantee of quality.

OTHER MEDIA

Kowalski Clockworks
Stephen Kowalski

Berkeley artist Stephen Kowalski combines mechanical knowledge and design training to produce clocks like you've never seen before, each created using antique architectural and mechanical parts from around the world.

A swinging pendulum gives motion to many clocks; others chime or ring. An antique toy airplane flies around the dial of one clock, another features flashing lights.

Kowalski's work has been published both nationally and internationally, and was recently featured in *The New York Times*.

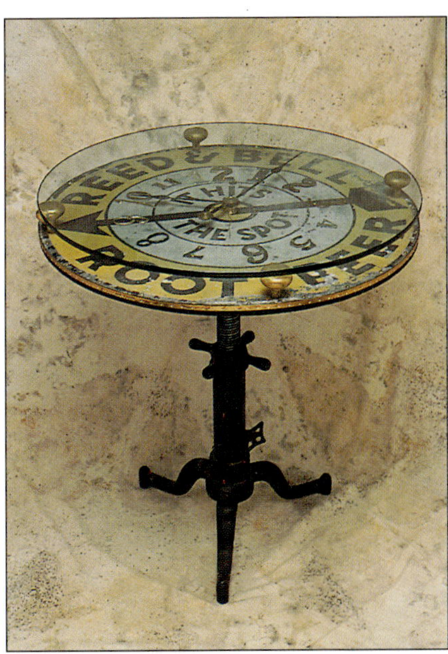

Timetable #2, 34"H x 30"Dia

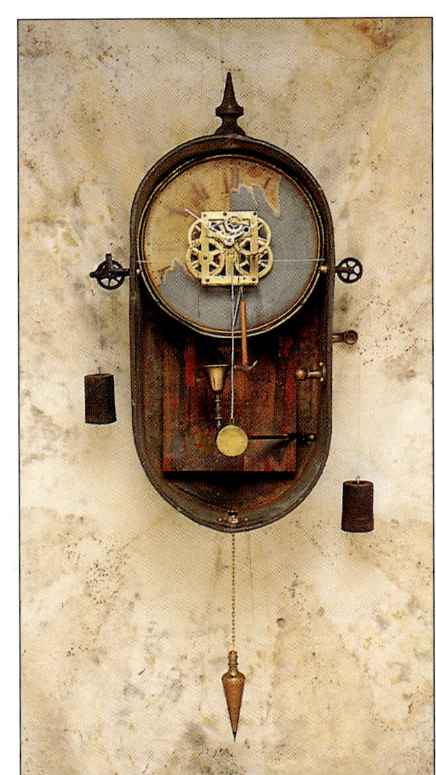

St. John, 48"H

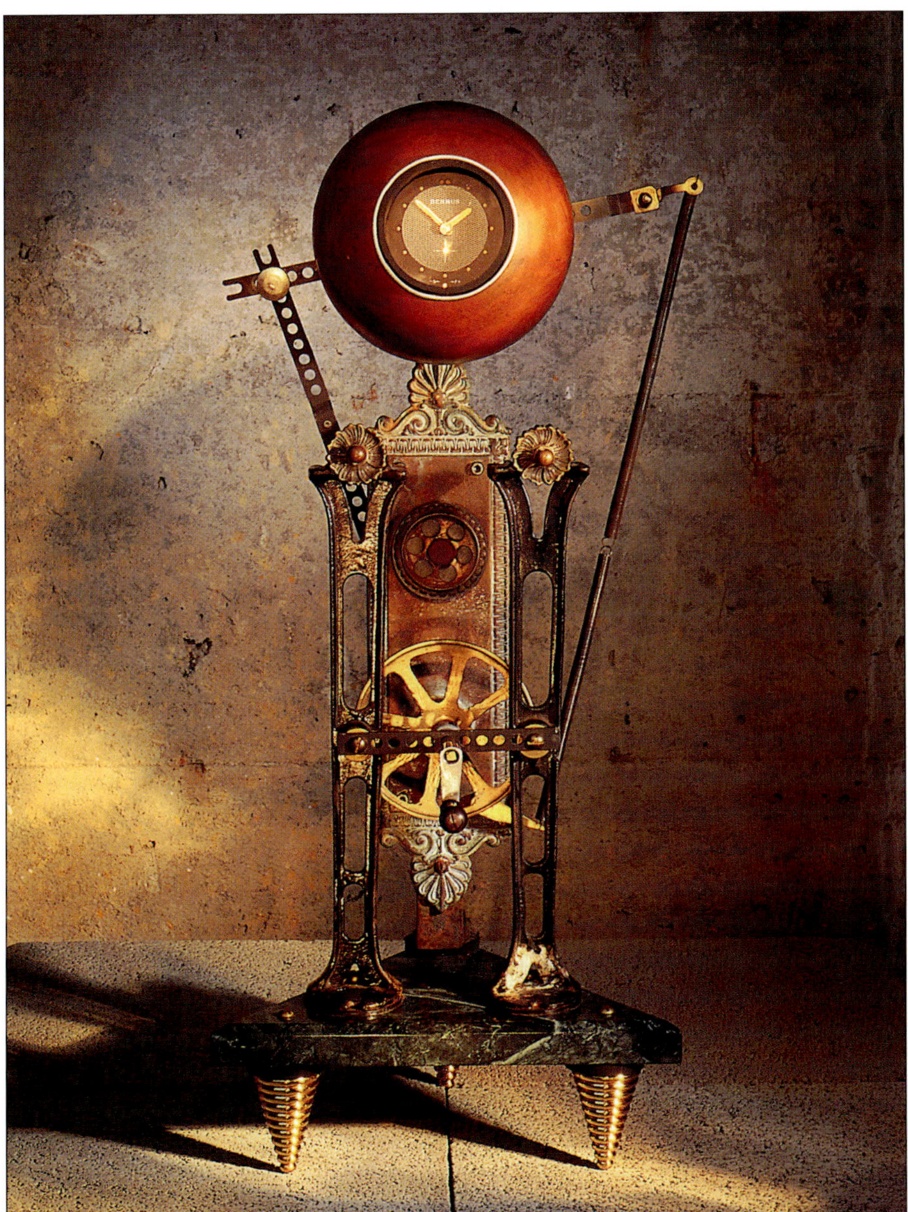

Perpetual Motion, 24"H

Photos: G. Post/D. Hayashida

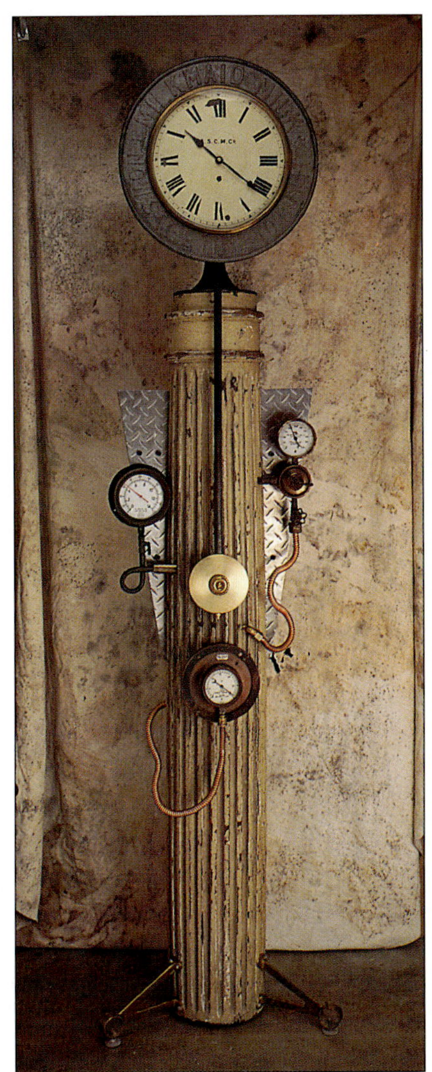

My Grandfather's Clock, 8'H

Silja Lahtinen
Silja's Fine Art Studio

The ancient Lapland shaman created good fortune and riches by using his drum. Now Silja (Talikka) Lahtinen draws ideas from her Scandinavian heritage in creating contemporary drums to bring us good fortune and riches.

The drums are strong and sturdy, with the fiber layers becoming almost one with the wood, in a unique working process. Available in any color and in abstract or realistic images, the drums can be installed in elegant groups in residential or commercial interiors. Many drums have images on both sides. The artist also creates large wall panels with fiber materials and handmade paper on canvas. She exhibits regularly in New York and other U.S. cities, as well as in Paris, France, and Helsinki, Finland.

Commissions accepted. For additional information, please contact the artist.

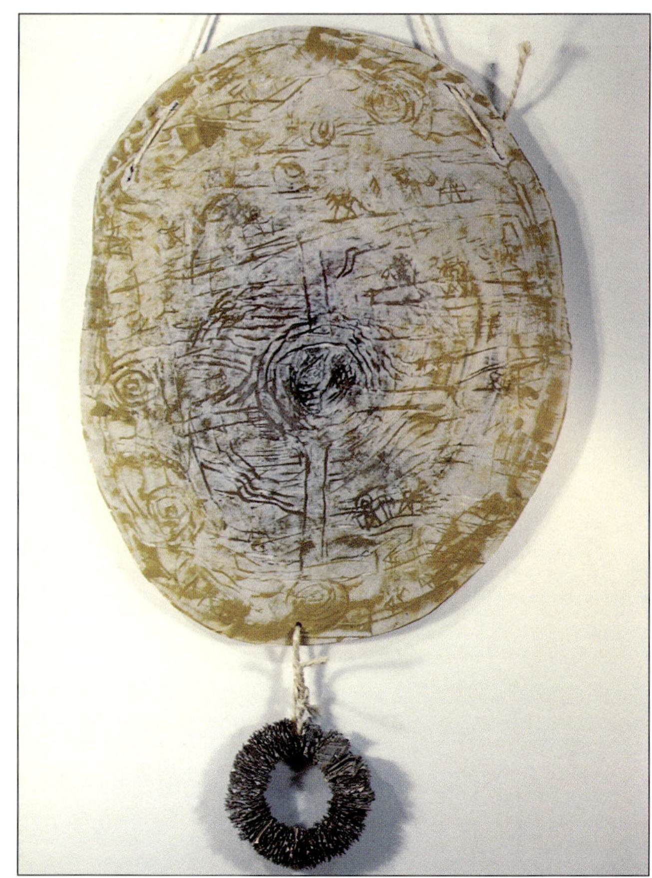

Drumming Talk (front), 1993, 40" x 23"

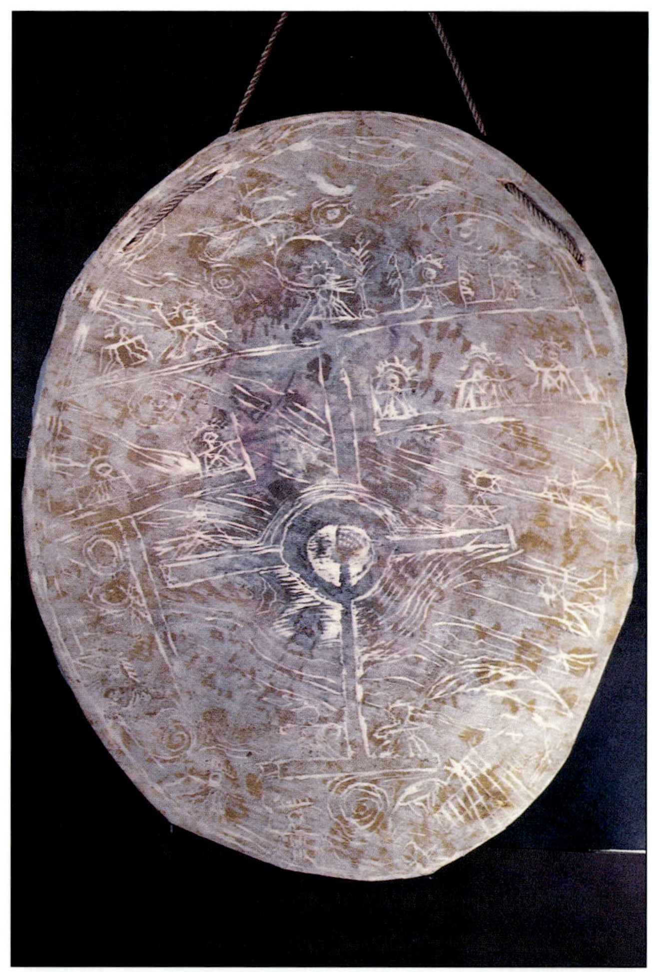

From The Earth, 1992, drum, acrylic, fiber, wood, rope, 29" x 26"

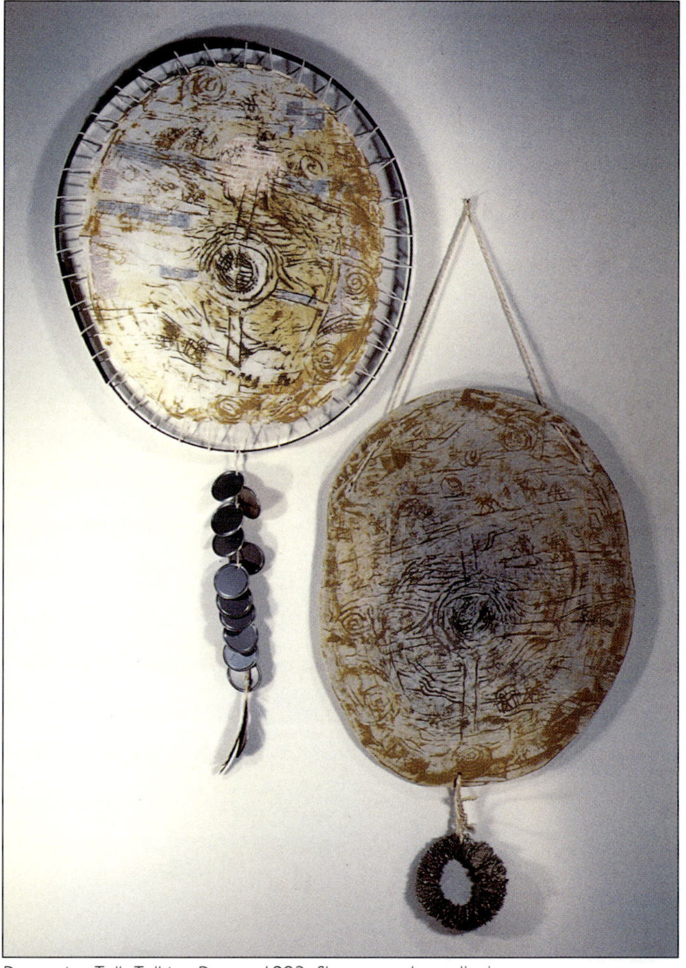

Drumming Talk-Talking Drums, 1993, fiber, wood, acrylic, iron, 54" x 26" and 40" x 23"

Designs in Leather

Cheryl Smeja

Cheryl Smeja, a self-taught leathersmith, has worked in this medium since the early '70s and first produced sculptural works in leather in the '80s. She began with wearable masks, which evolved into wall pieces. Her wall faces range from tranquil ladies to dramatic images of the elements, seasons and celestial beings. Sizes range from 15" x 15" to 24" x 36".

Color brochure and price list available.

SHOWN: wall face, 26"H x 24"W

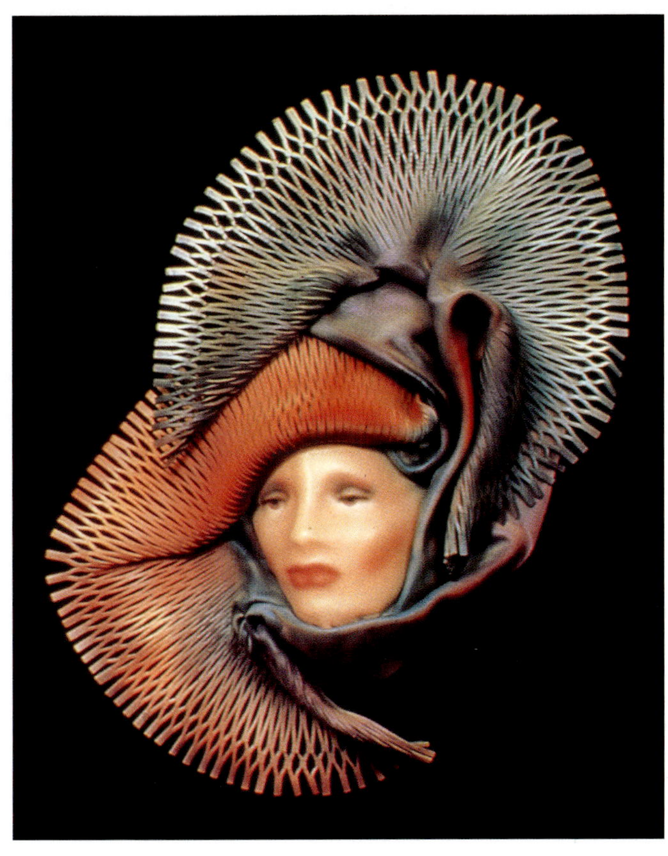

Kathleen Totter-Smith

Designer Products

Totter-Smith's career in papermaking began with her participation in the World Crafts Conference in Kyoto, 1978. Her sculptural paper reliefs have been exhibited in over 60 juried invitationals, national and international. Collections include the Champion Paper Company, Hartford, and the Ohio Crafts Museum.

SHOWN: *Big Horn Country*, 1994, a collage of natural materials on handmade paper, 32" x 40", from the *Spirit to Mother Earth* series

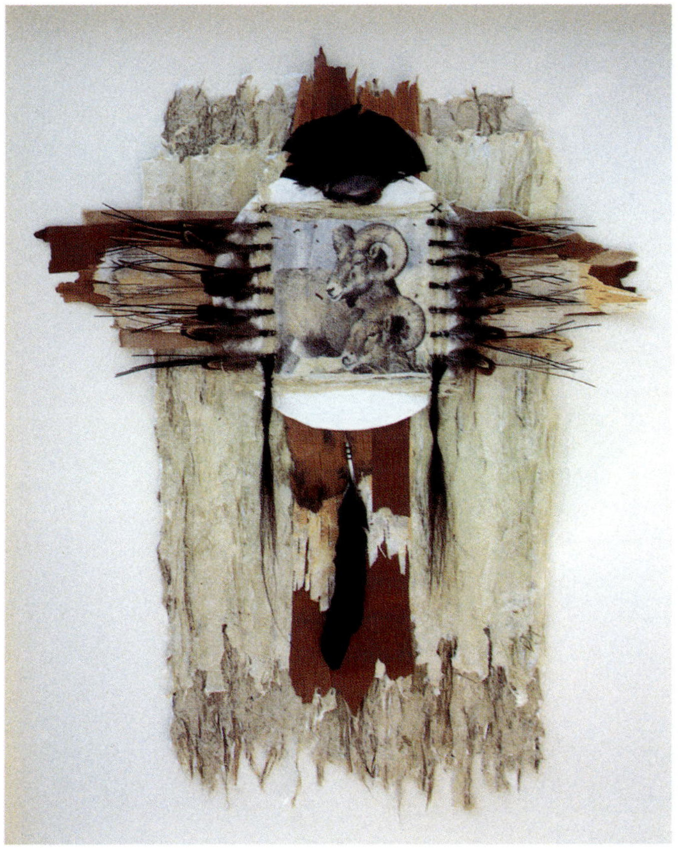

Jane Metzger

For over 20 years, Jane Metzger has created works of sculptural fiber inspired by nature. Recent work, including the wall relief featured here, mixes media such as branches, gut, handmade paper and paint, evoking illusions of movement.

Ms. Metzger's work has been exhibited widely and was recently selected as an Arizona Governor's Art Award.

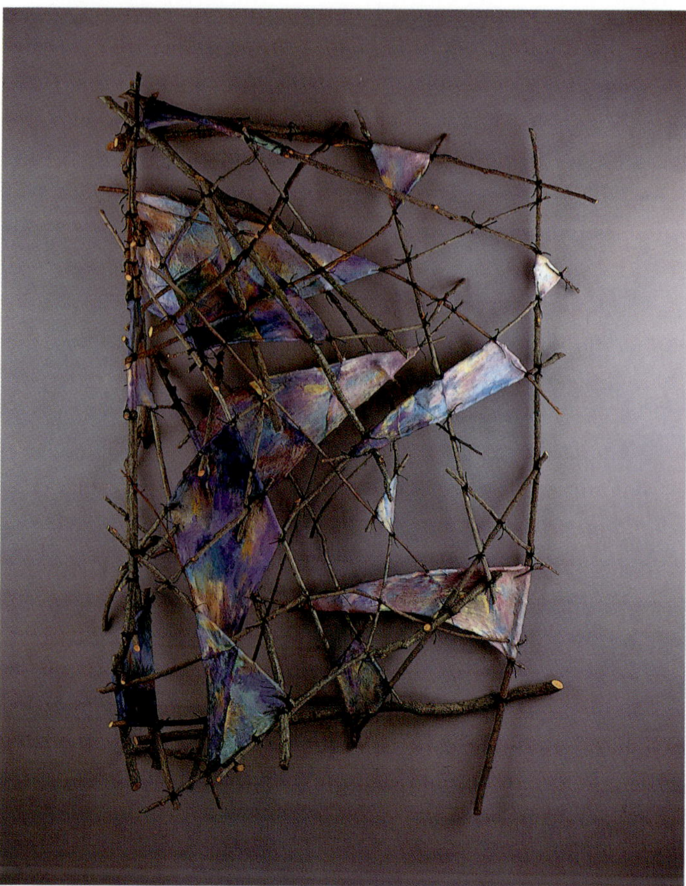

Ethereal Wing, 1993, mixed media, 36" x 24" x 11"   W. Scott Mitchell, Chandler, AZ

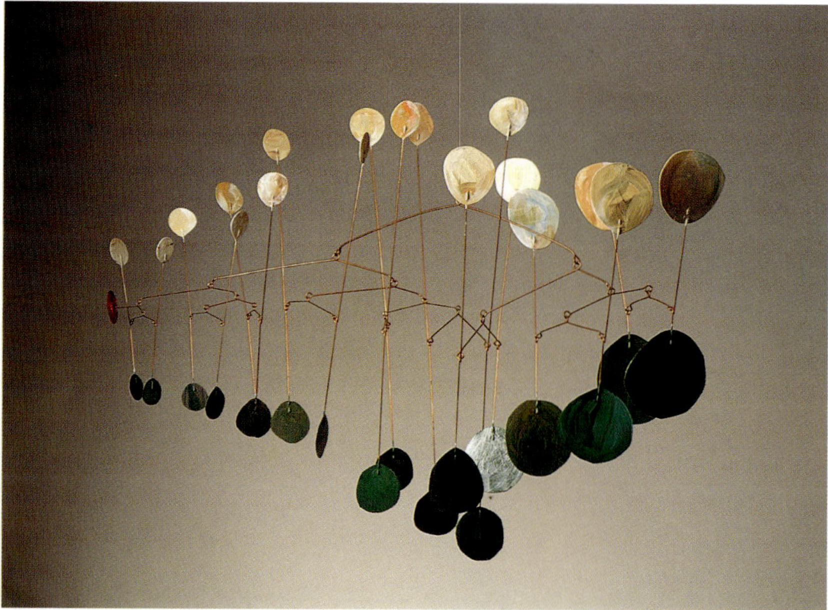

Will Mosgrove, Sausalito, CA

Timothy Rose
Timothy Rose Mobiles

Finding inspiration from movement and color, Timothy Rose has been designing and constructing mobile sculpture in the San Francisco Bay area for over 25 years. In addition to his one-of-a-kind pieces, he has sold replicated work to the Whitney, Guggenheim, Seattle, LA MOCA, and Carnegie museum stores. His commissions include work for the Chula Vista Nature Center, San Francisco Emporium and the Paris *Herald-Tribune*.

Resume and photos of current work are available upon request.

Also see these GUILD publications:
The Gallery & Retail Edition: 1
THE GUILD: 2, 4, 5
The Designer's Reference: 7

SHOWN: *Pan Mobile*, 1994, sheet metal, plywood, wire, and acrylic paint, 36"H x 52"L x 24"W

OTHER MEDIA

Susan Gardels

For over 15 years, Susan Gardels has created archival-quality paperworks for corporate and private clients. Pieces are constructed of handmade rag papers, painted with acrylic glazes, and sewn together for texture and durability. Information and slides are available.

Also see these GUILD publications:
The Gallery & Retail Edition: 1
*   The Designer's Reference: 8*

SHOWN: *Book of Scrolls*, 1993, 11" x 13"

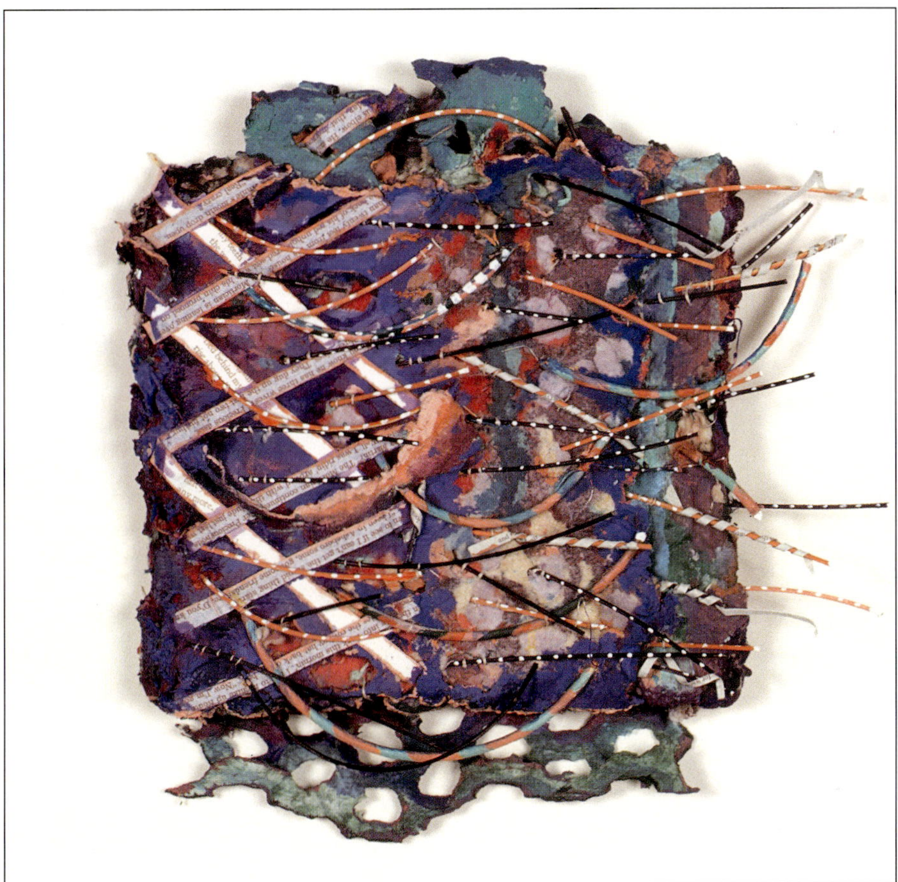

FIBERARTS
50 COLLEGE ST
ASHEVILLE, NC 28801
FAX 704-253-7952
TEL 704-253-0467
TEL 800-284-3388
$21/year

Five annual issues of *FIBERARTS* focus on contemporary textile art, including clothing, quilts, baskets, paper, tapestry, needlework and surface design. Features include artist profiles, critical essays, book reviews, and extensive listings of opportunities, events and resources.

Tim Walker
Pop Cat Studio

Artist Tim Walker creates extraordinary two- and three-dimensional mixed media sculptures that are humorous and refreshing in attitude. Sophisticated in style, satirical in content, and clever in approach, Tim's sculptures express his unique perception of the human condition.

Tim incorporates many technical innovations to achieve archival longevity, internal and external strength, and surface smoothness, and has chosen to draw inspiration from many different sculptural mediums. The result is a hybrid approach to his craft.

The goal is to redefine the medium and to put a whimsical spin on life.

Also see this GUILD publication:
The Designer's Reference: 9

A *Luciano Pavarotti*, mixed media,
   55" × 60" × 9", 2D©

B *Rabbit Magic*, mixed media,
   50½" × 33" × 5½", 2D©

C *Stage Fright*, mixed media,
   70" × 50" × 9", 2D©

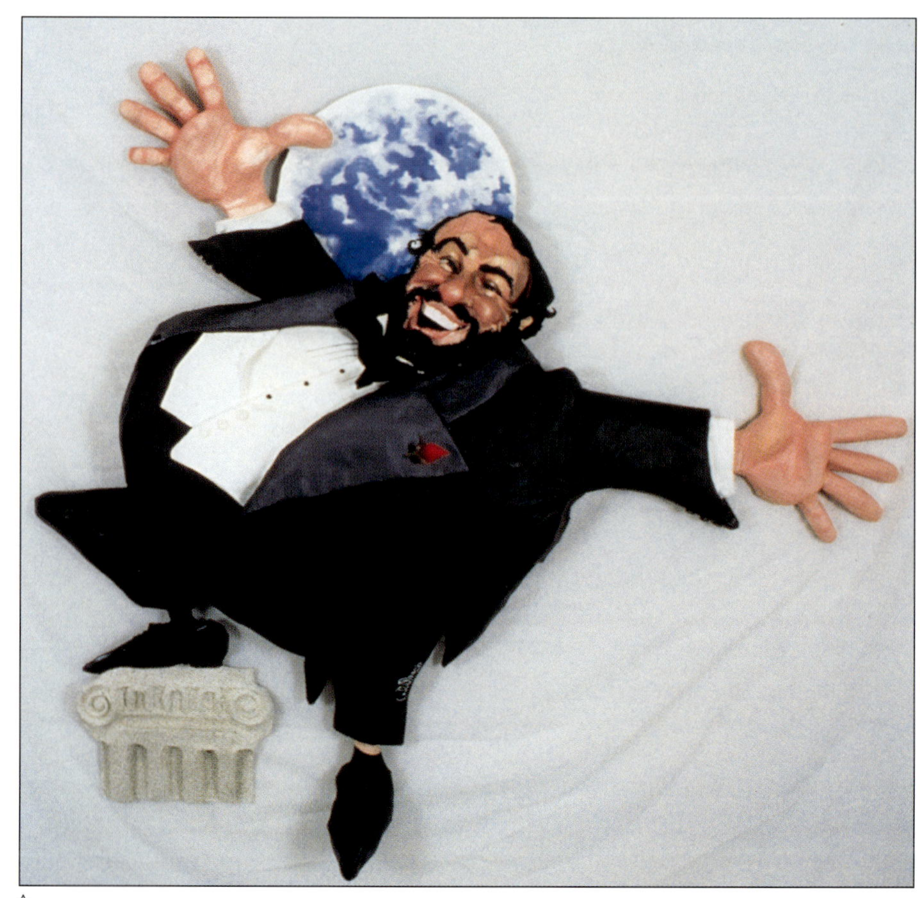

A

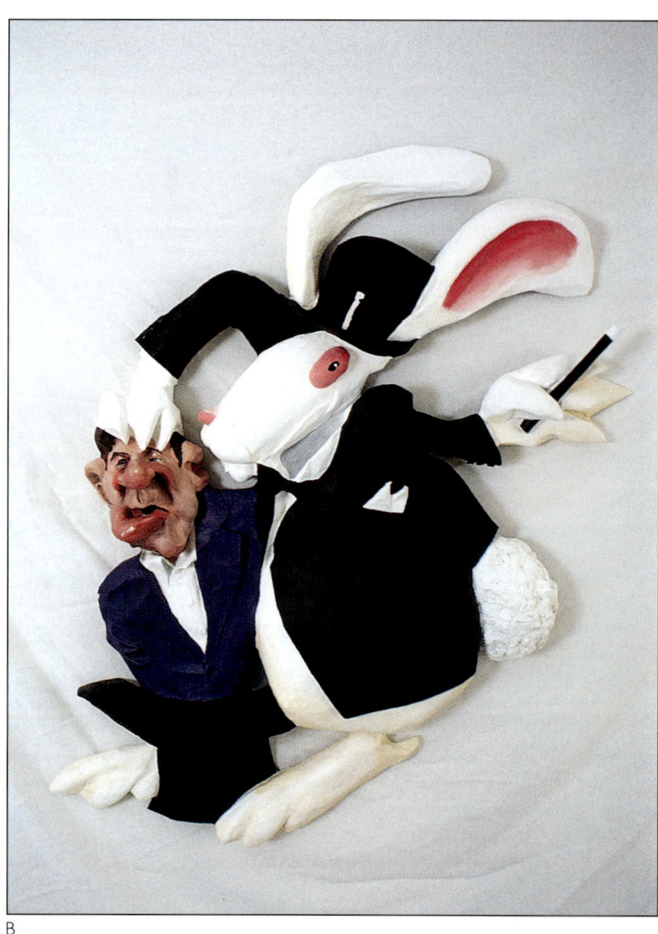

B

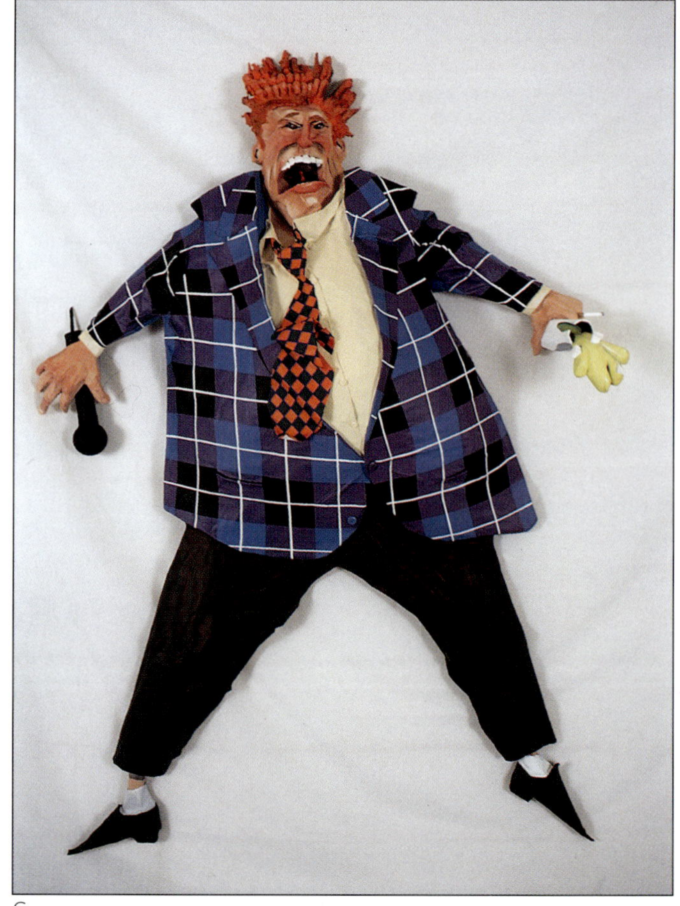

C

Itala Langmar
Itala

I have been a professional artist since 1984 and my work has been regularly shown in galleries, but I have been creating papier mâché vessels, vases and wall pieces only in the last three years. It was a trip to Venice, Italy, that inspired me; over there objects in papier mâché (carta pesta) are much sought after and are much more expensive than their clay counterparts.

I want to bring to mine the degree of beauty, elegance and uniqueness that I found in Venice.

SHOWN: papier mâché vessels, 10" to 14"Dia x 5"D, gold leafed and decorated with crochet and beads; *Fragments*, 1994, wall sculptures, handmade papers, papier mâché, mixed media, 11" to 13" x 1"D

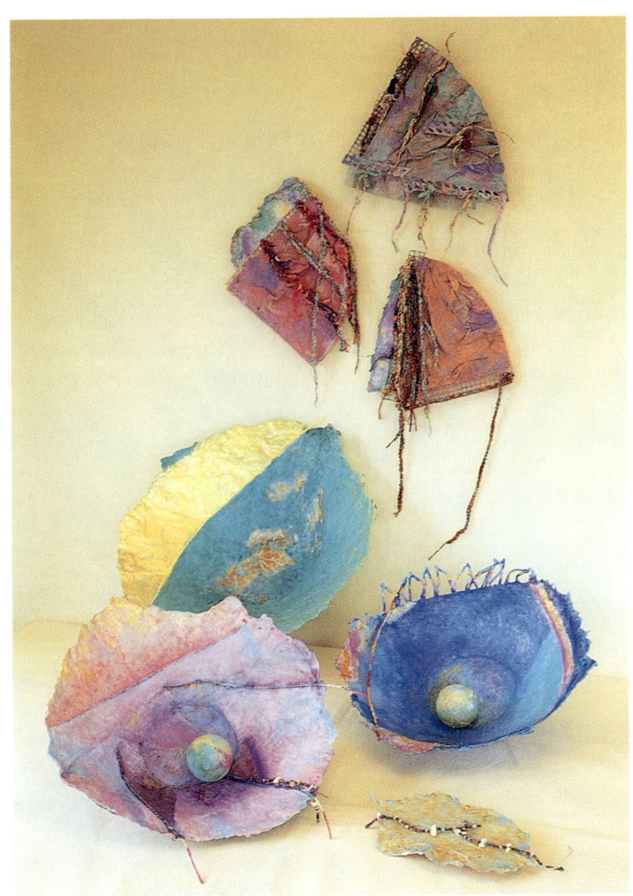

Carol Glassroth

Nancy J. Young

Young creates original, colorful and durable hand-cast paper wall art and 3D vessels. Included in *Who's Who in American Art* since 1984, her commissions and collections include the U.S. Department of State, AT&T, IBM and American Express.

Also see these GUILD publications:
The Gallery & Retail Edition: 1
THE GUILD: 1, 2, 3, 4, 5
The Designer's Reference: 6, 7, 8, 9

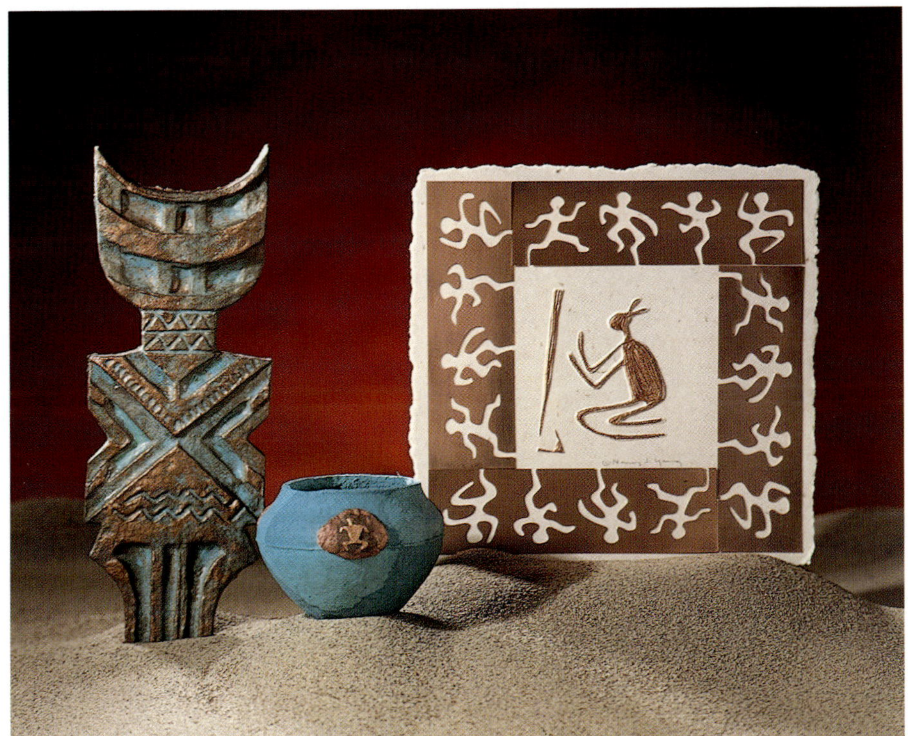

Pat Berrett

Hand-cast paper with a patinated bronze finish
(l. to r.) *Okalu*, 13"H x 4½"W x 5"D; small vessel, 3"H x 4"Dia; *Spirit Weaver*, 15" x 15"

Carole Alden
Doubek
Doubek & Doubek Studios

Ms. Doubek's creatures have been seen at the National Museum for Women in the Arts and the Royal Museum in Brussels, Belgium. Whether based in nature or the imagination, each fiber sculpture has its own distinct personality. In addition to individual pieces, Ms. Doubek enjoys creating complete environments. She is currently building a rainforest from recycled polyester double knits for the Red Butte Garden Arboretum at the University of Utah. Custom work includes freestanding sculptures, wall hangings, and educational exhibits. All work is primarily fabric, hand sewn, painted, and airbrushed.

Additional information available upon request.

A *Red-Eyed Treefrog*, 1995, polarfleece, dimensional fabric paint, 2½' × 3½'

B *MAW*, 1994, fiber, dimensional fabric paint, cast resin, 2½' × 2½'

C *Oriental Firebelly Toad*, 1995, recycled poly double knit, dimensional fabric paint, 2' × 2'

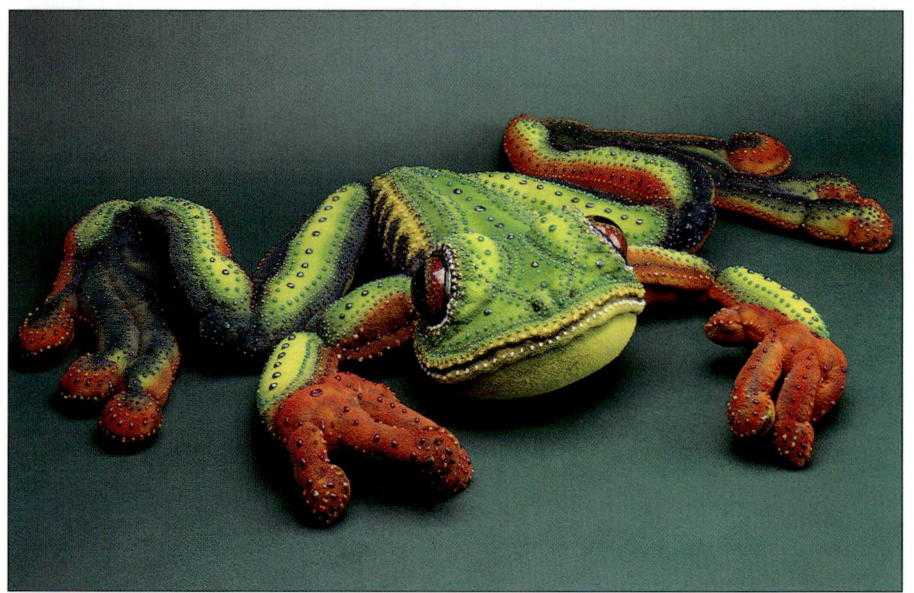

A

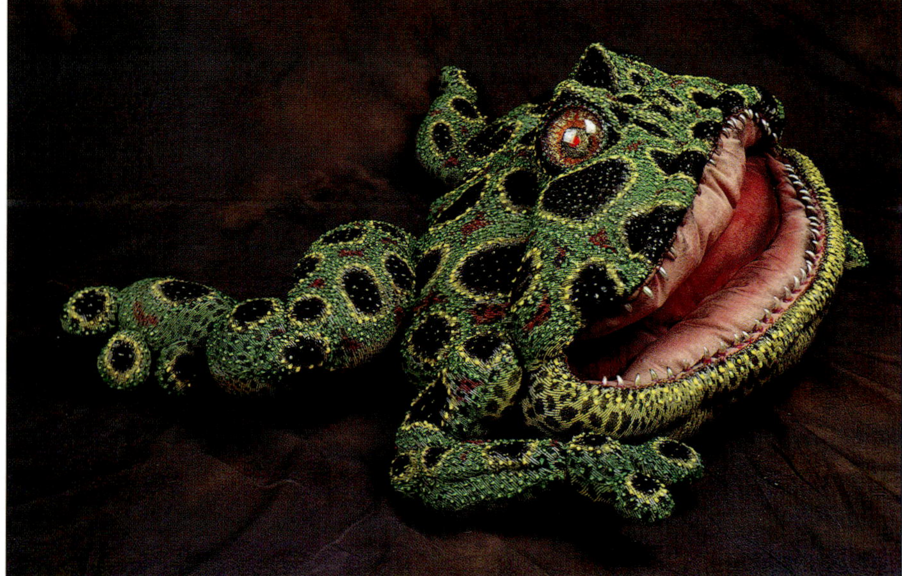

B

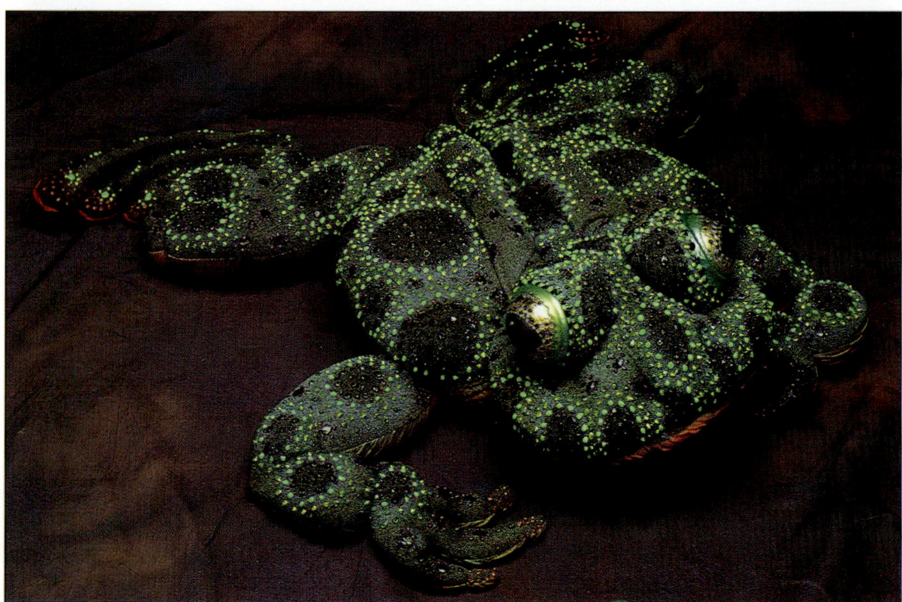

C

Photos: Gary Ott

OTHER MEDIA

Librus Studio
Linda Bruce Salomon

With a degree from Pratt Institute, this artist had a successful career in fine art. Started six years ago, the *Librus Studio Animal Dolls* are now in many collections. Most are fictional or imaginary, but some are commissioned pet portraits. The head and paws are porcelain. The bodies are textiles, beads and feathers. Most come with a chair or prop.

Also see these GUILD publications:
The Gallery & Retail Edition: 1
The Designer's Reference: 8

SHOWN (left to right): *Violette Cat*, 16"H; *Marsha Mouse Faery*, 6"H; *Madeline Marble Cat*, 13"H; *Francine Frog*, 10"H

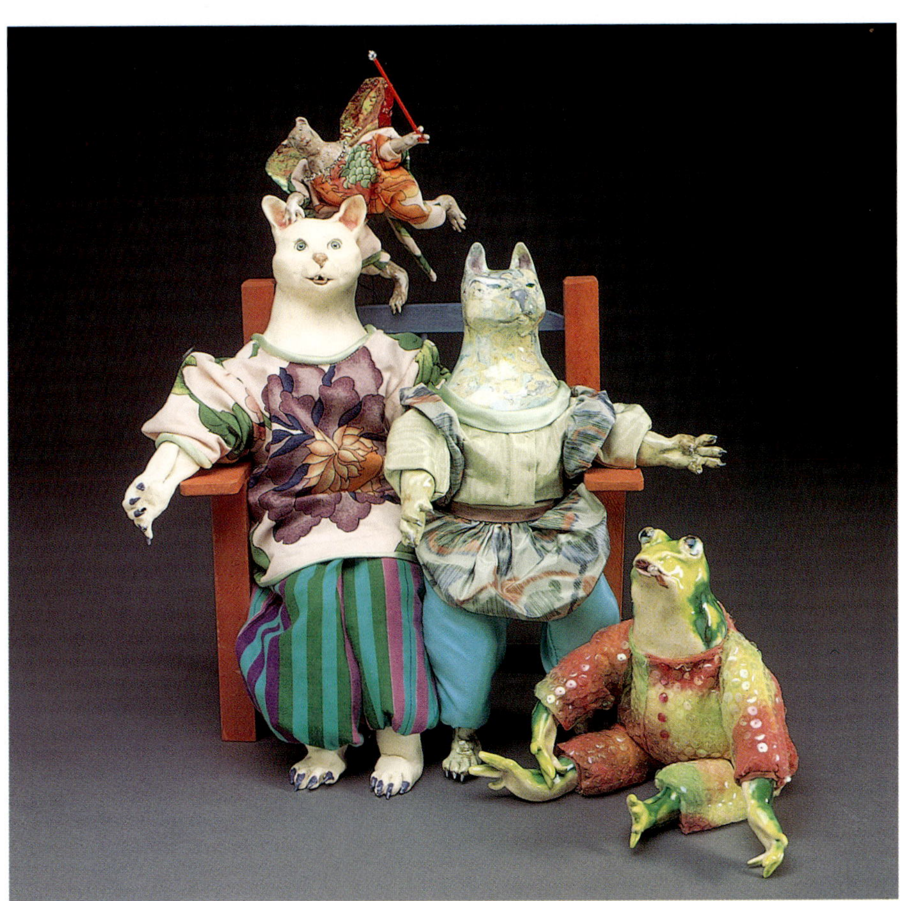

Oak Run Studios
Arthur Higgins

CRANK ART™: Tabletop sculptures with a toy vocabulary. Mixed-media sculptures featuring wood and metal with moving parts. Arthur Higgins has blended contemporary sculpture concepts, toyness and simple mechanical engineering into unique sculptures. A crank, lever or wheel is turned, pulled or pushed to activate the components of the sculpture. The viewer becomes a player.

SHOWN: *Swan*, turn the crank and the wheel turns and the head bobs back and forth; wood, aluminum, 12"H x 16"L x 16"W

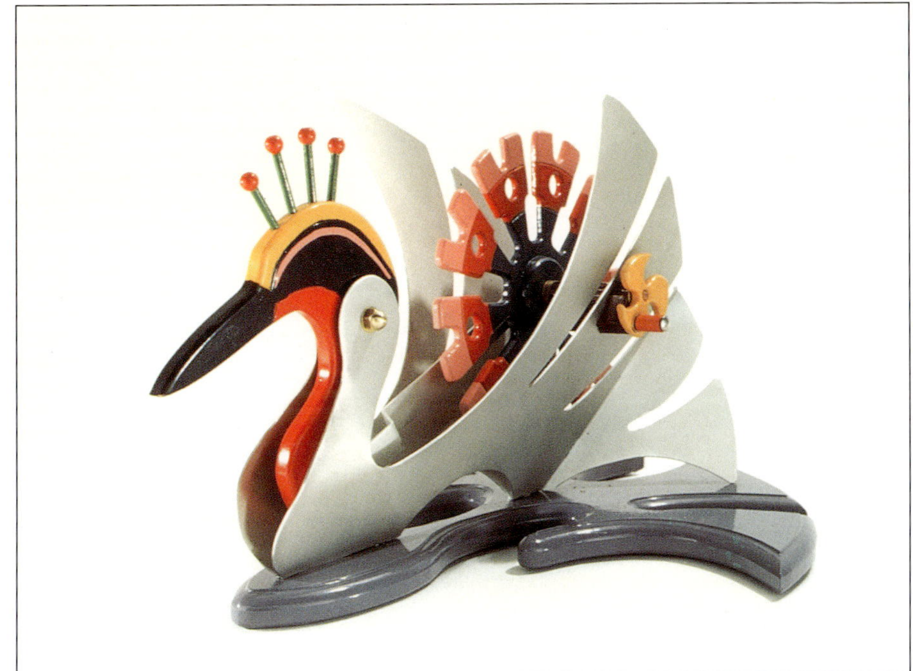

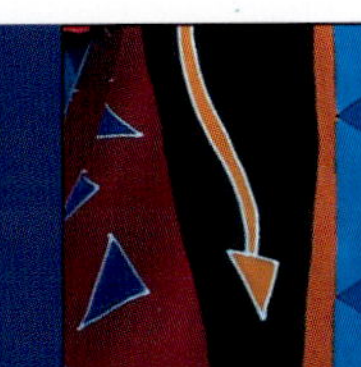

r fiber fiber fiber fiber fiber

Edward Mordak

Edward Mordak's figurative weaves have a 24K gold leaf with crystalline flake finish on plastic, vacuumed-formed masks. Vera-form bodies are mounted on a painted, textured background, with Fimo clay beads by the artist, and international handmade beads.

All weaves are 100% rag paper painted on both sides with metallic, metal flake, or luster and acrylic paint, and covered with a clear acrylic box. Paper is cut into eighth- and quarter-inch strips and knotted, braided or woven.

Mordak has exhibited at Virginia Brier Gallery in San Francisco and Wita Gardiner Gallery in San Diego and he is collected by private collectors.

SHOWN: figurative weave, 70½" × 40½" × 11¼"

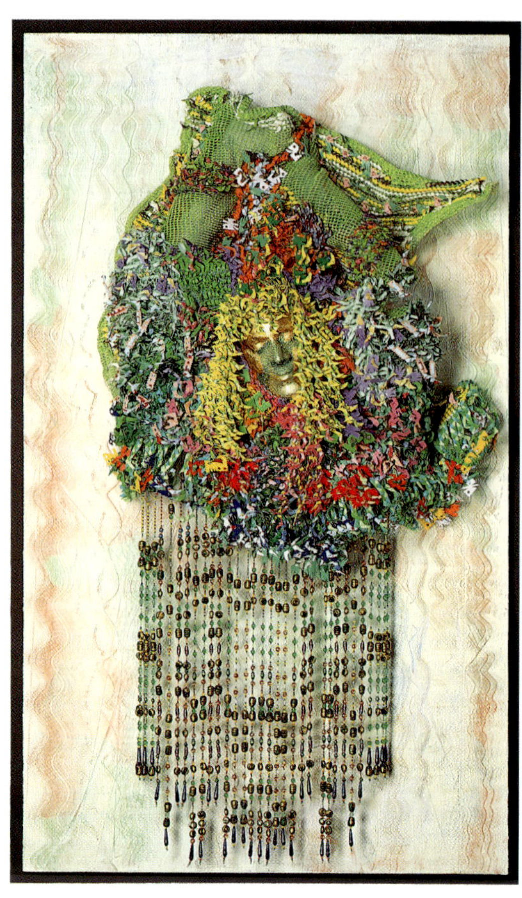

Nancy Moore Bess

The internationally known baskets and wall pieces of Nancy Moore Bess capture details of ancient armour, Japanese folk art and packaging, and African jewelry. Display for the vessels includes Japanese river stones, and bamboo and copper stands. Custom-made lucite boxes frame the wall art, allowing for easy installation and maintenance in public and private sites.

Also see these GUILD publications:
The Gallery & Retail Edition: 1
THE GUILD: 4, 5
The Designer's Reference: 6, 7, 8

SHOWN: U.S. Embassy commission, copper screen box, 24"

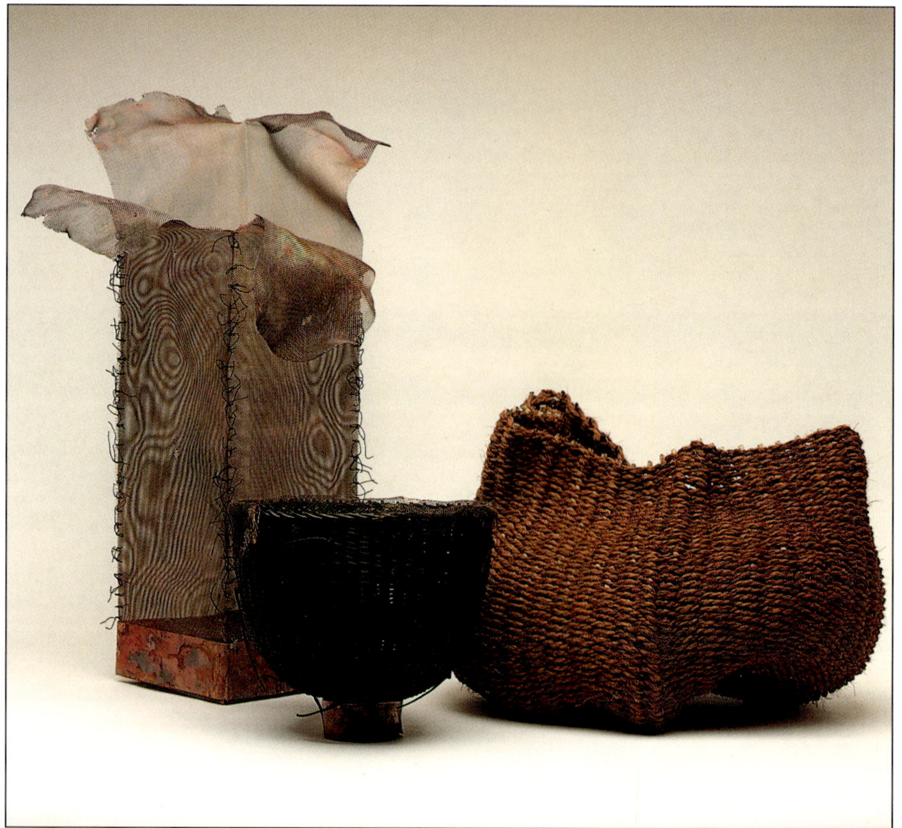

EKO
Ellen Kochansky

EKO's limited-edition pieced quilts combine durability (slipcover-weight textiles, and generous seams) with Ellen Kochansky's color artistry, in a unique blend of classic contemporary design, imaginative fabrication and reasonable pricing. EKO offers responsive customer service, a complete line of accessories, and a custom program.

Swatching and samples available.

Also see these GUILD publications:
The Gallery & Retail Edition: 1
THE GUILD: 1, 2, 4, 5
The Designer's Reference: 7, 9

SHOWN: queen-size comforter, 1994, mixed-fiber pieced quilt, style: *Nimbus*, color: canyon, 86" x 100"

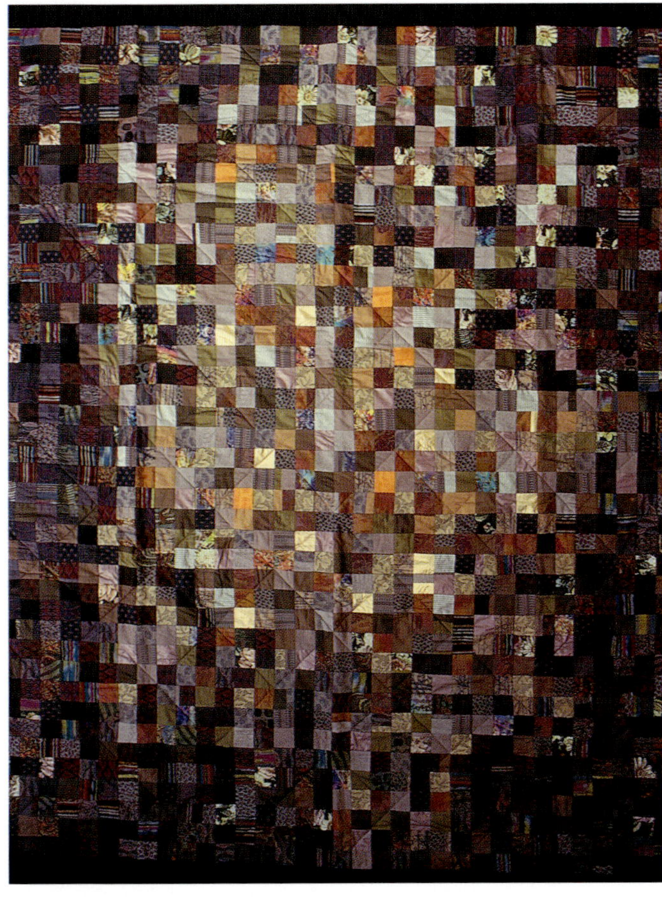

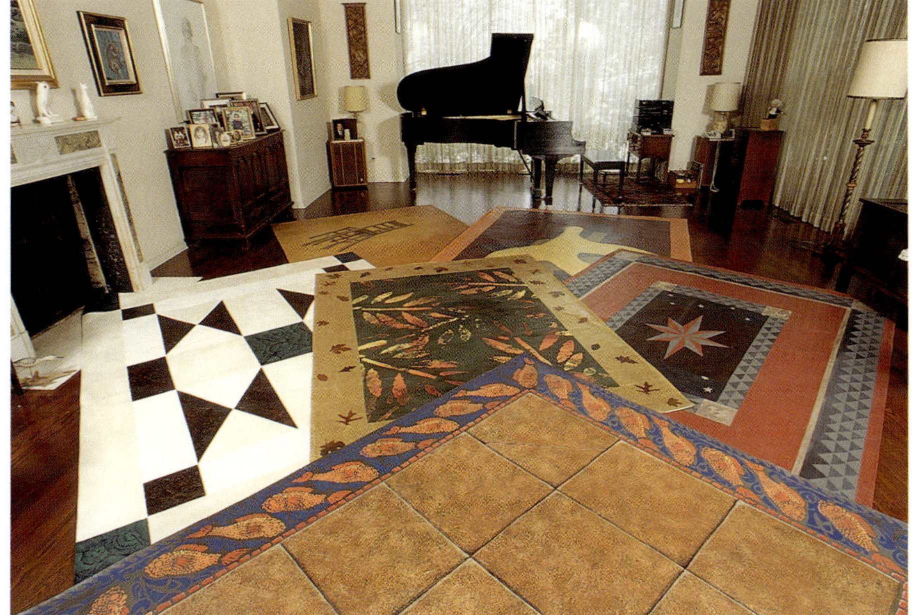

Marjorie A. Atwood

Marjorie Atwood creates distinctive floor and wall art that is meticulously crafted. These fabulous floorcloths often incorporate beautiful faux finishes, gilding and metallic effects. Designs can compliment fabrics and wallpaper. A protective sealer ensures easy cleaning, maintenance and durability. Commissions and collaborations are welcome. Atwood's designs are in galleries in California, Santa Fe and Tulsa. Information about pricing, sizes, and ordering is available.

Also see these GUILD publications:
The Designer's Reference: 7, 8, 9

Susan M. Oaks

Susan Oaks, an artist for over 20 years, utilizes the coiling technique to produce one-of-a-kind vessels made from a rich variety of materials, including silk, linen, wool and cotton.

These vessel forms look well under plexiglass, are unbreakable, and are easily freshened with a gentle shake or a light vacuuming.

Susan has exhibited her art nationally with past shows in New York, Chicago and Los Angeles. Her work has been featured in *Southwest Art* magazine.

A *The Internal Search*, man-made fiber over
   rush, 6¼"H x 9"Dia

B *A Time to Mourn and a Time to Dance*,
   linen over rush, 15½"H x 6"Dia

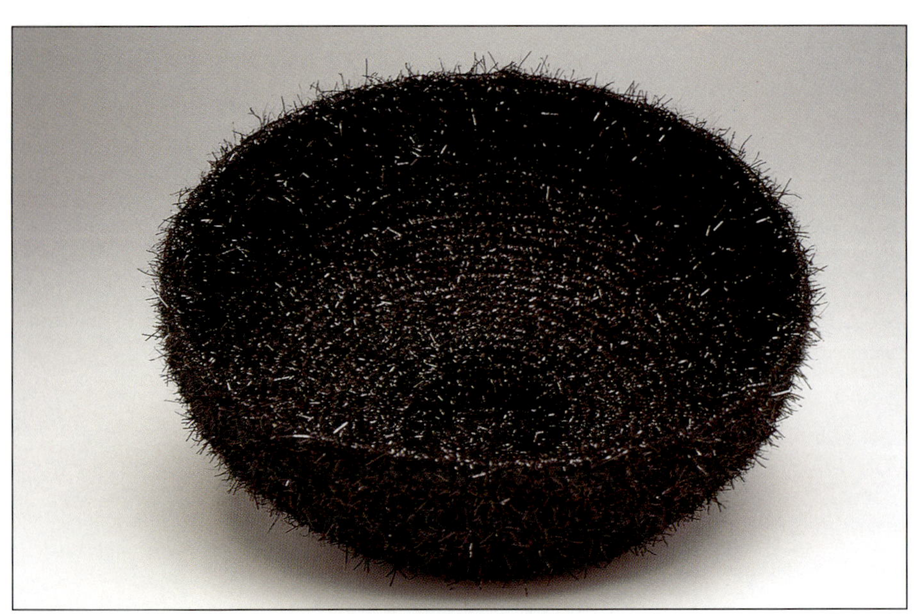

A

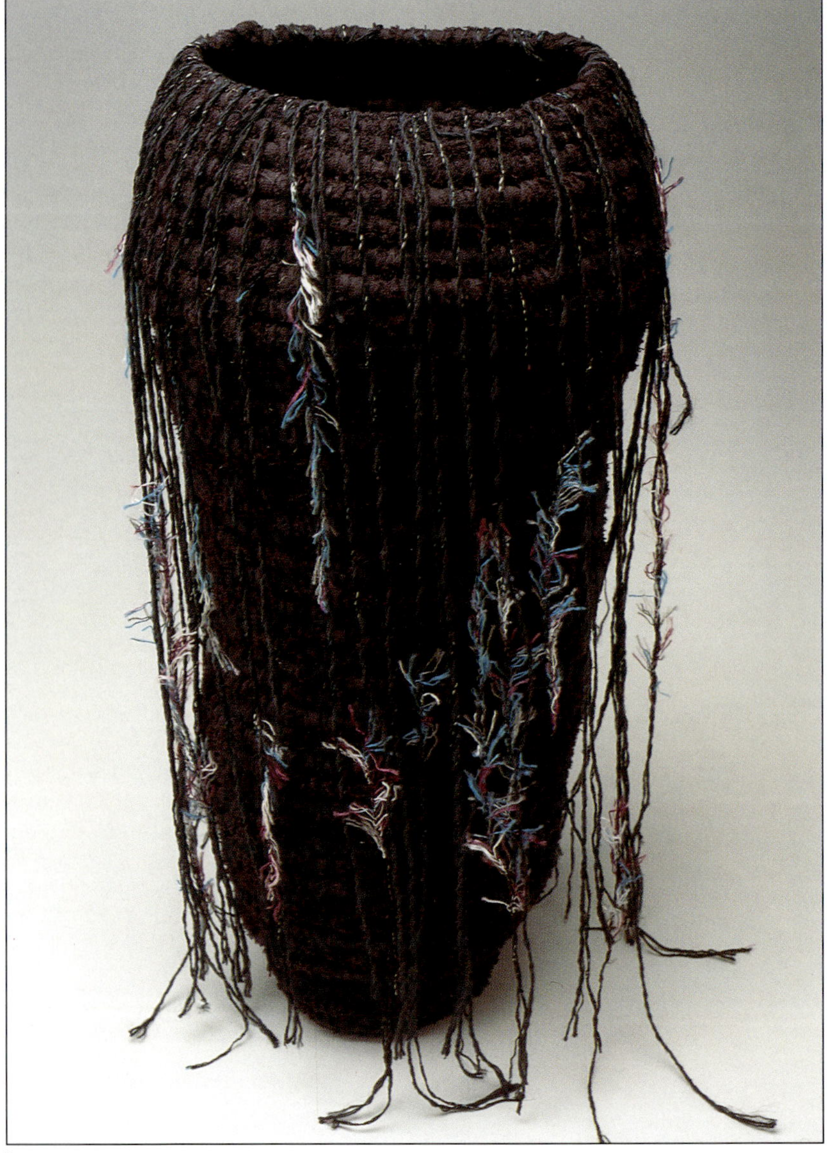

B

SMITTY BLANKETS

Elaine M. Wedge

Custom hand-woven saddle blankets offer something unique. English exercise blankets to Western show blankets, each is created as the rider's signature accessory. Many SMITTY BLANKETS, however, never see the back of a horse! They serve as color and texture accent pieces for interiors.

SMITTY BLANKETS throws are handwoven of natural fibers. Whether of a cotton/linen blend for a cottage porch or a wool/silk plaid for après ski, each adds pleasure to leisure time.

Elaine M. Wedge developed appreciation of textiles at the University of Michigan while earning her BA in History of Art.

A saddle blanket, ranuu weave with herringbone accent, 100% wool, 32" × 34"

B throw, Swedish rosepath pattern, 100% perle cotton, 45" × 72"

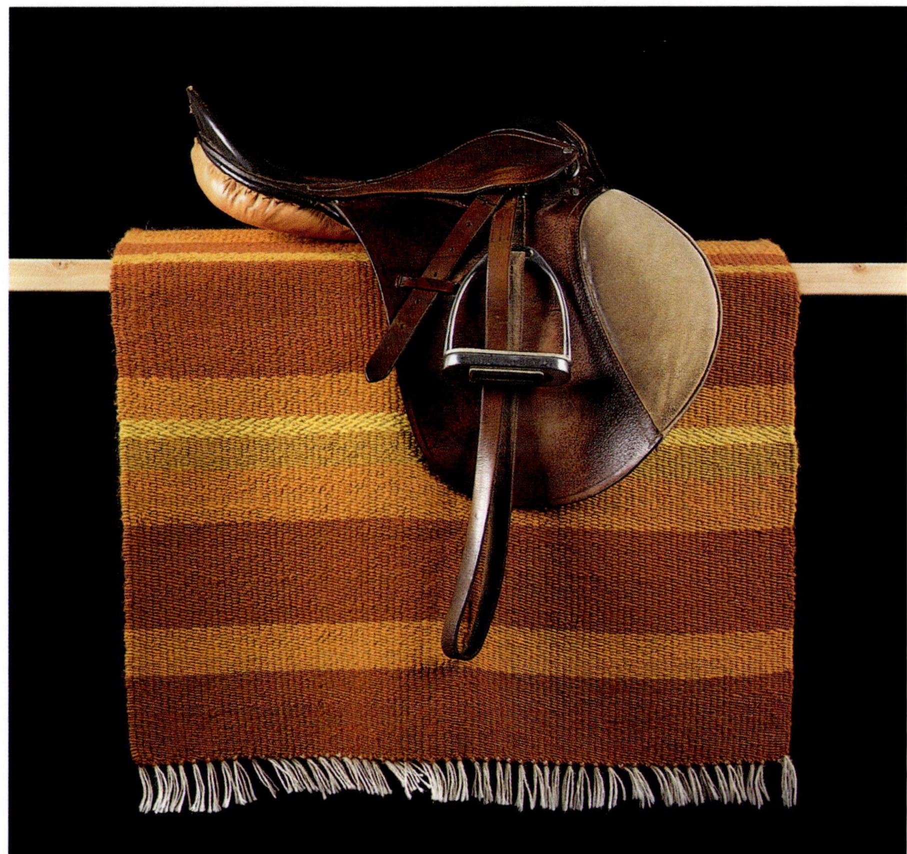

A

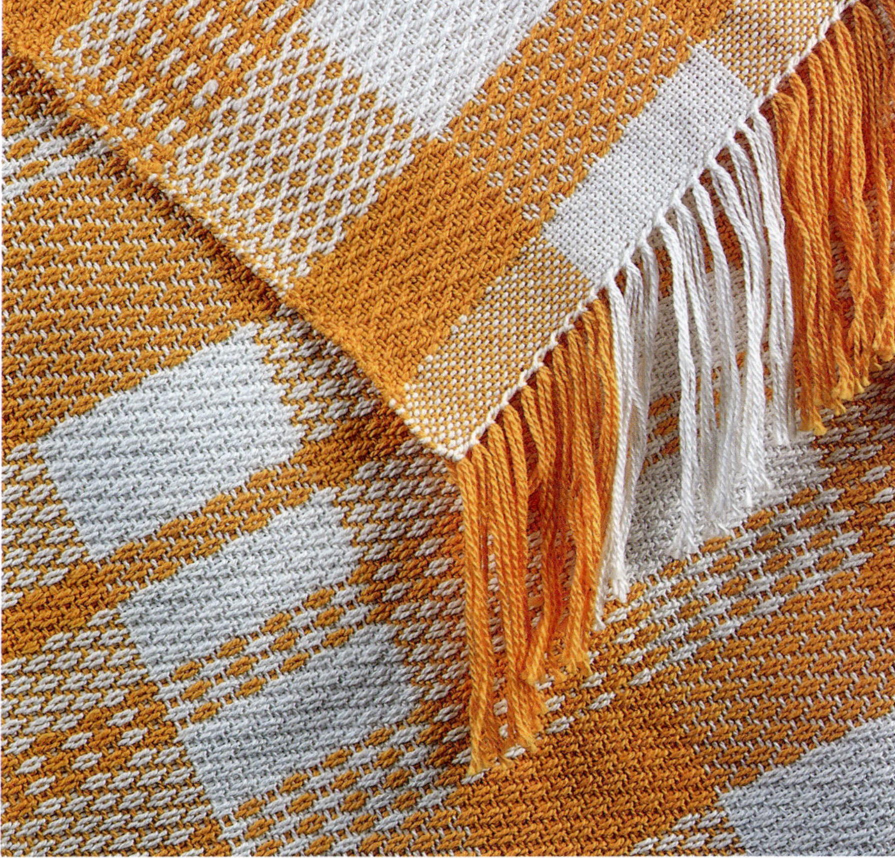

B

Victoria Potrovitza

**Bright Side Art to Wear
by Victoria Potrovitza**

Victoria Potrovitza is a fashion designer
with more than ten years experience.

Lately she enhances her creations by
designing exclusive patterns and textures
for the fabrics of her garments.

Her line of limited-edition clothing is
renewed annually and featured in a catalog
available by request.

Commissions are welcome. All ensembles
can be delivered in any combination of
designs and colors.

Also see this GUILD publication:
The Gallery & Retail Edition: 1

SHOWN: dress and two-piece suit, 1994, silk
and velvet, all hand dyed and resist painted

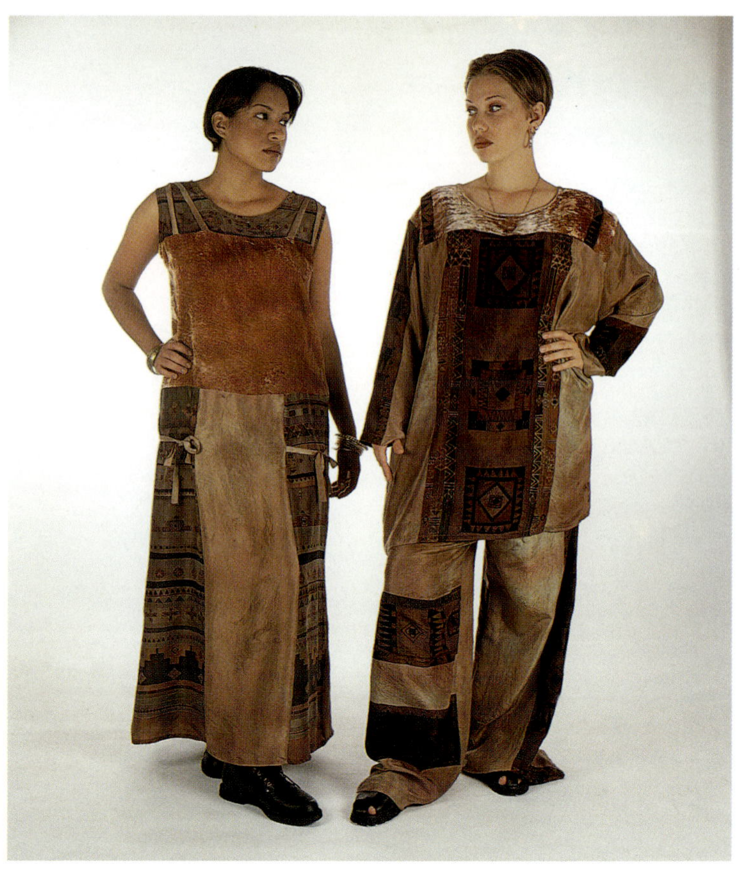

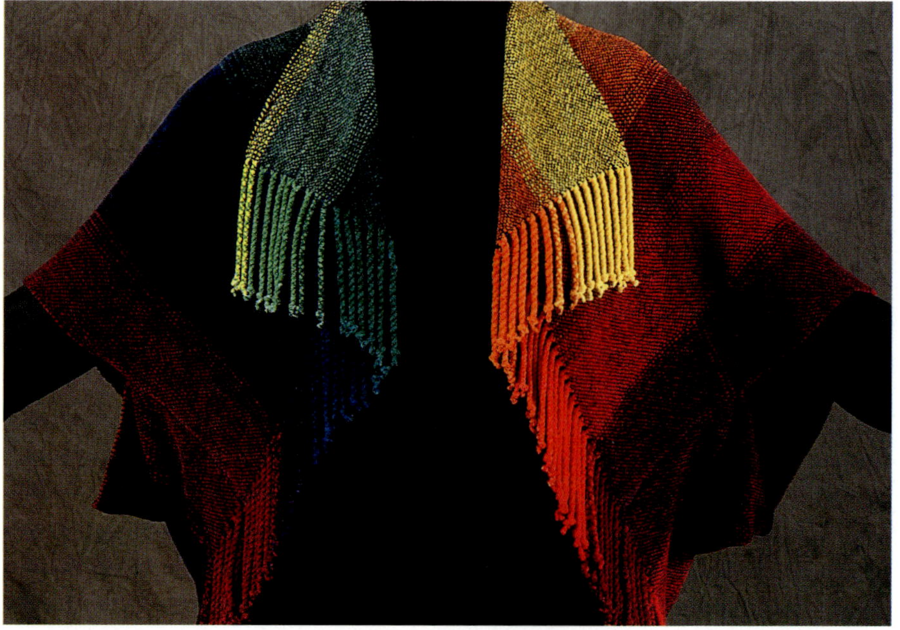

Stanley Blanchard, Schenectady, NY

Nettles and
Green Threads
Paula Chaffee Scardamalia

Seductive, rich colors and the luxurious feel
of rayon chenille make these hand-woven
wearables and throws by Ms. Scardamalia
irresistible. Whether limited edition, one-of-
a-kind or custom designed, each item is
prewashed for a soft, sumptuous hand, and
given a distinctive hand-plied fringe for
drape and durability.

Peggotty Handpainted Silk

Peggotty Christensen

Inspired by the colors and images of the Southwest, the brilliantly colored, hand-painted silks by Peggotty are timeless in design. Formerly a jeweler for 25 years, Peggotty has been a fiber artist for the last eight years and has incorporated many of the design elements used in jewelry-making into her unique garments. Each one-of-a-kind piece is painted with fiber-reactive dyes, which are extremely colorfast. Most garments are one size and can be either hand washed or dry cleaned. Peggotty's work includes scarves, neckties, blouses, tunics, jackets, skirts, shawls and dresses.

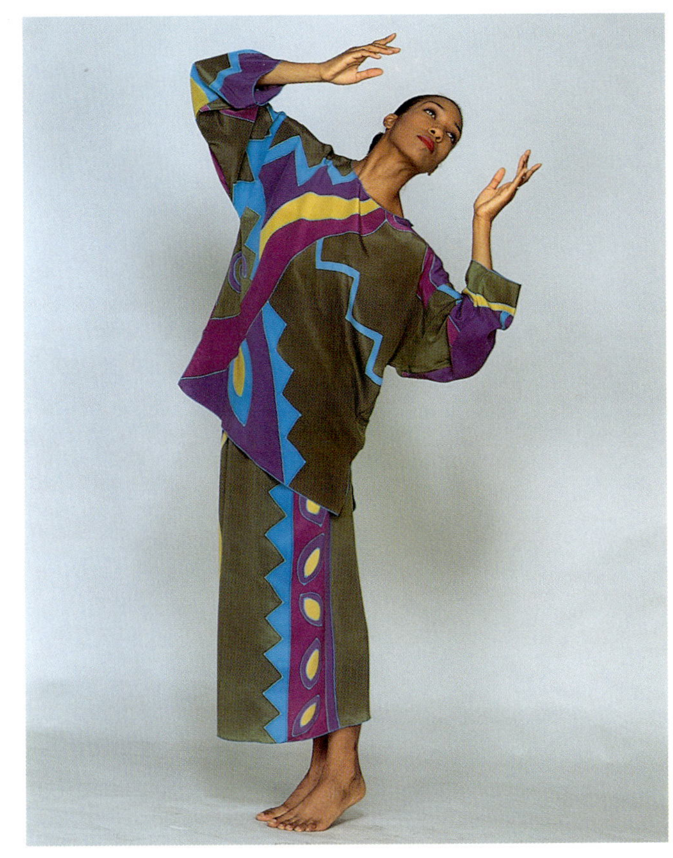

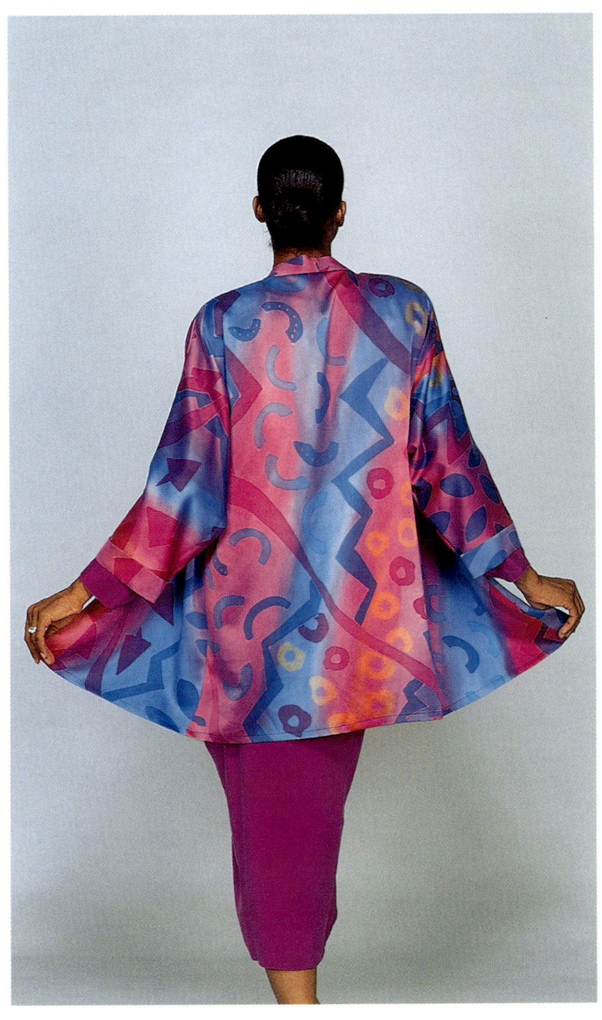

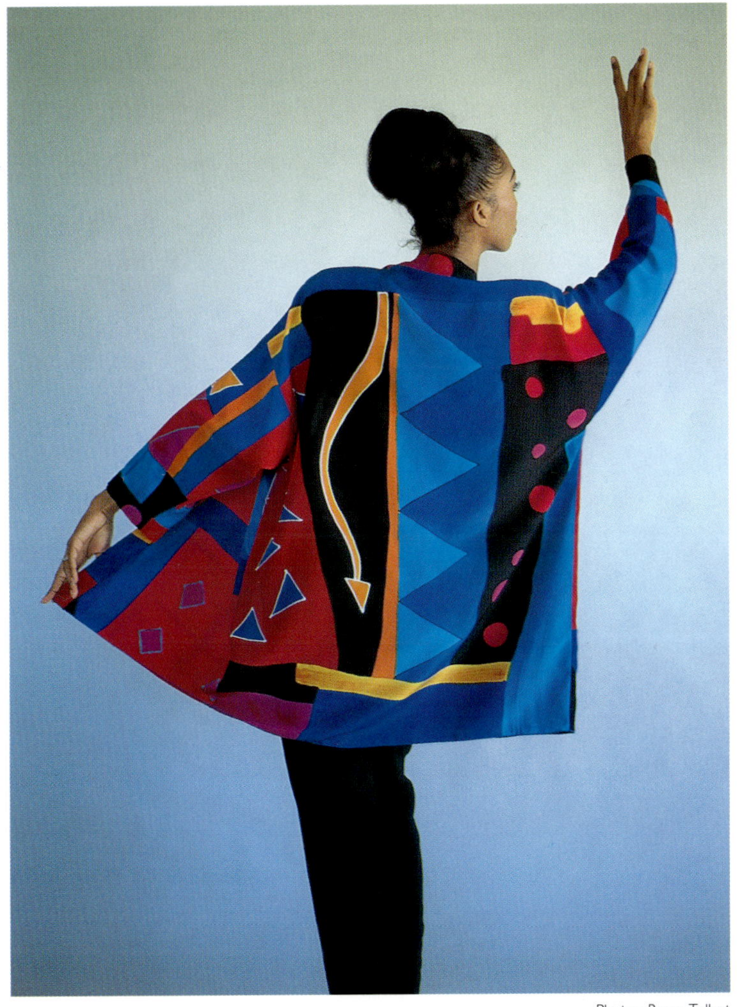

Photos: Bruce Talbot

jewelry jewelry jewelry jewelr

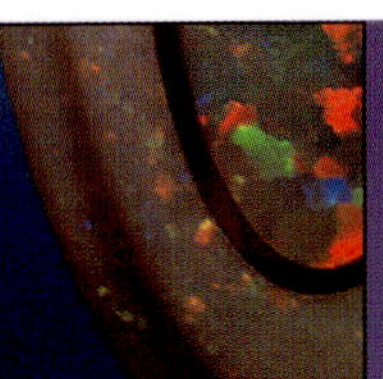

jewelry jewelryejewelry

Paulette J. Werger

Inspired by natural forms, Paulette Werger creates jewelry of silver, gold, pewter and unusual gemstones. Her award-winning jewelry is noted for its distinctive design and sensitive combination of materials. Ms. Werger exhibits nationally. Her work was recently featured in *Metalsmith* magazine.

Also see this GUILD publication:
The Gallery & Retail Edition: 1

SHOWN: *Boat in Slow Current*, brooch, fused and fabricated sterling, lapis, 4½"H x 2½"W x ¼"D

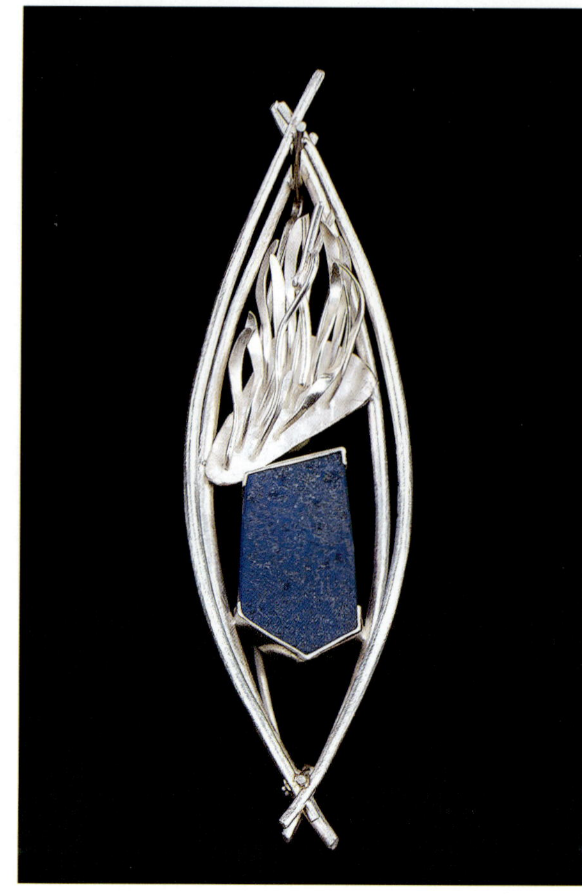

R. Trummer

METALSMITH

5009 LONDONDERRY DR
TAMPA, FL 33647
FAX 813-977-8462
TEL 813-977-5326
$26/year

Metalsmith, a four-color quarterly, includes artist profiles, critical essays and reviews. Its focus is on contemporary metal artists producing jewelry, small sculpture and objects. *Metalsmith* is published by the Society of North American Goldsmiths.

Tomoco Yamada
Ma Muse Collection, Inc.

Following in the tradition of her native Japan, Tomoco Yamada views art as an extended meditation on the natural world. Her elegantly simple designs derive from the powerful but momentary patterns formed by nature, which the artist arrests in time. Each hand-hammered piece in her *Wave Collection* is as unique as each wave in the sea. Beautiful pearls from the Sea of Japan and the South Pacific float upon her designs as if carried along by the force of nature.

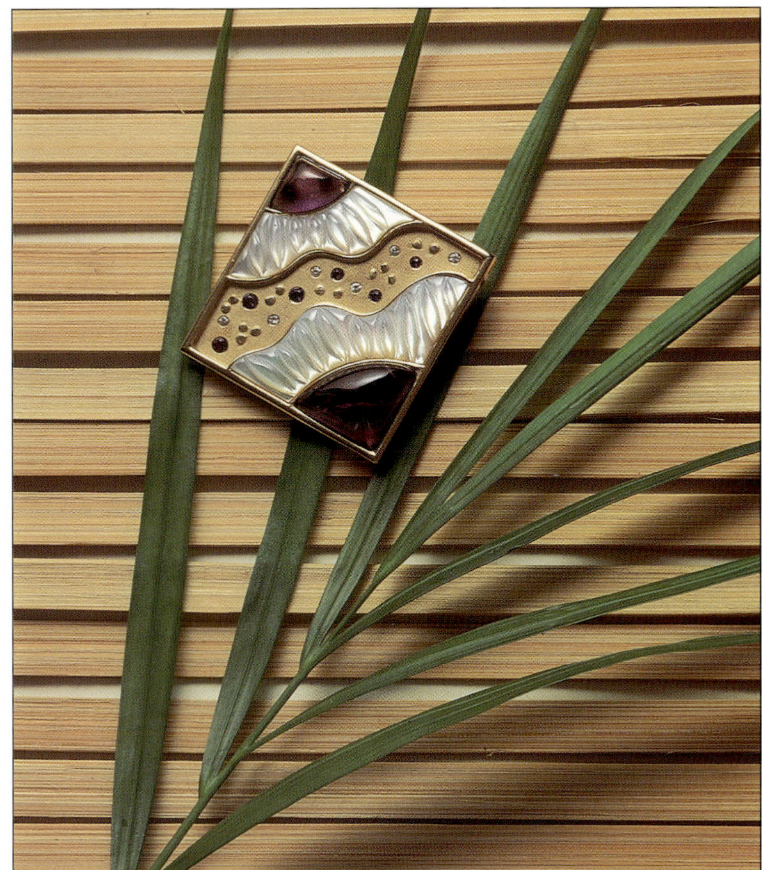

Zen Garden, 1994, brooch, amethyst, diamonds and mother of pearl, 18K gold

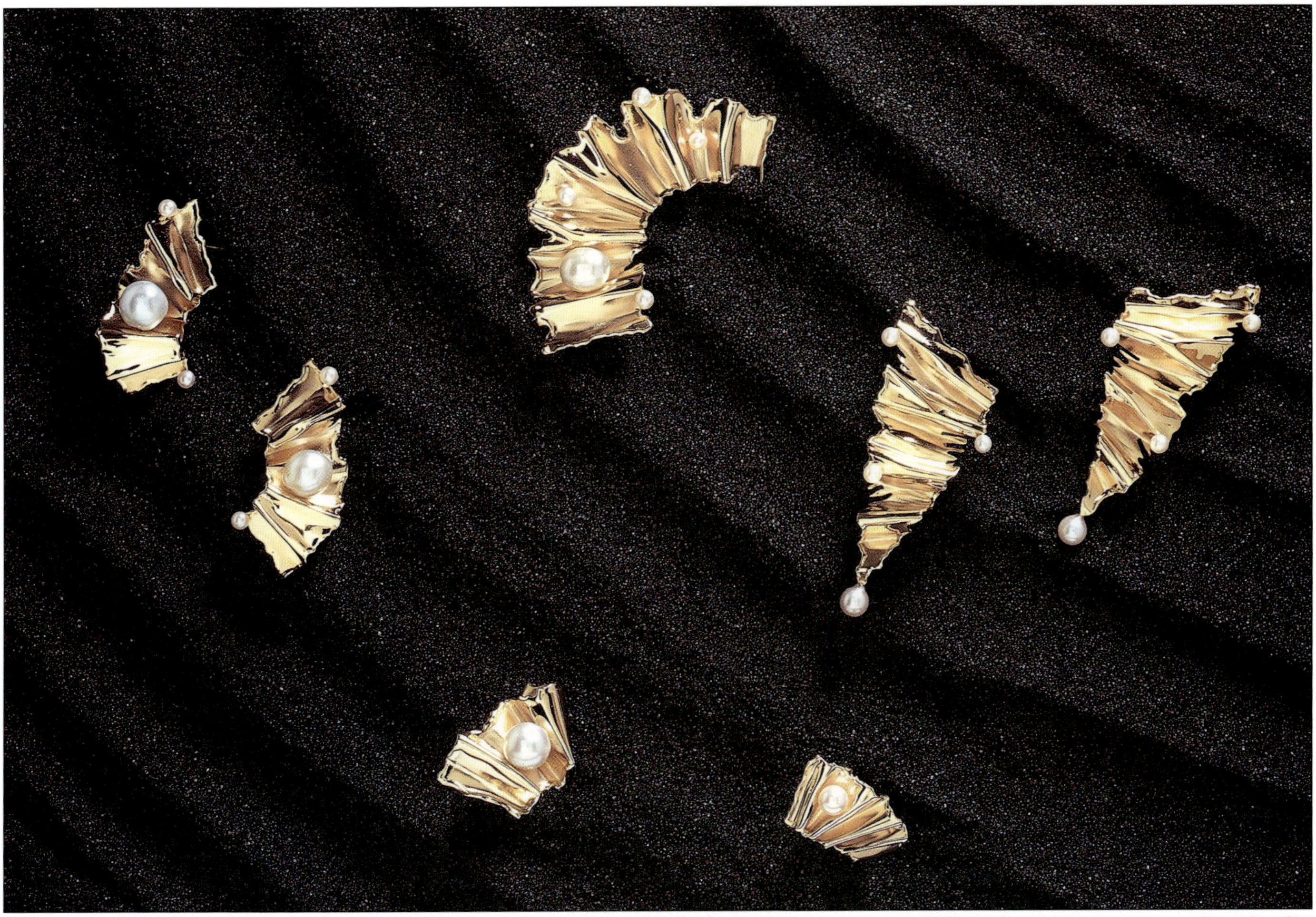

The Wave Collection, 1994, brooch, earrings and rings, 14K gold, Japanese and South Sea pearl, also available in 18K and sterling silver

Photos: Barry Blau

Circle 'Round the Moon
Jack Lalor

Circle 'Round the Moon has made jewelry from noble metals and fine gems since 1974.

Gimmel bands—interlocked rings that open to reveal hidden detail. They may be set with stones, engraved with a private message, and made of contrasting alloys or in a single color.

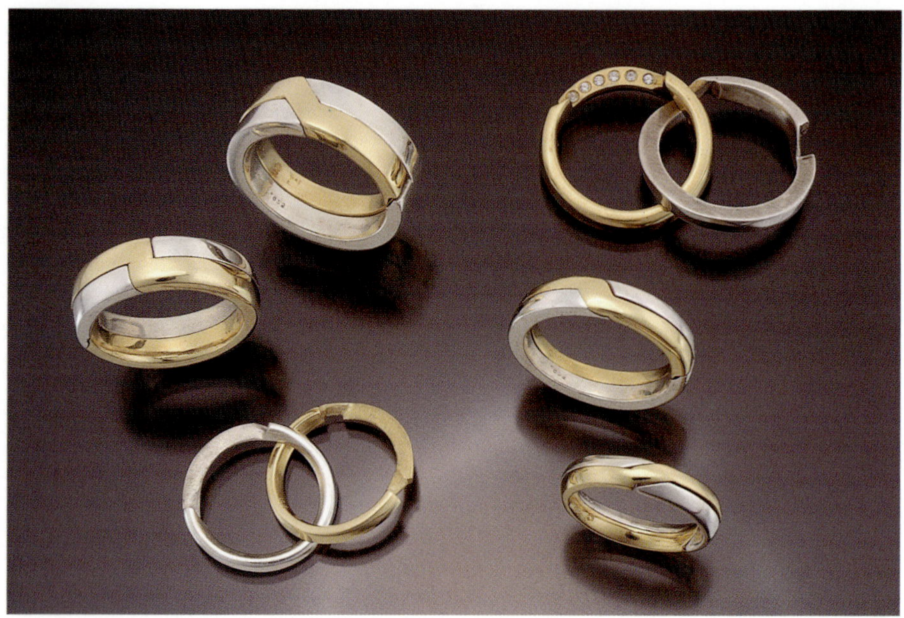

Ralph Gabriner

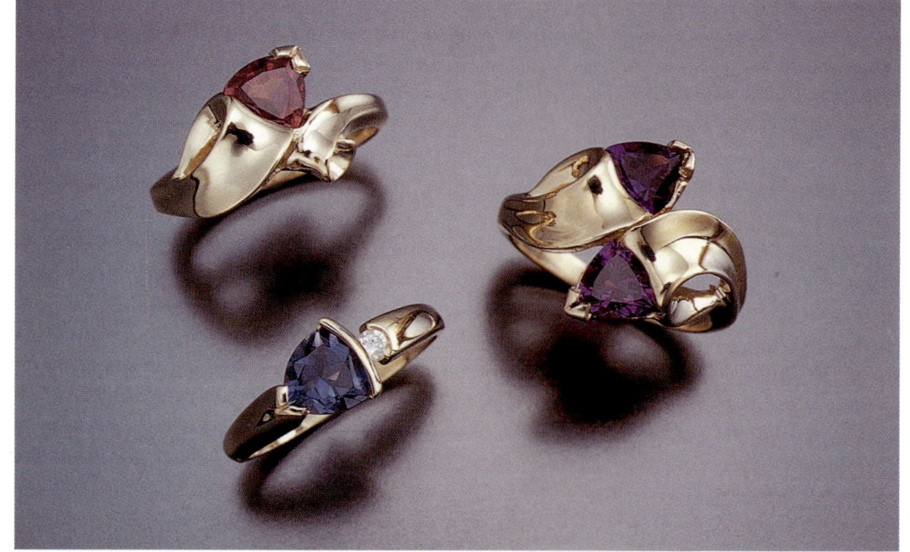

Allen Bryan

Artisans Accord
John Di Gregorio/Rick Butcher

John and Rick bring 35 years of experience in jewelry design to you. Beautiful, wearable, visible and totally unique contemporary jewelry of precious metals and gems.

Designs feature sweeping organic curves with a strong sense of movement and style.

Holly E. Churchill
Holly E. Churchill, Jeweler

Three-dimensional drawings in fine metal is what Holly calls her jewelry pieces. She hand fabricates each piece in either sterling silver or 14K gold. She has been making jewelry since 1987 and has shown her work from coast to coast and in Europe as well.

SHOWN: two brooches in 14K gold and sterling silver, each 1⅜" Dia

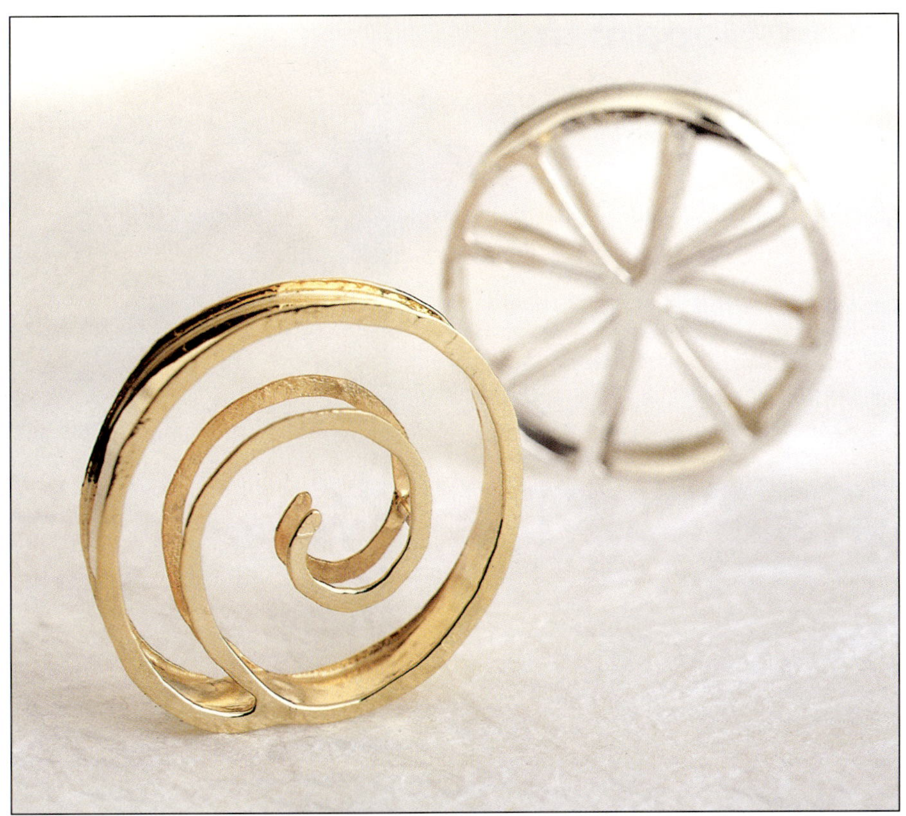

Kevin Brusie, Portland, ME

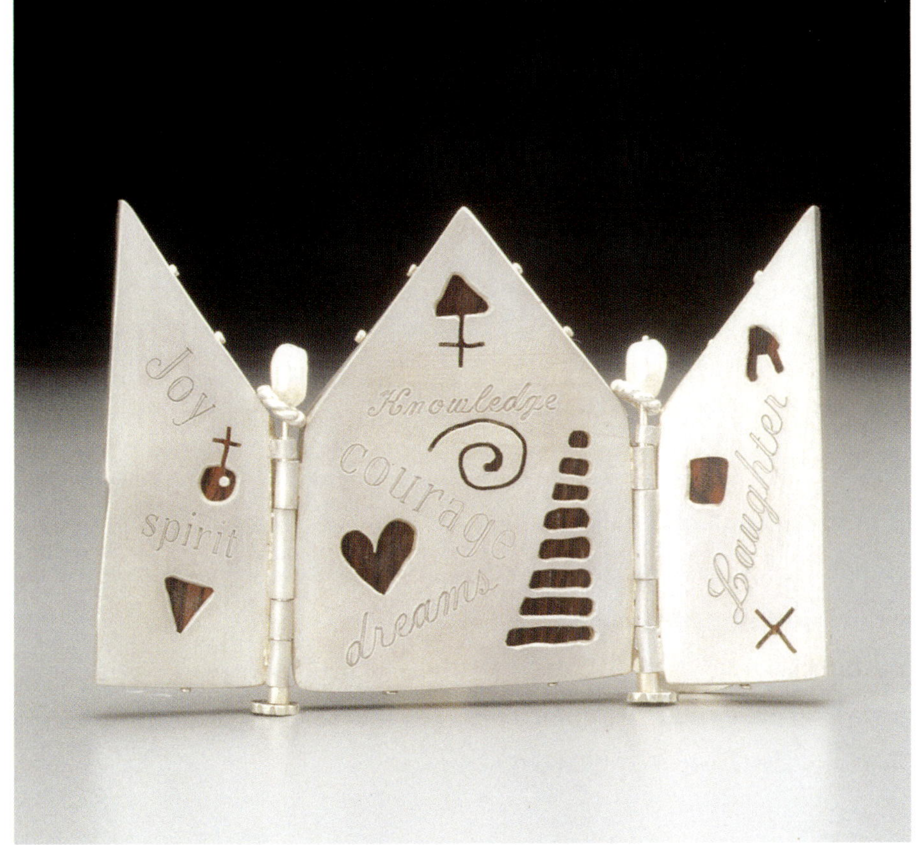

Gael A. Sloop
A. Sloop Design

The *Women Icon* triptych uses sacred symbols and engraved words such as 'courage,' 'laughter' and 'spirit' to emulate both men and women. Gael also produces a line of pins and earrings. Her exploration in design maintains simplicity combined with honest craftsmanship.

SHOWN: *Women's Icon, #3,* sterling silver, wood and pearls, 2½" × 2¾" × ½"

Barry Goodman and Son Jewelers

Barry incorporates sterling silver and 24K vermeil in 'Botanical' style neckpieces, earrings, pins, bracelets and rings. His pieces achieve an earthly form with romantic lines. Barry, a 25-year veteran jeweler, has international recognition and regularly shows at The Buyers Market of American Crafts, Beckman's Handmade, and Handmade in USA shows.

Also see these GUILD publications:
The Gallery & Retail Edition: 1
THE GUILD: 1

SHOWN: *Botanical Creations*, sampling of ten flower collection, sterling & vermeil

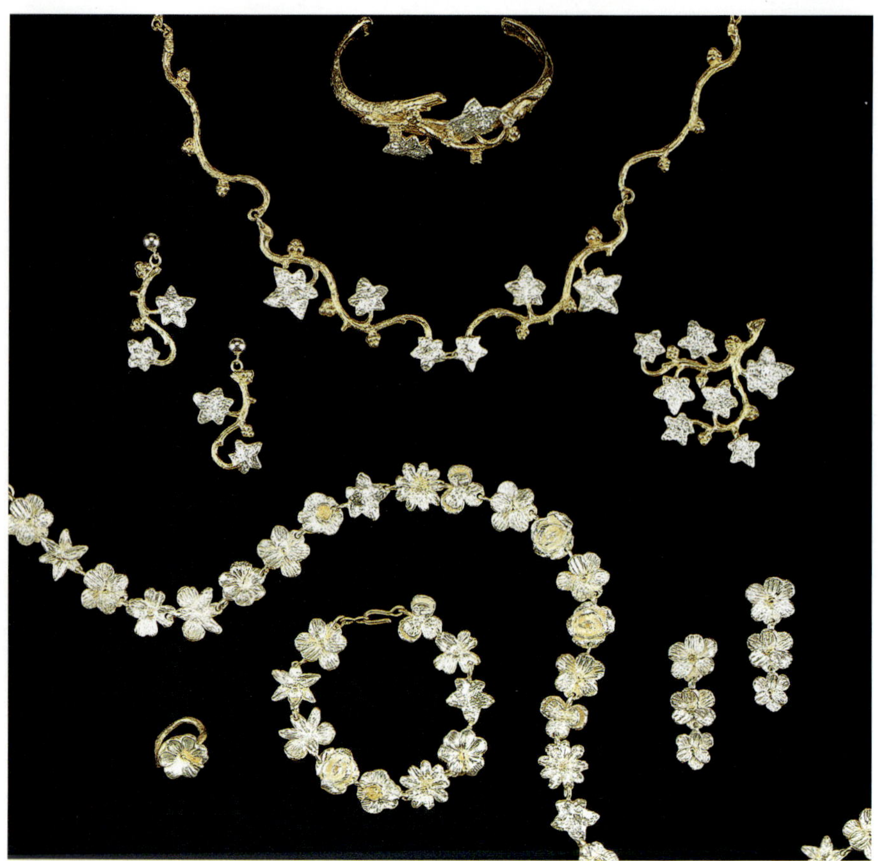

SOCIETY OF NORTH AMERICAN GOLDSMITHS

5009 LONDONDERRY DR
TAMPA, FL 33647
FAX 813-977-8462
TEL 813-977-5326
Bob Mitchell, Executive Administrator

The Society of North American Goldsmiths (SNAG) was founded in 1970 to promote contemporary metalwork and jewelry. Through its publications, services and advocacy, the Society serves the fine art and jewelry communities with publications and conferences for members, practitioners and teachers of metalwork. Professional metalsmiths, students, collectors, gallery owners and enthusiasts form the dynamic mix of the Society.

Rita Baker Design

The jewelry presented here introduces the *Rhythm Collection*: elegant surface-embellished metal jewelry based on original designs by Rita Baker, designer of contemporary jewelry, located in eastern Pennsylvania.

Inspired by Rita's background in graphic design, as well as her longtime interests in interior design, architecture and industrial design, *Rhythm* jewelry is both dynamic and understated.

Designs are produced in 14 karat gold, sterling silver, and lacquered brass, with the highest quality standards. Even the silver and brass earrings have 14K posts. Some styles also feature precious and semi-precious stones.

SHOWN: *Shield I*, earrings, 14K gold with amethyst, green tourmaline and pink tourmaline; *Shield II*, pendant, 14K gold with iolite, green tourmaline and pink tourmaline

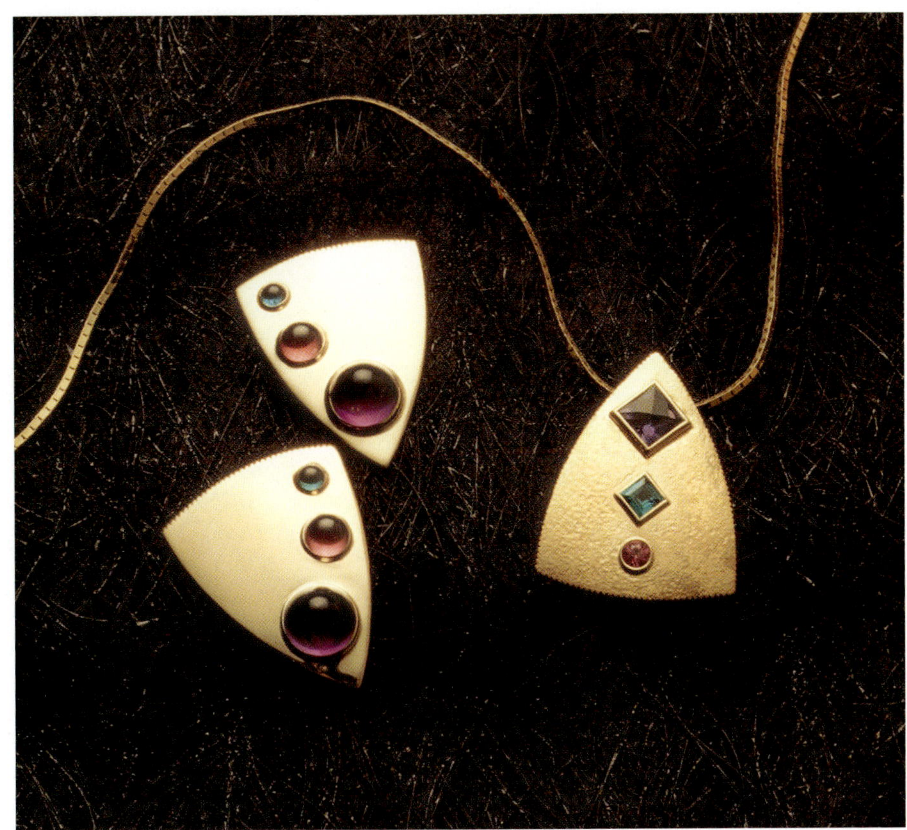

Kurt Wilson

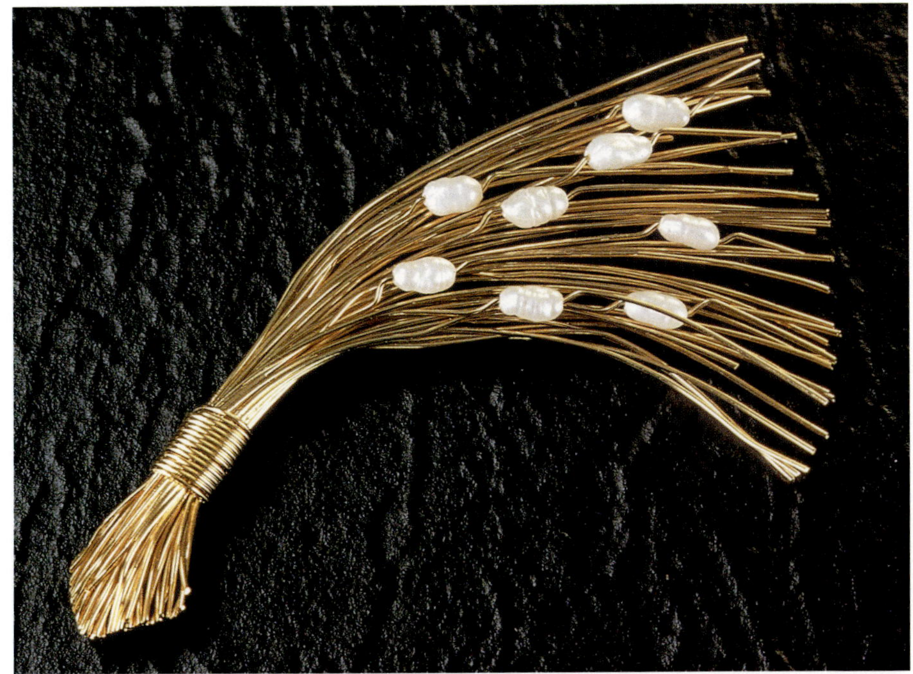

Kallima Jewelry
K. Kathryn Pearce

Known for their clean lines and classic appeal, the elegant designs of Kathryn Pearce are always in style. Employing fine metals, precious stones and pearls, Kathryn's work is an inspired fusing of earth and art. The vermeil pin shown aptly demonstrates her bold design approach, which gives rise to a breathtaking collection. Small wonder then, that the creations of Kathryn Pearce are perennial favorites at finer galleries and craft stores everywhere.

Kreg Scully
Peterson-Scully Studios

Kreg Scully creates unique and beautiful 'gemstone settings,' delicately carved inlay composites, bas-relief gem engravings, and other original work expressing a fresh and strongly individual style. His graceful compositions embody high standards of quality, artistic integrity and originality, reflecting a depth of understanding of design elements and visual harmony.

SHOWN: pendant, sculpted white opal with semi-black opal inlay, 22K gold, approx. 2.4" x 1.1" x .4", weighing 96 carats

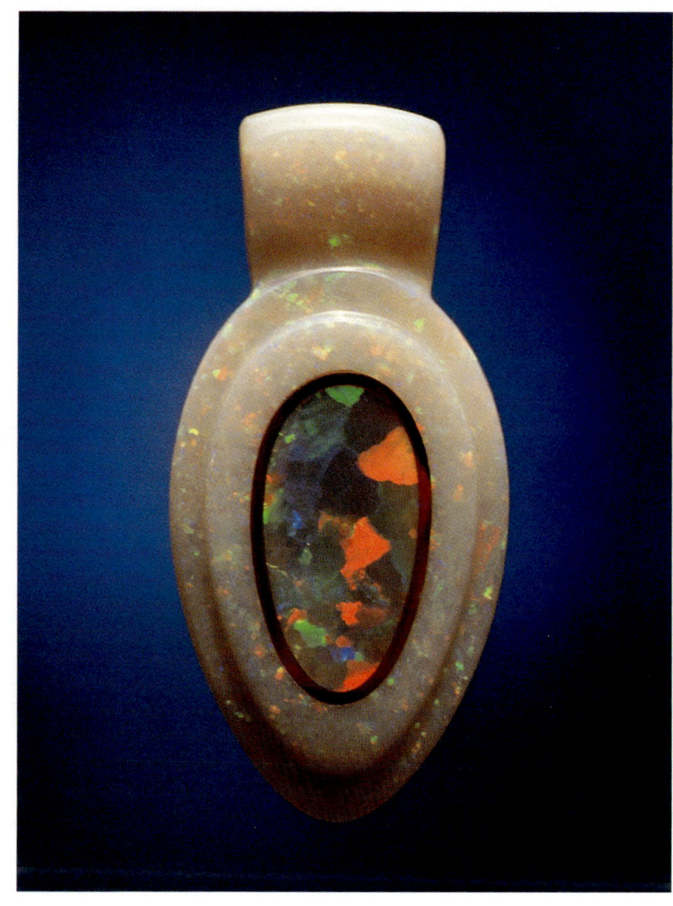

Mary Beth Rozkewicz Jewelry
Mary Beth Rozkewicz

Mary Beth's brooches, earrings and bracelets are a compelling blend of classical design with echoes of Victorian and vintage Mexican jewelry, filtered through her own wry sensibility. Her sterling and vermeil work with semi-precious stones has been featured in magazines and films, museum shops and galleries worldwide.

SHOWN: whimsical *Garden Pin*, sterling silver with bracciated jasper

Ralph Gabriner

Betsy King

Betsy King creates one-of-a-kind, commissioned, and limited-edition jewelry and miniature sculptures. Her award-winning pieces have been exhibited in numerous museums and galleries nationally and internationally. She has several works included in the *Helen Drutt Collection of 20th Century Jewelry*. Betsy recently participated in *American Dreams, American Extremes* and *Brilliant Stories*, two invitational exhibitions of narrative jewelry.

Her work is very personal in nature and incorporates elements of humor, nostalgia, and surrealism. Brooches, boxes, frames, neckpieces and earrings combine traditional precious metals with fragments of plastic, mylar, rubber, photographs and postcards to form an integration of popular iconography and technical expression.

Prices and information available on request.

A *Where Have All the Flowers Gone*, frame sculpture, sterling silver, bronze, paper, plexiglass, 4½" x 2½" x ½"

B *Return to Sender*, two pins, sterling silver, copper, paper, plexiglass, 1½" x 2"

C *Planes, Trains and Automobiles*, brooch, sterling silver, plastic, plexiglass, paper, horsehair, 4½" x 3½" x ¼"

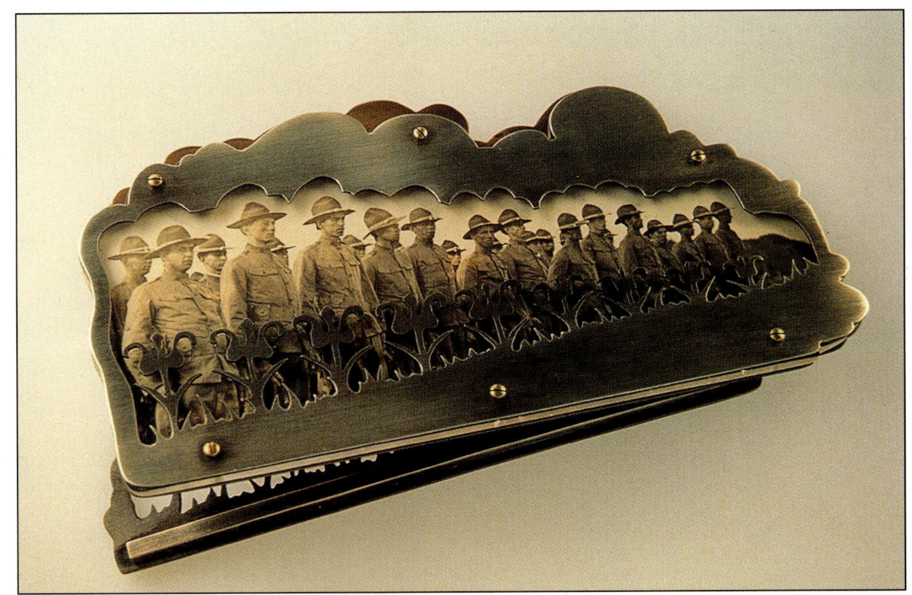

A

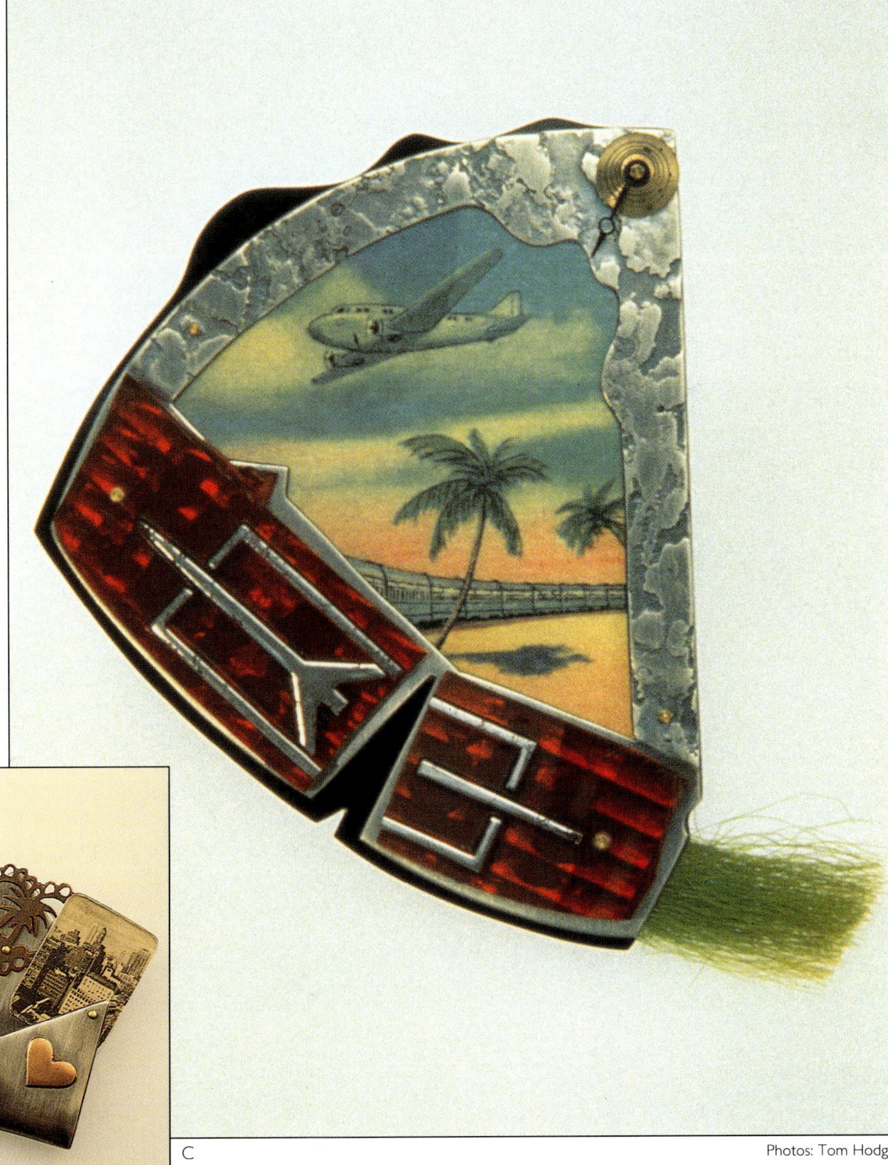

C

B

Photos: Tom Hodge

Ann Allen Jewelry
Ann Allen/Mary Winstead

The collaboration of designers Ann Allen
and Mary Winstead has produced handcrafted creations in sterling and vermeil.
Allen and Winstead's lines of necklaces,
earrings, pins and bracelets utilize techniques of hollow forming and hand engrav-
ing. Their innovative use of semi-precious
stones and hand-blown glass creates a
unique look that has made them the choice
of fine galleries and museums.

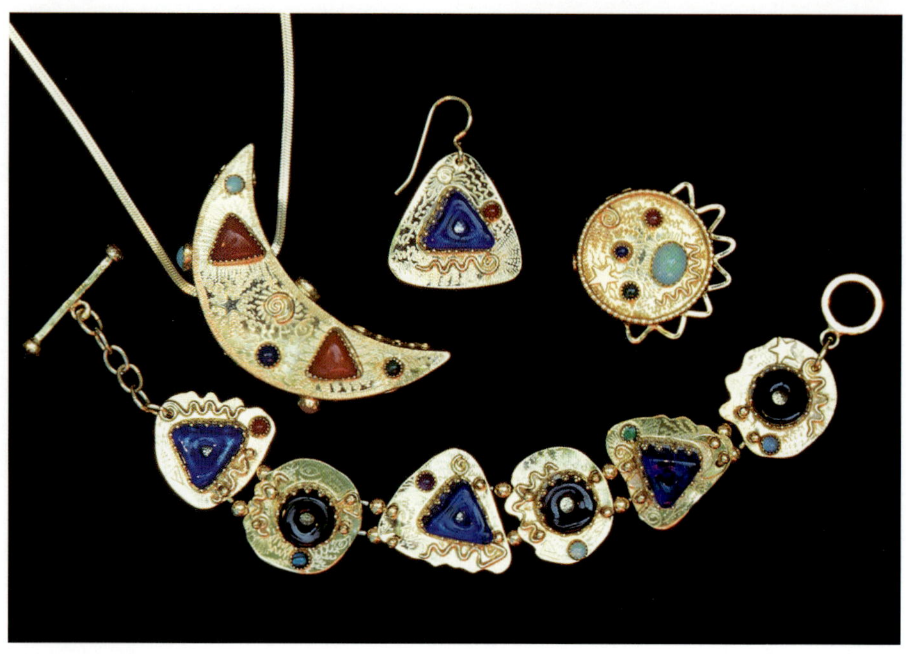

Barbara A. Hirschfeld
handmade jewelry

Barbara Hirschfeld's jewelry is inspired by
the symbols and patterns of ancient
cultures. She creates her jewelry using a
combination of casting and hand-fabrication
techniques, designing first in wax to achieve
a fluid line quality. Matte finishes and oxida-
tion enhance the graphic nature of her
work. Her jewelry is available in sterling
silver and 18K vermeil.

Ralph Gabriner

Jessica Felix
Jessica Felix Designs

Jessica Felix has been professionally expanding her jewelry techniques since 1970. She has an uncanny ability to take simple ideas and transform them into powerful images that incorporate the spirit worlds of Alaska, the Canadian Northwest Coast and Africa, along with her own free-form designs. Feathers, stones and beads are sometimes included. Her works have been shown at the Smithsonian Museum, as well as prominent galleries across the country.

The sterling silver whistles and bell shown here are some of her latest designs, along with the mask pin.

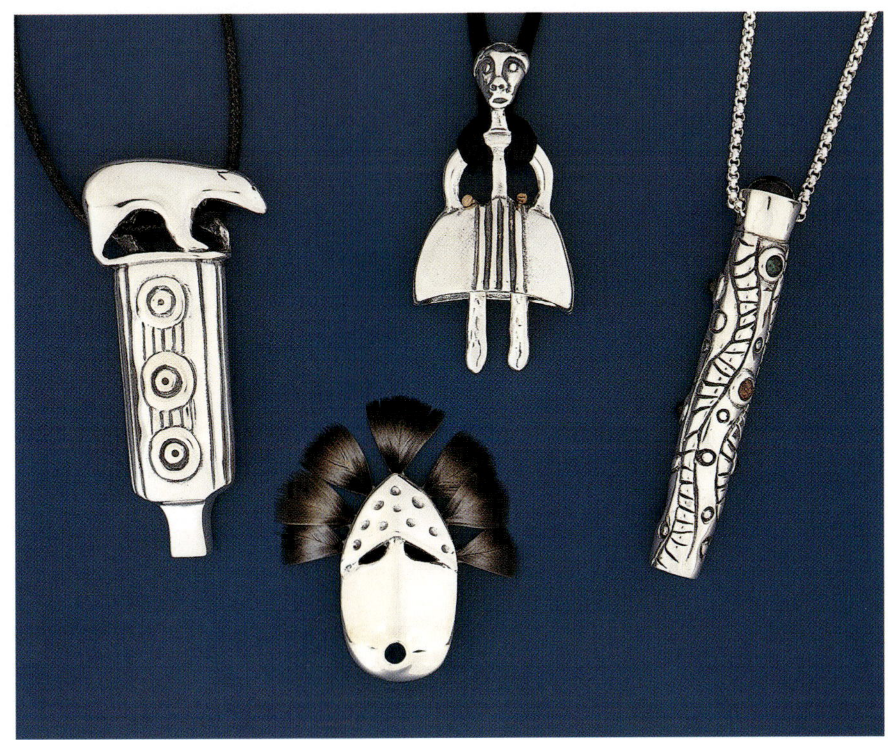

George Post

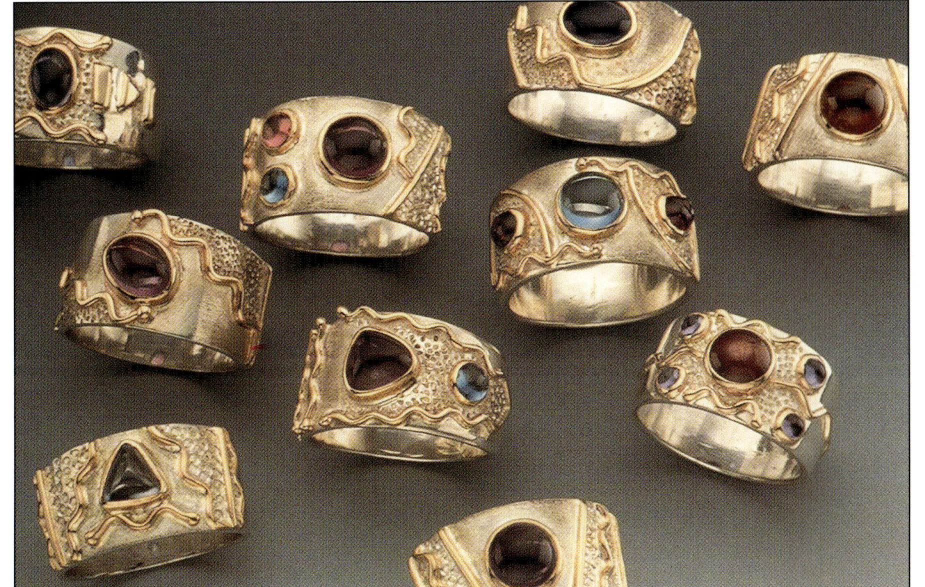

Peter Groesbeck

Rona Fisher
Rona Fisher Jewelry Design

'Primal Elegance in Precious Metals' are the words that best describe the warm, personal feeling of these rings, mixed with clean contemporary styling and fine craftsmanship.

The intensity of the colored stones is further enhanced by their 14K gold settings, contrasting subtly with the textured sterling band.

SHOWN: rings, elegantly crafted in sterling silver, 14K gold and high-quality cabochons such as blue topaz, amethyst, iolite and rhodolite

Mark Ehrmann
Jewelry Designs
Mark Ehrmann

Mark has found that it is important to develop a relationship of trust with each account. His willingness to work on an individual basis, giving special attention to each buyer, has formed deep and lasting relationships.

He sells to many stores in both the United States and Japan. Accounts requesting quality, large-volume orders, as well as galleries and boutiques, carry his unique, handcrafted jewelry.

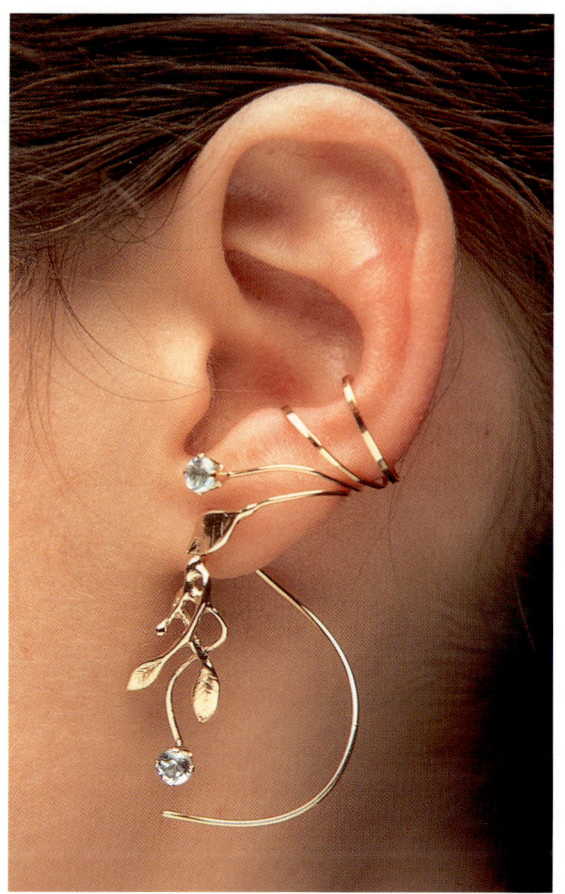

ORNAMENT
PO BOX 2349
SAN MARCOS, CA 92079-2349
FAX 619-599-0228
TEL 619-599-0222
$26/year
$23/introductory rate

The full-color quarterly publication *Ornament* focuses on personal adornment, with an emphasis on jewelry and clothing. Features include profiles of contemporary artists; critical reviews of books, videos and exhibitions; a news section; and articles of technical, ethnic and historic information.

Donna Murakami

Inspired by nature, Donna Murakami's jewelry designs combine metals and natural stones, creating a rich, organic quality in her work and reflecting her fine arts background. Her work is known throughout California, and in 1994 Donna was the featured artist and model for the 16th Annual Celebration of Craftswomen in San Francisco.

SHOWN: pendant and earrings, sterling silver, copper, amber, green diopside, 1994

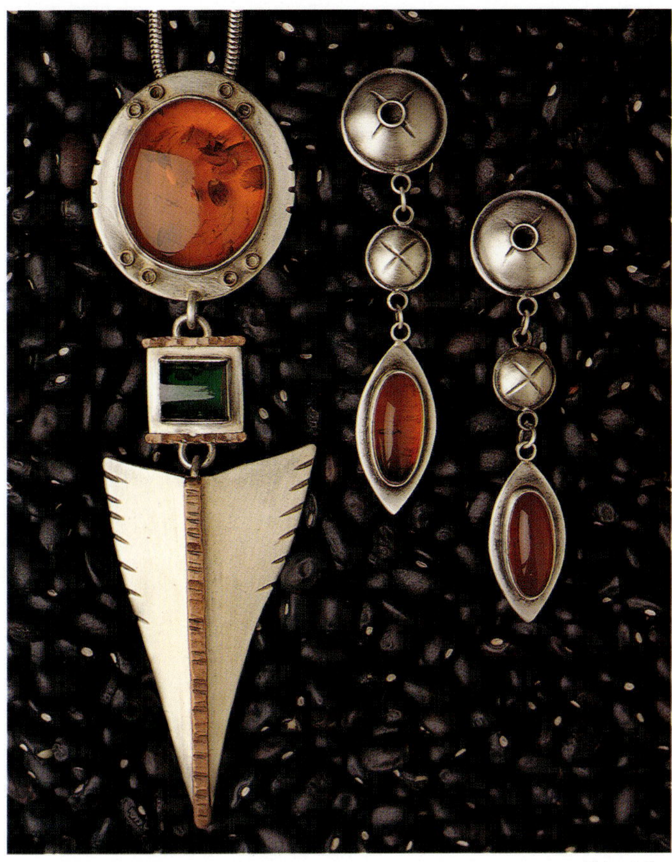

Chloe Atkins

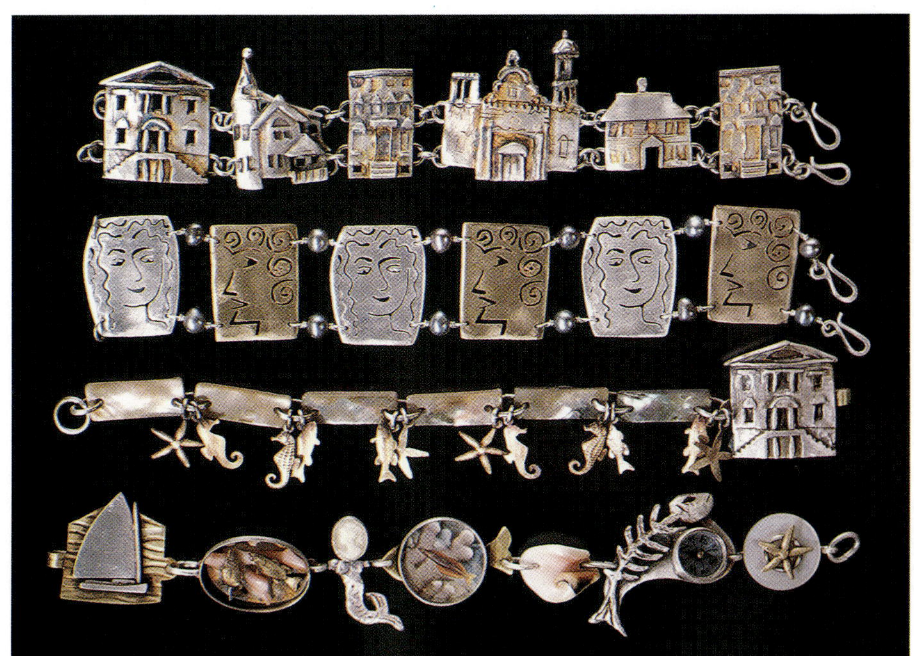

Deborah Sabo
Deborah Sabo Designs

Deborah's *Home and House* series of handcrafted jewelry (bracelets shown) touches on architecture and domestic life with humor and fantasy. Trained as a fine artist, she approaches metalworking from a printmaking, collage perspective. Her work is comfortable, durable, essentially care free, and priced competitively.

The series also includes a line of table top 'treasures'—candlesticks, picture frames and mirrors.

Judy Ditmer

Judy Ditmer has been turning for eight years. Her contemporary jewelry has a classic quality that works with dress and casual wear. Light in weight, it is finished with clear lacquer for a moisture- and oil-resistant finish.

Her book, *Turned Wood Jewelry*, has just been published by Schiffer Publishing, Ltd.

SHOWN: earrings, 1994, lathe-turned wood, cut, shaped and reassembled with beads and findings. Clockwise from upper left: ebony, grasstree root, beads, 2¼"H x 1⅜"W; bocote, beads, 1¾"H x 1⅛"W; greenheart, 1¾"H x 1½"W

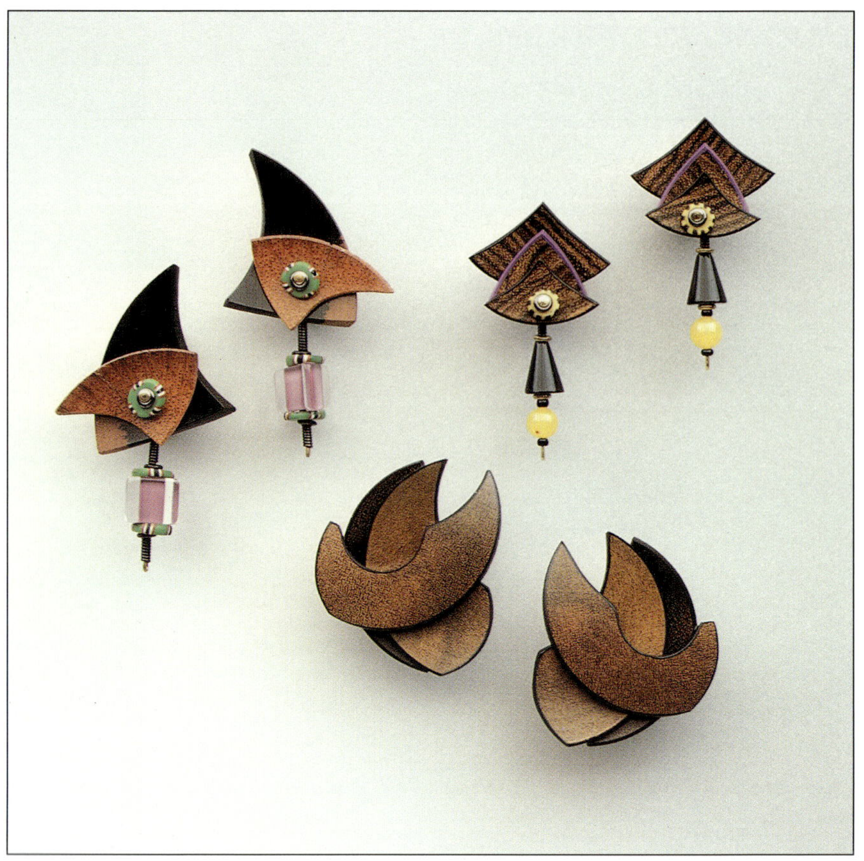

Susan Eileen Burnes

Susan Burnes creates needle-made fiber jewelry of fine cotton, silk and metallic threads. Each piece is created individually, completely stitched by hand, including hand-knotted cords on the necklaces.

Susan's original designs reflect the exuberant abundance of form and color which surround us, appealing to the senses, encouraging joy.

Completed brooches and necklaces are available and custom orders accepted.

Also see these GUILD publications:
The Gallery & Retail Edition: 1
The Designer's Reference: 8, 9

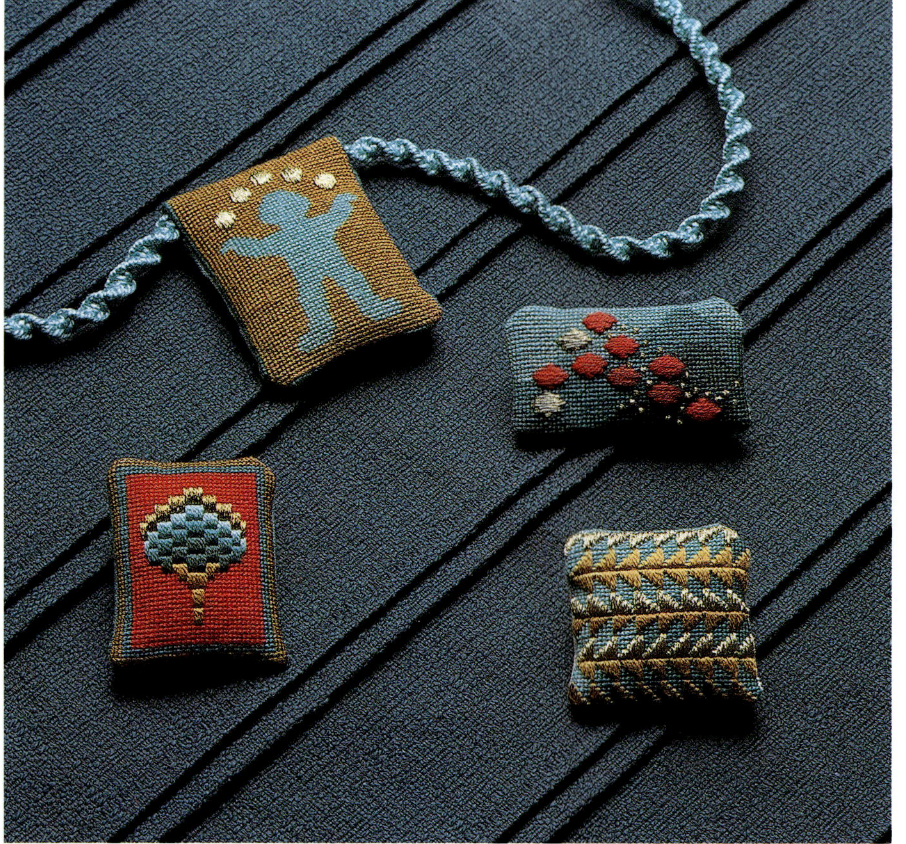

Audrey Forcier
Gaudie Audie

Audrey Forcier began working with clay while living in Volcano, Hawaii. In this idyllic setting, her first clay inspirations were transformed into jewelry realities. Audrey's studies in historical body decoration and keen interest in cultural diversity have influenced her work into a rich tapestry of shape, pattern and color.

Chosen by the Apparel Board of Chicago as one of the city's brightest new designers, Audrey's jewelry has become a favorite of collectors and shop owners. Sold under her trade name, Gaudie Audie, this unique line of extraordinarily detailed, wonderfully finished jewelry is offered at select galleries and boutiques.

A *Totem Pendant*, 1994, polymer clay, brass and glass

B *Blue Nude*, 1994, polymer clay, amber, brass and glass

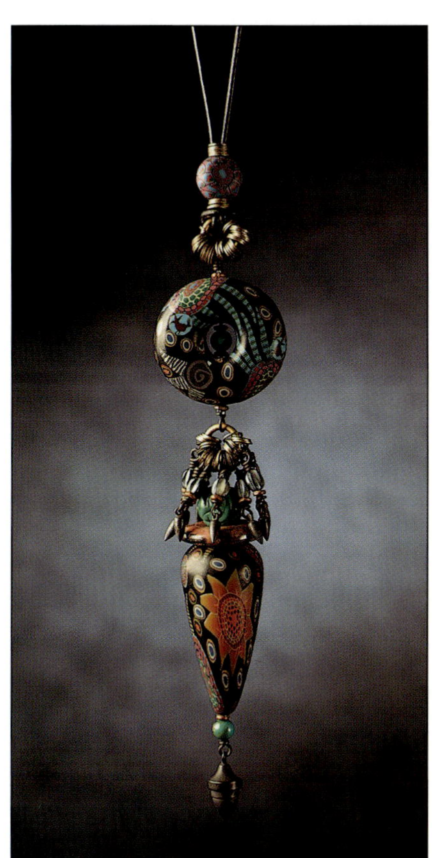

A

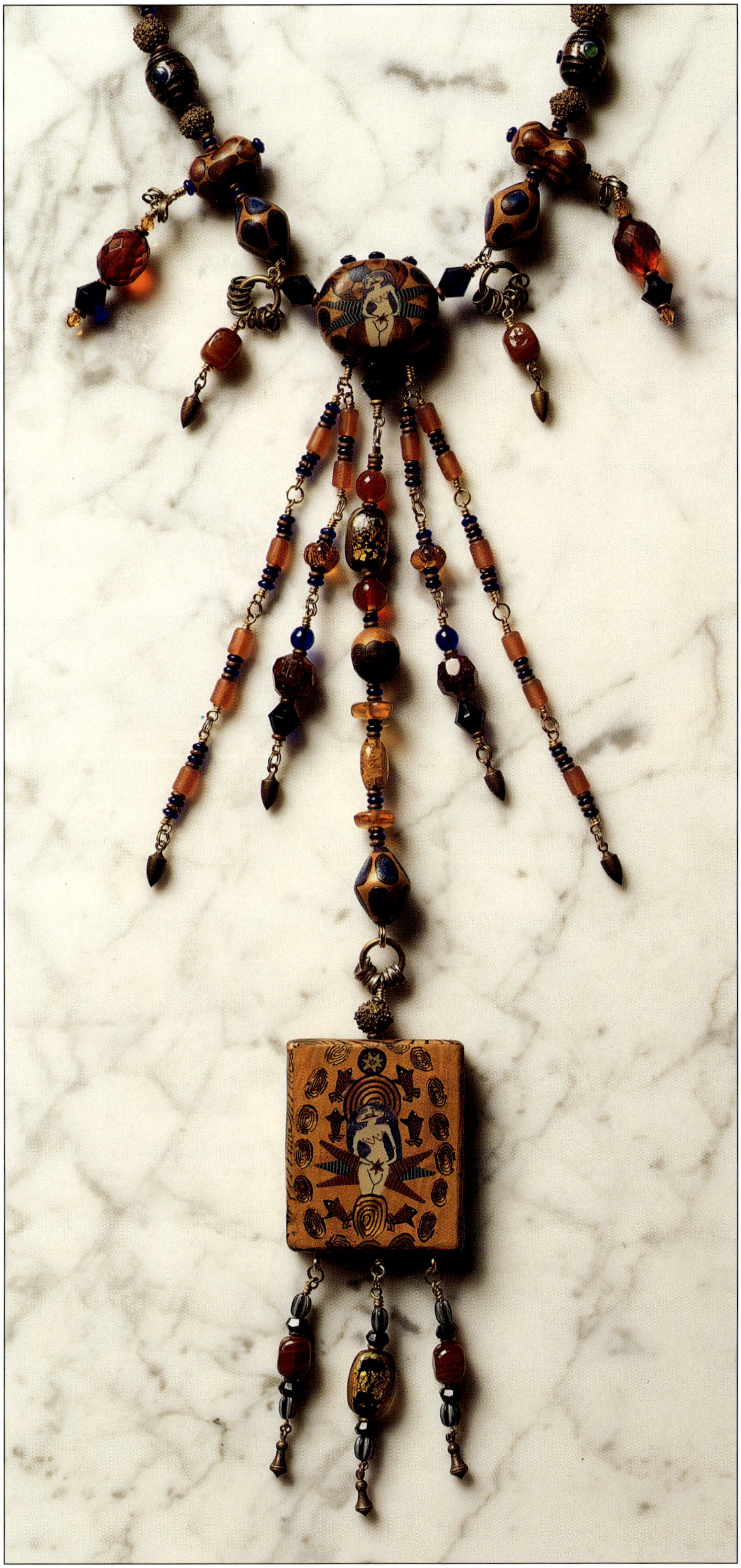

B

Photos: Kenji Kerins, Chicago, IL

Steff Korsage Browne

Despite being born into a third-generation silver mining family in Silverton, Idaho, Steff Korsage Browne's prominent use of sterling in her jewelry designs is more than an expression of her heritage. For whereas her ancestors thrived upon separating silver from stone, Steff thrives upon reuniting stone and other elements with silver. This natural recombination provides the creative spark for her distinctively original, award-winning designs: from wearable sculptures in sterling and gold, to a full range of metal and stone creations.

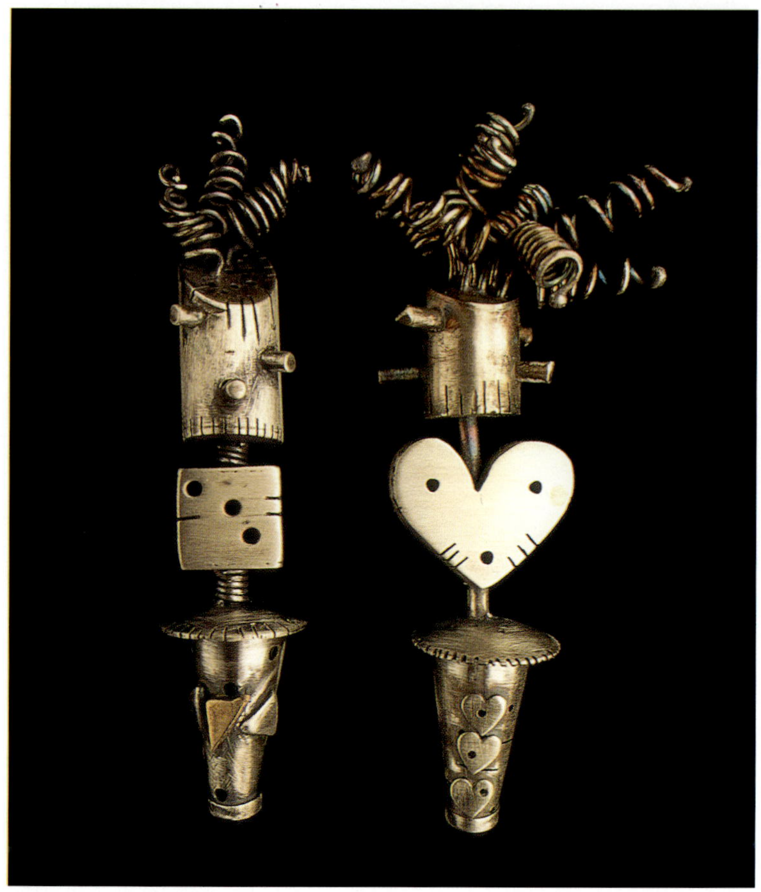

Oilcan Erl and Mabel: Wedding Photo, 1994, brooches, sterling silver and 18K gold, each 1½" × 3½"

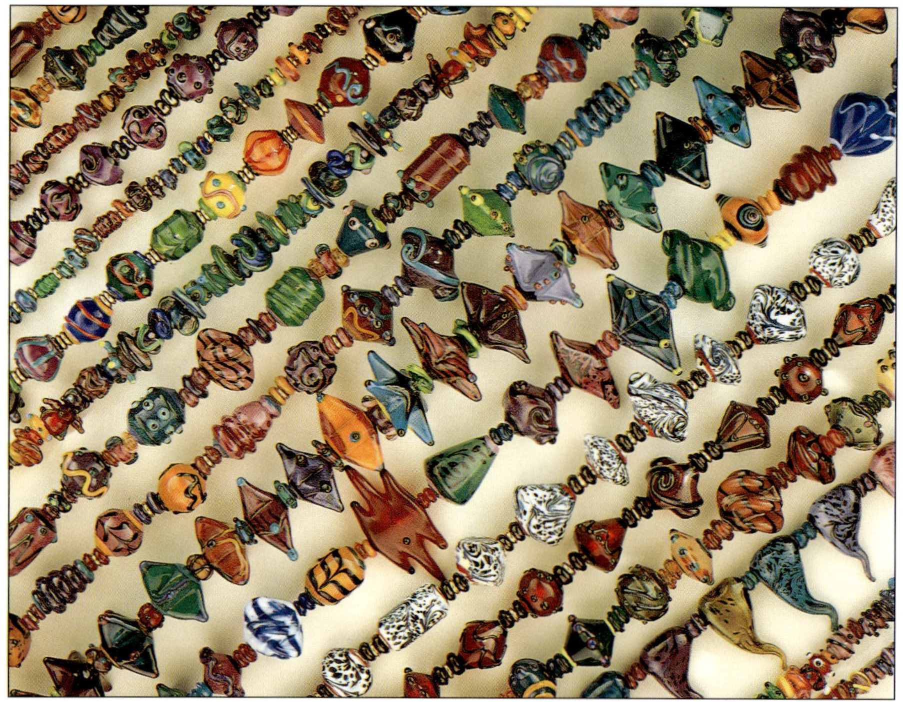

Nathan Ham Photography, Topeka, KS

Alison Sheafor
Alibaba Glass Works

Alison Sheafor has been blowing glass and making glass beads for the past ten years. Making her own glass cane gives her necklaces a unique look and an unlimited range of color. Bracelets and necklaces are strung on heavy steel foxtail cable with sterling silver clasps soldered to each end for ultimate durability.

Beth Piver Designs
Beth Piver

Beth Piver's creations in silver, bronze, copper and brass, joined together with rivets and screws, create a bold statement in contemporary body adornment. This ever-changing collection of rings, pins, pendants, earrings and other specialty items can be worn fashionably for any occasion. A wide range of production and one-of-a-kind pieces are available.

Also see this GUILD publication:
The Gallery & Retail Edition: 1

SHOWN: rings, mixed metals, semi-precious stones

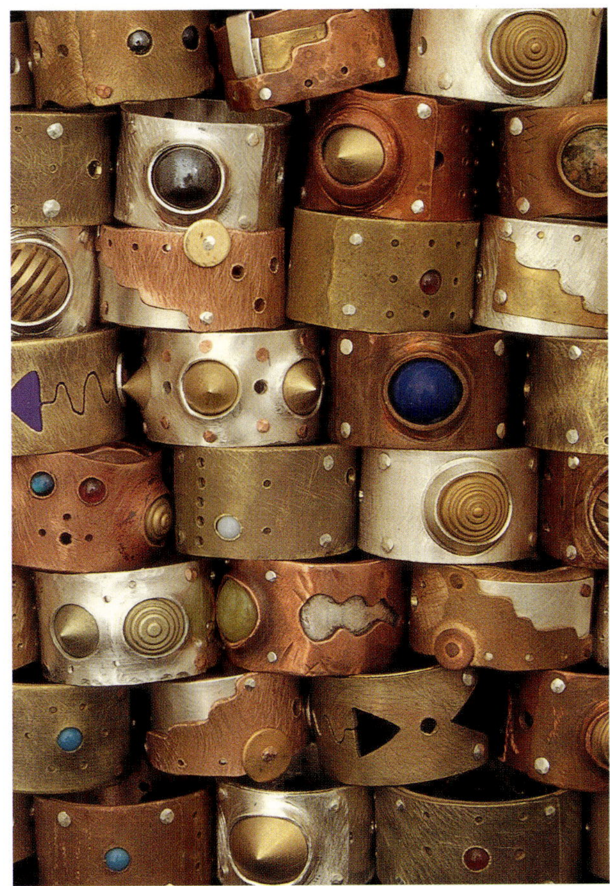

Jana Cooper
Jana Designs

Jana Cooper's whimsical jewelry incorporates a unique blend of the lost wax casting process and fabrication of silver and exotic metals. A metalsmith for almost 20 years, Cooper exhibits in many museums and galleries. Her new work concentrates on jewelry in sterling silver for the gardener.

SHOWN: small spade pin, 1⅛"H; garden club pin, 2"H x 1⅝"W; small shovel pin, 1⅛"H

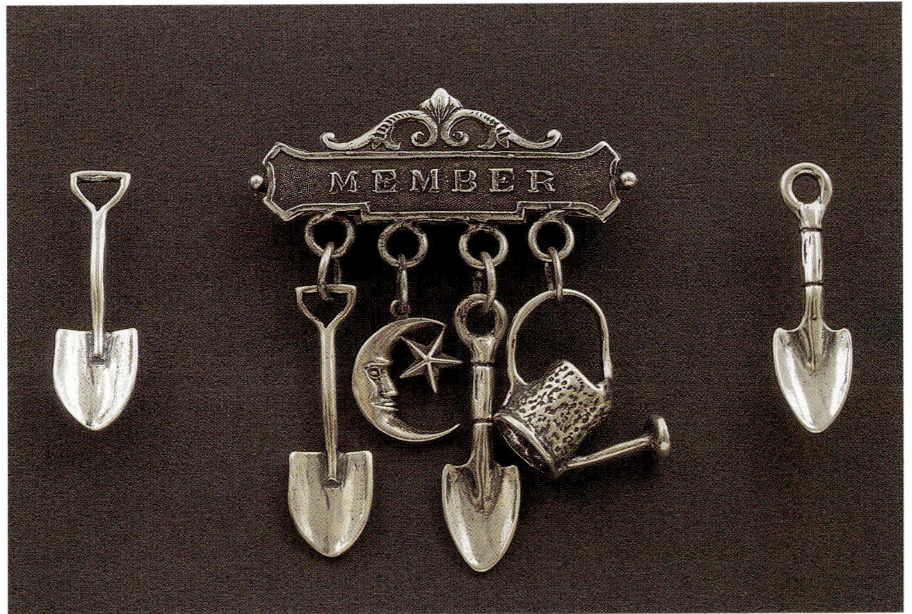

Richard Nichols

Lynn Shansky
The Bead Pallette

Lynn has been creating with beads for ten years. Her work is woven with needle and thread, incorporating glass beads, gemstones and crystals. Lynn's creations are both contemporary and elegant. She is recognized for her unique designs and craftsmanship.

SHOWN: rose quartz and sugilite bracelet, rose quartz and charoite earrings and brooch

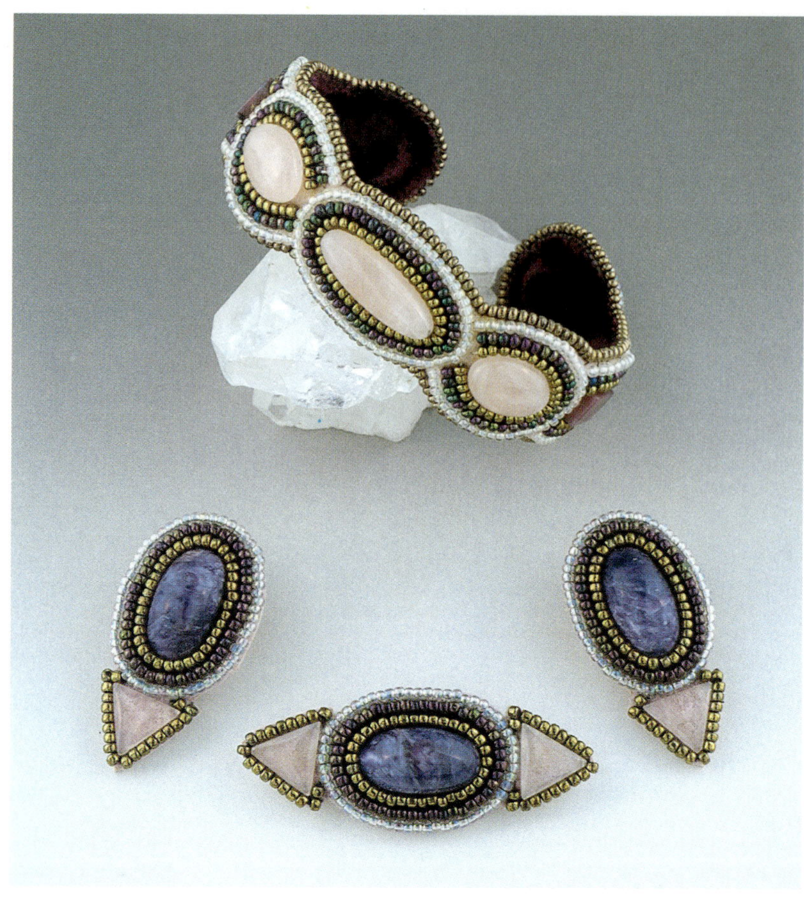

David Marson
Woodwear By David

David's combination of wood and sterling silver forms an unmatched style of contemporary jewelry. His inspiration comes from varied sources, ranging from studies in geological stratigraphy to romantic journeys through the Southwest. Multiple lamination techniques are used in his designs.

SHOWN: *Ebony Silver Rainbow*, barrette, 4" × 1" × $\frac{3}{16}$"; earrings, 2" × $\frac{3}{4}$" × $\frac{3}{16}$"

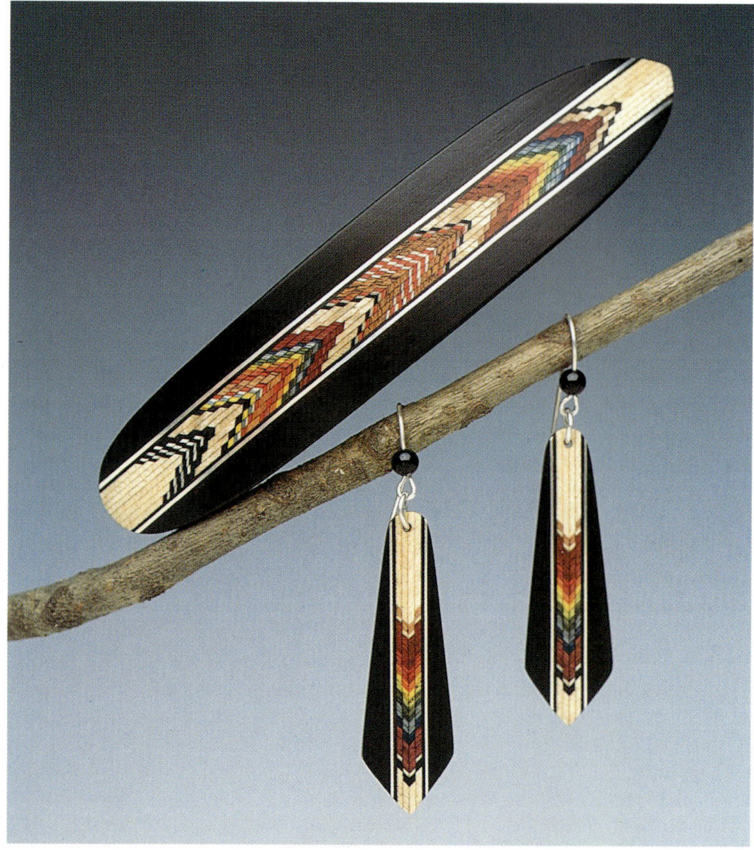

Cynthia Chuang
Erh-Ping Tsai
Jewelry 10, Inc.

Husband and wife team Cynthia Chuang and Erh-Ping Tsai have created a distinctive, unique line of three-dimensional procelain jewelry and sculpture.

Their works of art capture the beauty and fascination of the natural world in imaginative interpretations, including 'creature' pins and one-of-a-kind pieces, that can be worn or displayed. They have earned recognition and many honors for their art.

SHOWN: scorpion, wearable sculpture, porcelain, metal and semi-precious beads, 3½"H × 5½"L × 4½"W

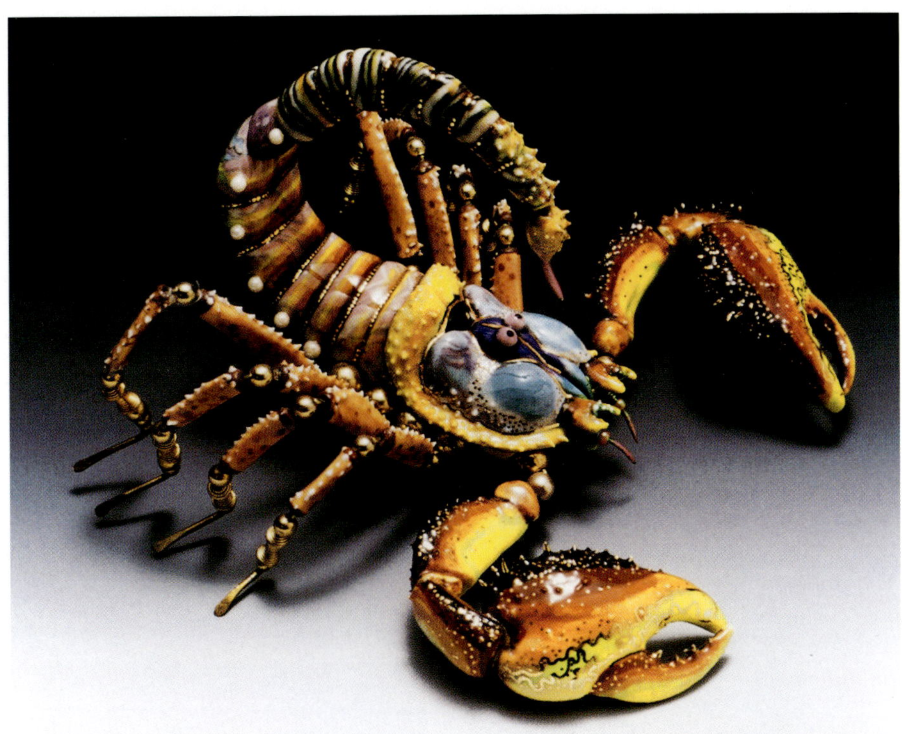

Jerry L. Anthony

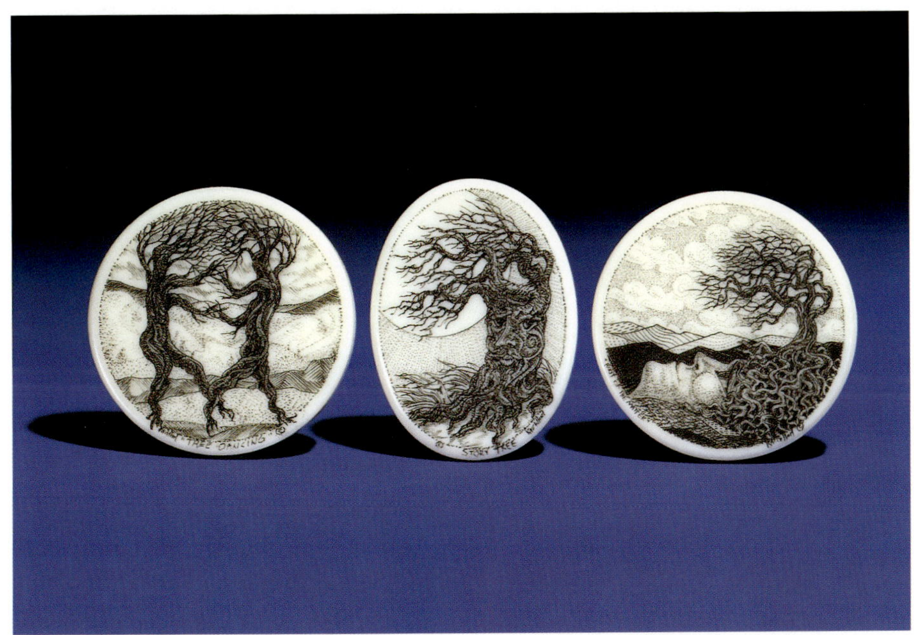

Left to right: *Tree Dancing*, *Story Tree* and *Root of the Matter*, engraved resin jewelry, 1½" ovals

Tree of Life
Art Works
Kim McClelland

Kim McClelland—artist, innovator and full-time scrimshander for two decades—created resin castings of his coveted original scrimshaw jewelry in response to public environmental concerns. Each piece, carefully hand cast and inked, reflects the fidelity of the original. A wide variety of designs is available from series such as landscape fantasies (shown), cosmic, nature, cats and whimsy.

Rings of Passion
Randall C. Johnson

Randall's works are pieces of pure romance. His attention to detail is astonishing. Icarus is richly robed in hundreds of individually carved feathers. Each work is immersed in months of delicate concentration until it slowly emerges as a final product.

Every wearable sculpture is lovingly created in sterling silver, 14K gold or gothic bronze. Randall Johnson's fresh new visions are graciously exhibited in Chicago-area galleries and along the Magnificent Mile.

A *Lancelot and Gwyneviere*, one of seven fairy tale couples carved to circle the finger

B *Battered Heart*, a unique design allows one ring to fit all sizes

C *Tears of Atlantis*, sterling silver oxidized to hold shell-like golden colors

D *Icarus*, one of seven dramatic characters, set in playful interactive necklaces

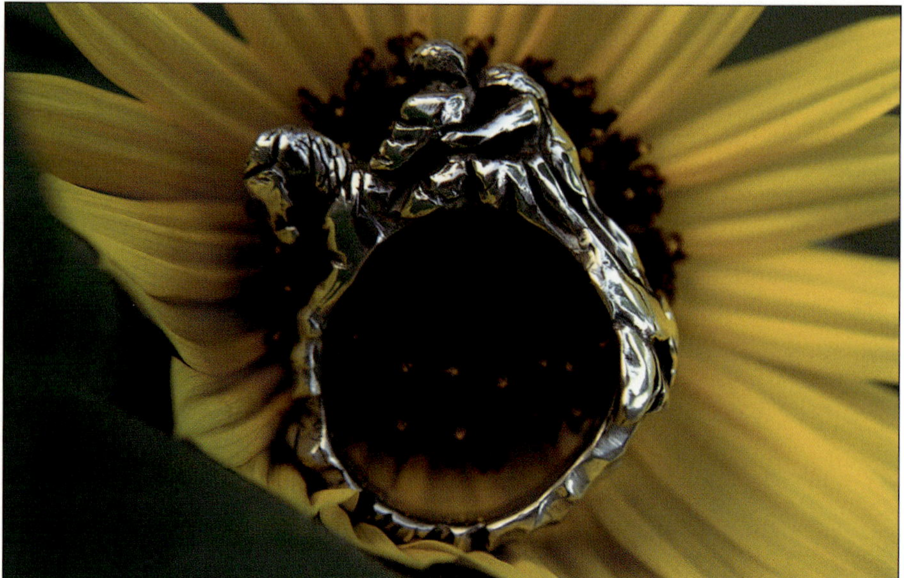

A

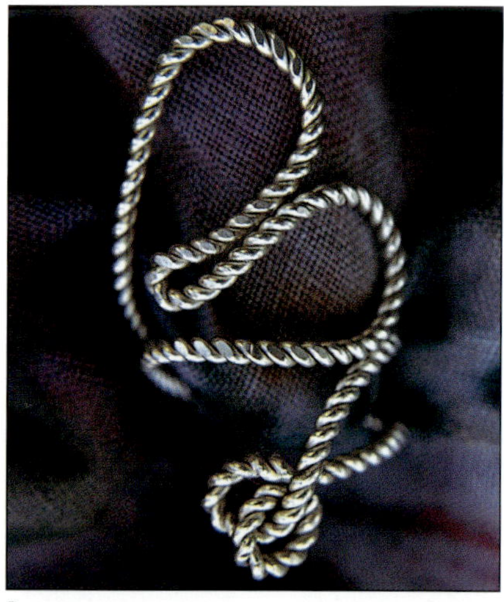

B

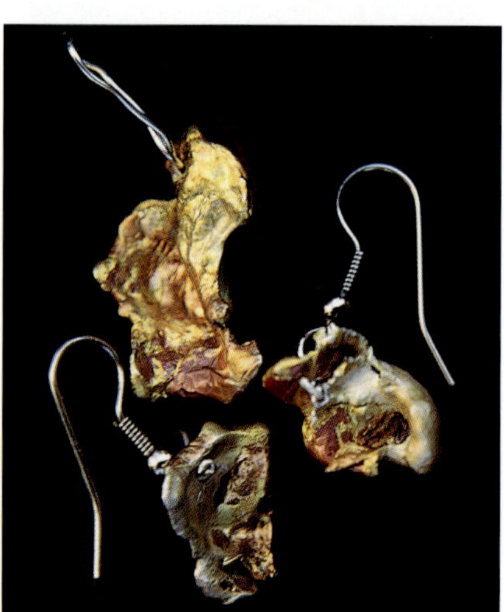

C

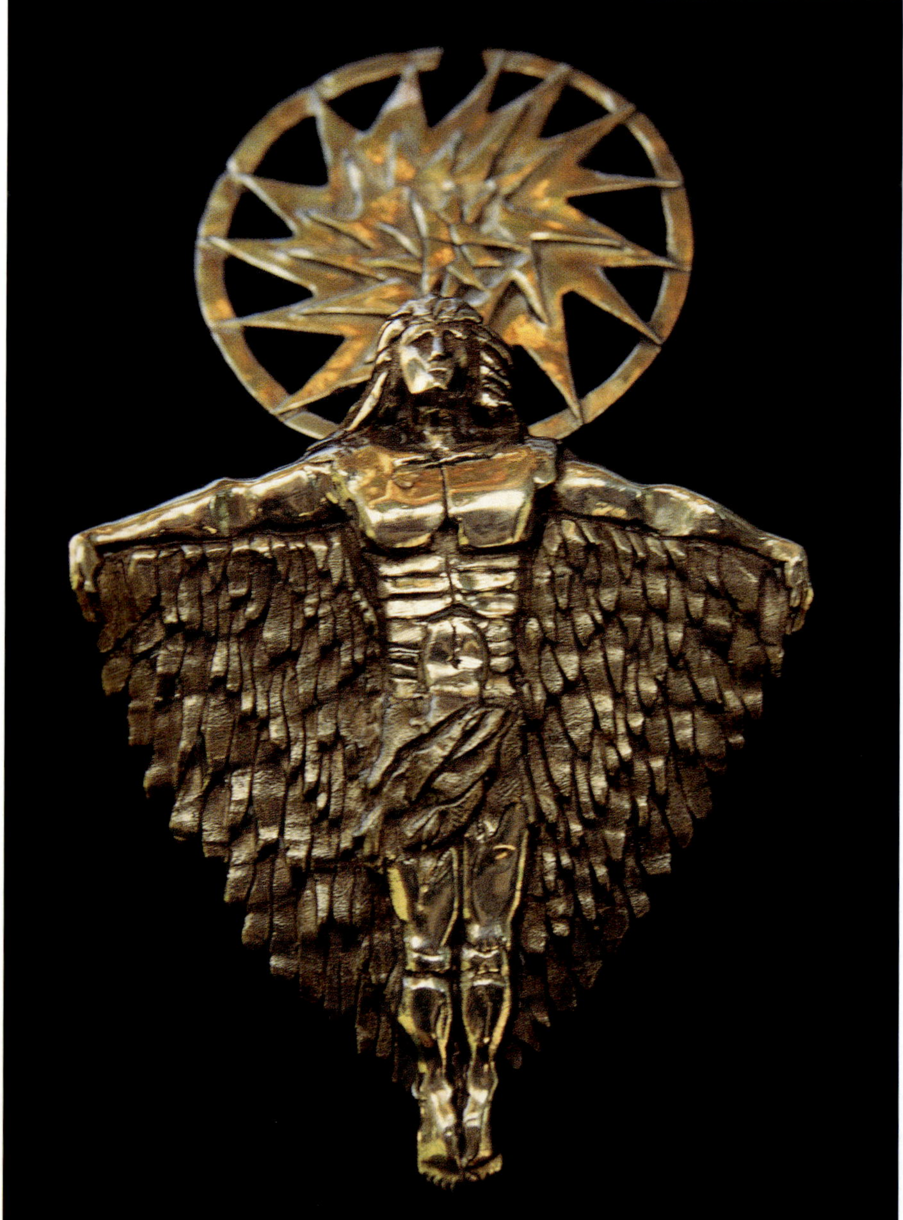

D

Debra Dembowski
Ethereal Adornment

Debra Dembowski's jewelry is primarily figurative. The human form becomes, for her, a vehicle in which to explore the complex ambiguities of human nature and existence. Symbolism and humor are important aspects of her work. Debra has exhibited extensively at museums and galleries throughout the United States. Her work may also be purchased at the Buyers Market and A.C.E.

Also see this GUILD publication:
The Gallery & Retail Edition: 1

SHOWN: *Guardian Necklace*, 1994, sterling silver

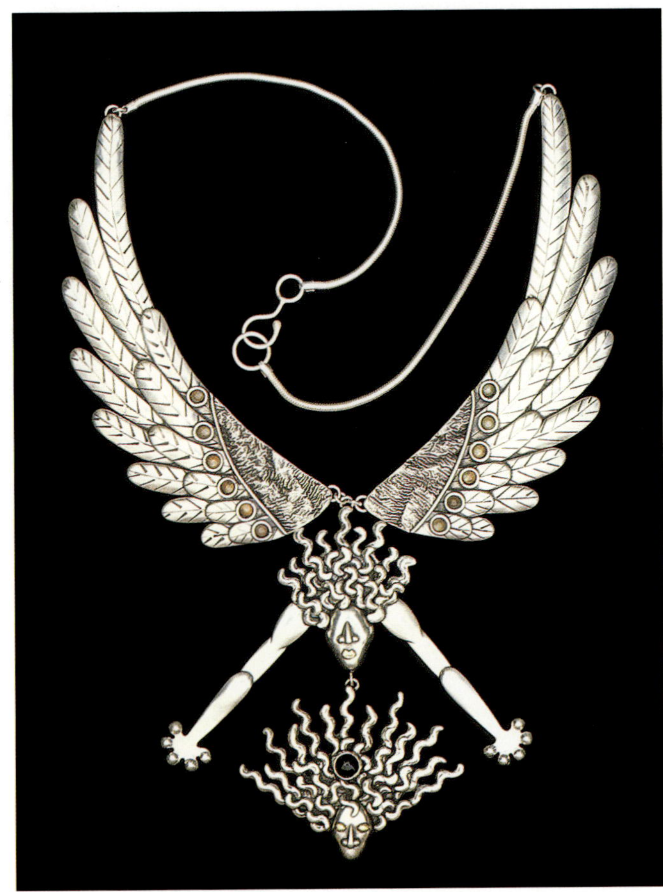

Gisela von Eicken
Gisela von Eicken Associates

With pliers and wires, she twists, coils and weaves her timeless art pieces. Using fine-gauge wire of sterling, gold-filled, 14K, brass, and natural and color-coated copper, she creates airy yet bold neckpieces, cuffs, rings, earrings and pins. Light as a feather, and often incorporating precious and semi-precious stones, her controlled tangles of wire have the appeal of sculptural art. Ms. von Eicken's work is collected by her peers and personalities such as Peggy Lee, Paul Simon, Joni Mitchell, John Cleese, Carrie Nye and Diane Feinstein.

SHOWN: *Lion's Head* pin, 2⅞" x 2½"; bronze beaded bracelet; abalone and 14K gold ring; *Sinai Fragments* bracelet

Jennifer Lévy

Jill Elizabeth
Scott MacLaren
LizTech Jewelry

Jill Elizabeth creates an enchanted realm
of ancient myths, legends and folklore by
combining the worlds of architecture,
industry and jewelry. Hand cutting laminated, mirrored chrome, then wrapping
and beading it with a dazzling array of
wires and beads, she and husband Scott H.
MacLaren have been selling LizTech Jewelry
that evokes personal self-discovery nationally and internationally for over ten years.

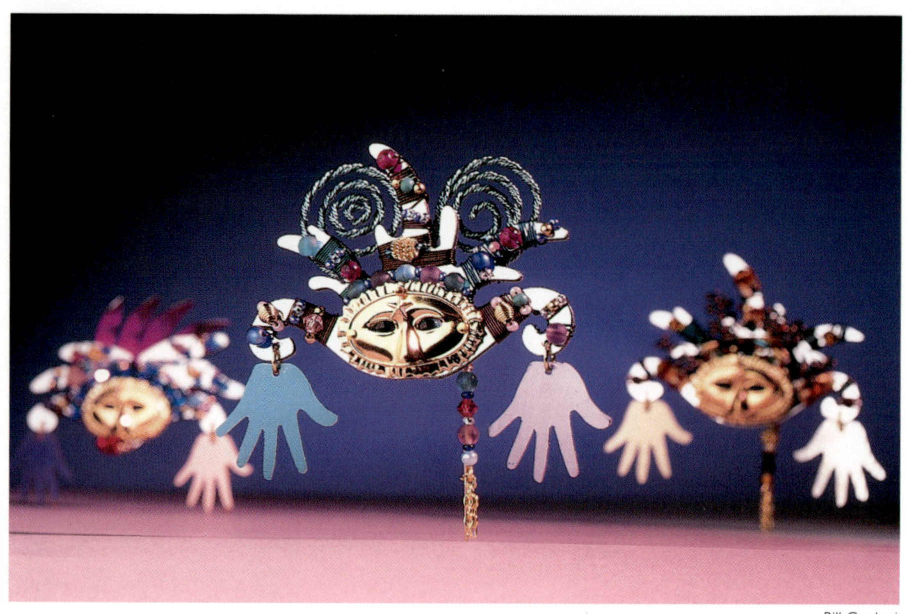

Bill Cardoni

Teri Bernard-Sokoloff
Bernard & Sokoloff Glass Studio

Teri has been creating award-winning glass
art for the past six years. She is best known
for her light-hearted approach and her
work is exhibited nationally. Teri's pins
are dichroic glass with embellishments of
anodized aluminum or kinetic sterling silver.
Each pin has its own individual character
and is signed, numbered and dated.

SHOWN: *Character Pins*

Kris Feldmann

Constance Kennedy Designs

Constance Kennedy

Constance Kennedy's background in graphic design and dance is reflected in her unique jewelry, which exudes both power and femininity. She hand-knots semi-precious, sterling silver and vermeil beads into wonderfully supple necklaces. A variety of earring styles complement the limited-edition necklaces. Her designs are modern and exotic, yet exude a timeless classicism.

Also see this GUILD publication:
The Gallery & Retail Edition: 1

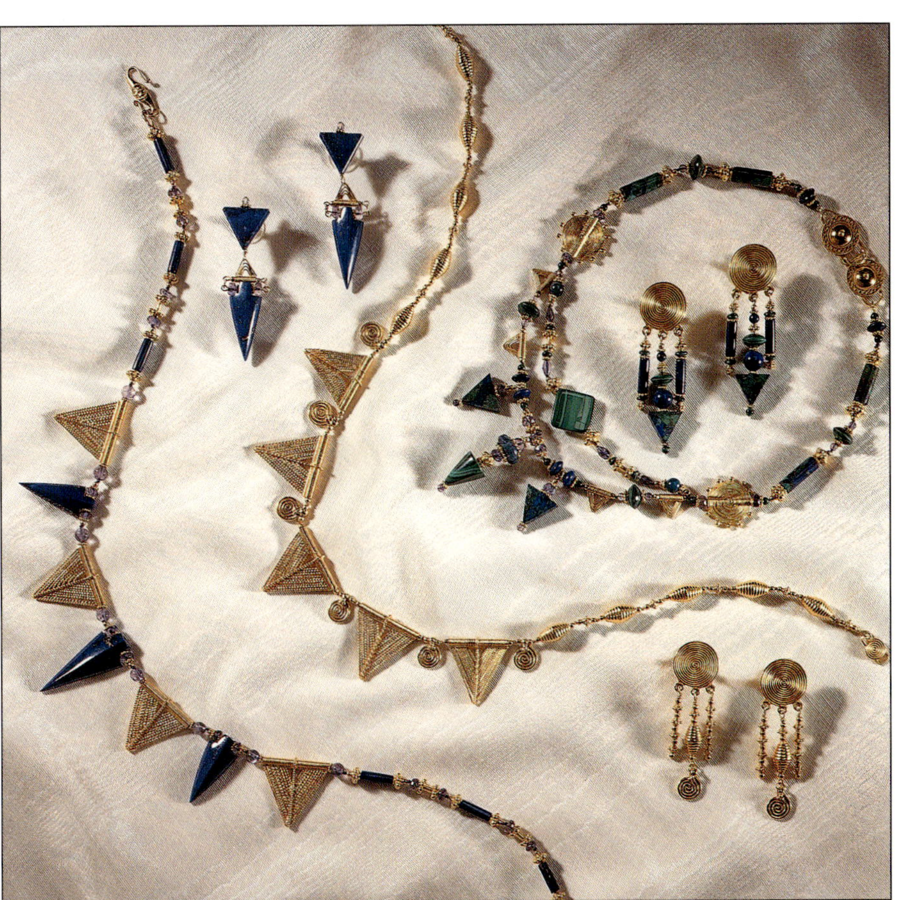

Bob Swanson, Swanson Images

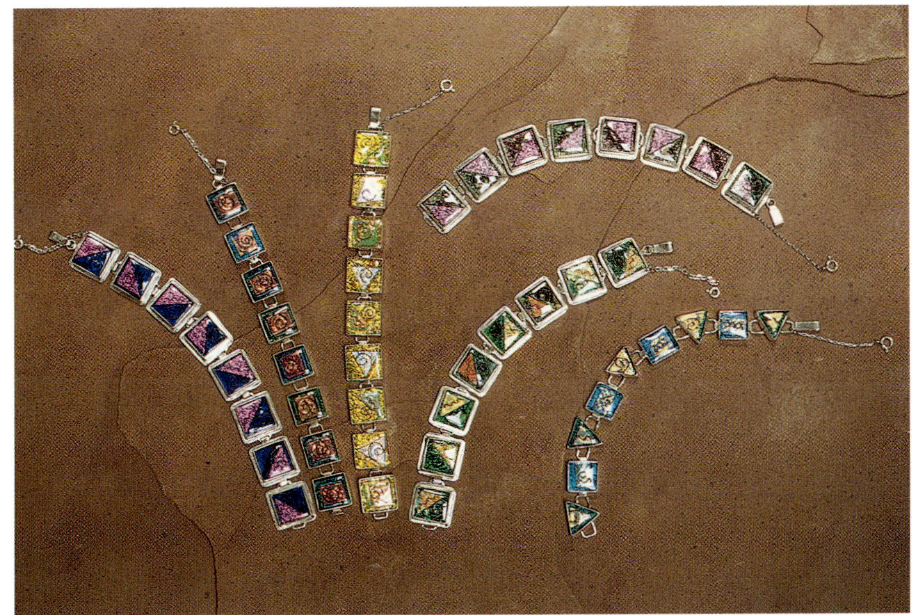

KROMA

Rupama and Murray Schwartz

These folks are the original source of dichroic jewelry, dancing their dance for 23 years.

Featuring glass with shifting colors, sometimes geometric, sometimes primitive, often etched, slumped, fused … but always simple, uncomplicatd and primary—timeless.

They have assembled a 28-page catalog presenting the dichroic evolution.

Also see these GUILD publications:
The Gallery & Retail Edition: 1
The Designer's Reference: 8

Helen C. Bunch
Helen Bunch Creations

Helen Bunch has passionately worked in silver for 16 years, hand constructing her jewelry with earth treasures and trade beads. Her creations symbolize feminine strength and the life forces of nature.

Ms. Bunch focuses on making jewelry that is unique and very wearable, equally at home on denim or with silks.

In the five years since Ms. Bunch entered the professional art world, she has shown in numerous well-established galleries in over 25 states.

SHOWN: 1995 catalog selections, fine sterling silver, accented with bronze, semi-precious stones and trade beads

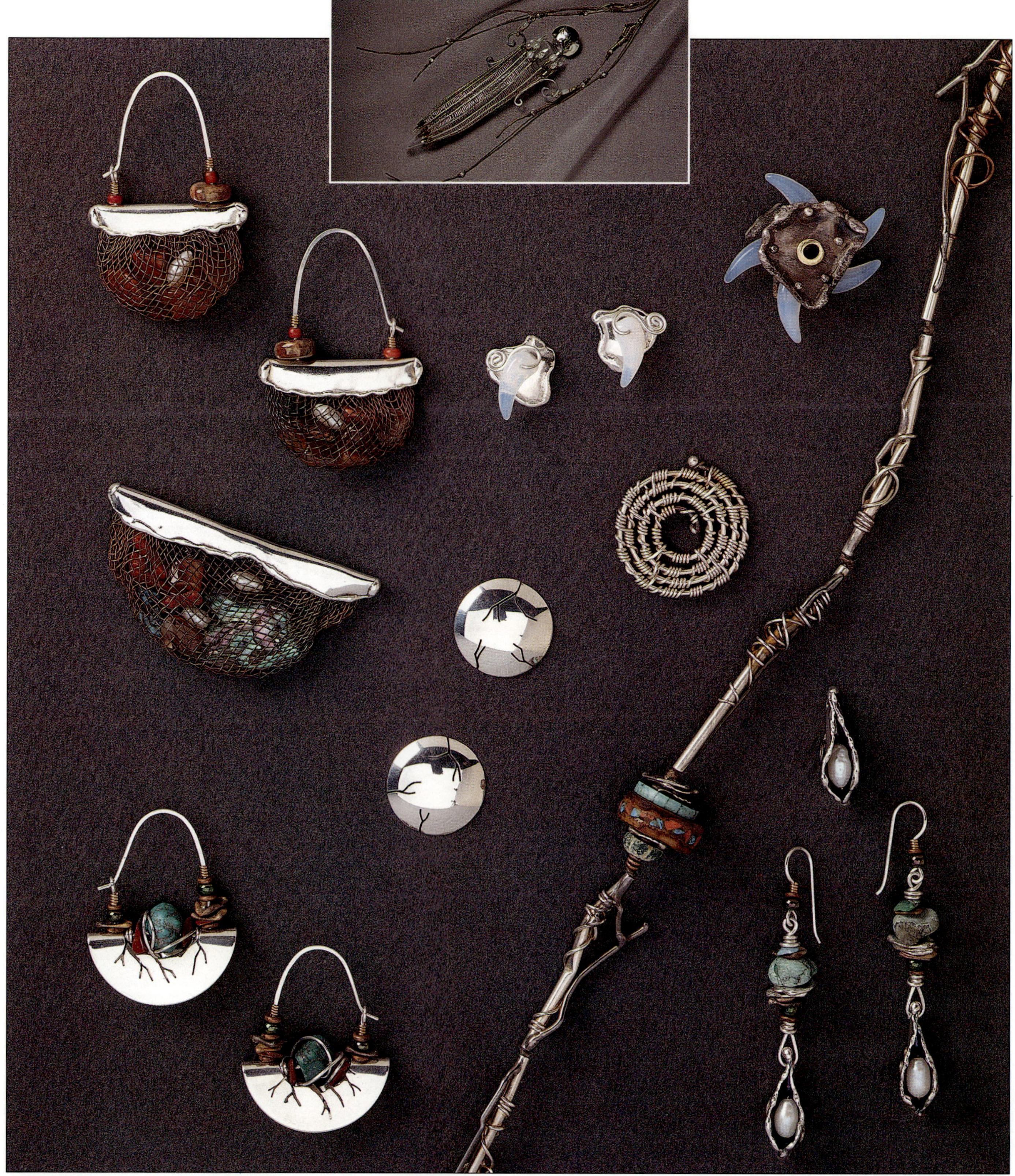

David Knox, Ann Arbor, MI

Finding the *Artwork*

FINDING THE ARTWORK

Yes, you're right.

THE GUILD's **Gallery Edition** is an exceptional portfolio of North American crafts. But please don't forget its other dimension, the one that really makes it a unique resource.

The following section includes phone numbers of the artists represented in this book, as well as the galleries which carry their work. We urge you to dial those numbers for the best possible reasons: to research and invest in the outstanding artwork of **Gallery Edition** artists.

Not every artist represented here lists a personal phone number: Some prefer to work with the doors barred and the phone cord pulled. Others are happy to fill individual phone orders or direct you to additional galleries close to home. Some artists also welcome studio visitors; use our phone list to inquire about policy and appointments.

Artists who haven't listed a personal number under their heading (and many who have, as well) include phone numbers and locations of the galleries which show their work. Do visit these galleries! They offer a quiet, reflective space to view artwork, and usually display several works from a represented artist. Gallery owners are knowledgeable and enthusiastic about the art forms they carry, and can facilitate special orders.

As you shop, remember that much of the artwork shown here is one-of-a-kind. That may well mean the vase you fell in love with on page 58 is unavailable. However, it also means that the artist whose work you love has made—or can make—a piece which will be uniquely yours.

That's the beauty of handmade work.

ANN ALLEN JEWELRY
See page 112

GULFPORT, FL
FAX 813-345-1528
813-345-1528

VERONICA'S ATTIC
ATLANTA, GA
404-257-1409

ACCENTRICS LTD.
MEQUON, WI
414-241-9292

DINA PORTER GALLERY
ALLENTOWN, PA
215-434-7363

SCOTT LAURENT GALLERIES
WINTER PARK, FL
407-629-1488

ARTISANS ACCORD
See page 106

RED HOOK, NY
518-423-0251

THE ARTFUL HAND GALLERY
BOSTON, MA
617-262-9601

CAPITOL CRAFTSMAN
CONCORD, NH
603-224-6166

CIONA GALLERY
WELLESLEY, MA
617-235-6230

DON MULLER GALLERY
NORTHAMPTON, MA
413-586-1119

GRAY AND COMPANY
ROCHESTER, NY
716-454-3300

P. CHURCH JEWELERS
CHELMSFORD, MA
508-256-1234

SELO-SHEVEL GALLERY
ANN ARBOR, MI
313-761-4620

WILD GOOSE CHASE
BROOKLINE, MA
617-738-8020

ARTISTRY IN WOOD
See page 57

HANSVILLE, WA
360-638-1335

THE WICKIUP WESTERN ART GALLERY
COEUR D'ALENE, ID
208-664-3001

ARTISTRY IN WOOD
HANSVILLE, WA
360-638-1335

QUEST GALLERY AND GIFTS
BOZEMAN, MT
406-586-0611

THE LANDING
BAINBRIDGE ISLAND, WA
206-780-1162

MARJORIE A. ATWOOD
See page 97

TULSA, OK
FAX 918-583-0886
918-583-0886

ROBERGE GALLERY
PALM DESERT, CA
619-340-5045

M.A. DORAN GALLERY
TULSA, OK
918-748-8700

ROBERGE GALLERY
SANTA FE, NM
505-820-2008

AXELSSON METALSMITH
See page 45
PLEASE CONTACT ARTIST DIRECTLY

CARMEL, CA
FAX 408-624-3940
408-624-3909

BRM DESIGN
See page 46

BURLINGTON, VT
FAX 802-658-3090
802-863-9553

FALCONER'S
CHATHAM, MA
508-945-2867

ABC BED, BATH & LINEN
NEW YORK, NY
212-473-3000

AMBITIOUS ENDEAVORS
BALA CYNWYD, PA
610-667-7377

AMERICAN CRAFTWORKS
BOCA RATON, FL
407-362-4220

PERLORA
PITTSBURGH, PA
412-431-2220

PLACE ON EARTH
VAIL, CO
303-476-2111

STUDIO 330
BLOOMFIELD HILLS, MI
313-851-5533

UNIQUE PRESENCE
CHICAGO, IL
312-929-4292

J. TODD BARBER
See page 81
PLEASE CONTACT ARTIST DIRECTLY

ALBANY, NH
603-447-2881

BARRICK DESIGN
See page 80

LANCASTER, PA
FAX 717-295-4812
717-295-4800

AN AMERICAN CRAFTSMAN
NEW YORK, NY
212-727-0841

CLARKSVILLE POTTERY
AUSTIN, TX
512-478-9079

ELEMENTS OF MINNESOTA
MINNEAPOLIS, MN
612-827-5911

HERO'S JOURNEY
NEW YORK, NY
212-874-4630

KNORR BEESWAX
DEL BAR, CA
619-755-2051

LIVING ARTS
KENNEBUNK, ME
207-967-8460

MELTING POT
MENDOCINO, CA
707-937-0173

OVERWHELMED
BOCA RATON, FL
407-368-0078

BARRY GOODMAN AND SON JEWELERS
See page 108
PLEASE CONTACT ARTIST DIRECTLY

COLUMBUS, OH
800-336-1833

CHERYL BATTAGLIA
See pages 78-79
PLEASE CONTACT ARTIST DIRECTLY

BOSTON, MA
617-859-0675

MICHAEL BAUERMEISTER
See page 59

AUGUSTA, MO
FAX 314-228-4663
314-228-4663

GROVEWOOD GALERY
ASHEVILLE, NC
704-253-7651

M. LAVINE DESIGN WORKSHOP
COLD SPRING, MN
612-685-3071

ROCHE BOBOIS
PHILADELPHIA, PA
215-972-0168

SANDRA COLLINS, INC
BIRMINGHAM, MI
313-642-4795

CURTIS BENZLE
See page 84

HILLIARD, OH
614-876-5340

ODC SHOW OF HANDS
COLUMBUS, OH
614-224-7119

LIVING ARTS
SIESTA KEY, FL
813-346-2681

SANDRA C.Q. BERGÉR
See page 25
PLEASE CONTACT ARTIST DIRECTLY

BURLINGAME, CA
FAX 415-340-0198
415-348-0310

FINDING THE ARTWORK

TERI BERNARD-SOKOLOFF
See page 124

SHERWOOD GALLERY	LAGUNA BEACH, CA 714-497-2668
ART OPTIONS	SAN FRANCISCO, CA 415-252-8535
GALLERY 912½	SANTA MARIA, CA 805-922-5005
INTERNATIONAL GLASS AND BEAD	CLAREMONT, CA 909-626-0877
KITTRELL AND RIFFKIND	DALLAS, TX 214-239-7957

NANCY MOORE BESS
NEW YORK, NY
FAX 212-633-1844
212-691-2821
See page 96

BROWN/GROTTA GALLERY	WILTON, CT 203-834-0623
BANAKER GALLERY	SAN FRANCISCO, CA 415-397-1397
COUNTER POINT	EL PASO, TX 915-545-5073
GAYLE WILLSON GALLERY	SOUTHAMPTON, NY 516-283-7430
KATIE GINGRASS GALLERY	MILWAUKEE, WI 414-289-0855
THE WESTMAN COLLECTION	BIRMINGHAM, MI 810-645-6212

BETH PIVER DESIGNS
FAIRFAX, VA
FAX 703-968-9561
703-968-9561
See page 119

AMERICAN HAND PLUS	WASHINGTON, DC 202-965-3273
AN AMERICAN CRAFTSMAN	NEW YORK, NY 212-399-2555
CLARKSVILLE POTTERY	AUSTIN, TX 512-478-9079
ITCHY FINGERS	PORTLAND, OR 503-222-5237
MELI-MELO	ST. LOUIS, MO 314-725-4285
METALWORKS	PHILADELPHIA, PA 215-625-2640
MINDSCAPE	EVANSTON, IL 708-864-2660
OFF THE WALL	SANTA FE, NM 505-983-8337

DAVID TERRETT BEUMÉE
LAFAYETTE, CO
FAX 303-665-4229
303-665-6925
See page 28

AMERICAN HAND PLUS	WASHINGTON, DC 202-965-3273

MARK BLESHENSKI
See page 24

MOUNTAIN CRAFT GALLERY	WHISTLER B.C. 604-932-5001
COURTYARD GALLERY	NEW BUFFALO, MI 616-469-4110
WOODWARD GALLERY	BIRMINGHAM, MI 313-642-1357

JUDIE BOMBERGER
NOVATO, CA
FAX 415-898-5627
415-898-8191
See page 44

WHYEVERNOT	MYSTIC, CT 203-536-6209
A. MANO	NEW HOPE, PA 215-862-5122
ACCENTRICS LTD.	MEQUON, WI 414-241-9292
DON DRUMM STUDIOS AND GALLERY	AKRON, OH 216-253-6268
GRAPHIC'S GALLERY	BALBOA ISLAND, CA 714-673-2220
IRON ROSE	KENWOOD, CA 707-833-1153
LANGMAN GALLERY	WILLOW GROVE, PA 215-657-8333
NEW MORNING GALLERY	ASHEVILLE, NC 704-274-2831

BARBARA BRAVO
See page 28

BLANC DE BLANC	WAYZATA, MN 612-473-8275
COUNTRY CLASSICS	NORRISTOWN, PA 610-275-3666
GLASS GOWER'S GALLERY	ERIE, PA 814-453-3758
GUESS WHAT? LTD.	ALBANY, NY 518-458-8383
LATITUDES	PHILADELPHIA, PA 215-482-0417
PENNIMAN SHOWCASE	PLYMOUTH, MI 313-455-5531
PIECES	HIGHLAND PARK, IL 708-432-2137
PRESENCE	BETHESDA, MD 301-986-4710

BOB BROWN
JUDY DYKSTRA-BROWN
BOULDER CREEK, CA
408-338-7505
See page 74
PLEASE CONTACT ARTIST DIRECTLY

PHIL F. BROWN
BOWIE, MD
301-262-8597
See page 57

SANSAR	WASHINGTON, DC 202-244-4448
HIGHLIGHT GALLERY	MENDOCINO, CA 707-937-3132
LEAGUE OF MARYLAND CRAFTSMEN	ANNAPOLIS, MD 410-626-1277
SNYDERMAN GALLERY	PHILADELPHIA, PA 215-238-9576

STEFF KORSAGE BROWNE
CHICAGO, IL
312-338-2101
See page 118
PLEASE CONTACT ARTIST DIRECTLY

JACK BRUBAKER
NASHVILLE, IN
FAX 812-988-7830
812-988-7830
See page 48

AN AMERICAN CRAFTSMAN	NEW YORK, NY 212-399-2555
ARTFUL HAND GALLERY	BOSTON, MA 617-262-9601

<table>
<tr><td>GLASS REUNIONS</td><td>RICHMOND, VA
804-643-3233</td></tr>
<tr><td>LUMA</td><td>COLORADO SPRINGS, CO
719-577-5835</td></tr>
<tr><td>NATIONAL ORNAMENTAL METAL MUSEUM</td><td>MEMPHIS, TN
901-774-6380</td></tr>
<tr><td>NEWBILL COLLECTION</td><td>SEASIDE, FL
904-231-4500</td></tr>
<tr><td>RIVER RUN GALLERY</td><td>KETCHUM, ID
208-726-8878</td></tr>
<tr><td>SERENDIPITY</td><td>ANACORTES, WA
206-293-9433</td></tr>
</table>

THOMAS BUECHNER III
See page 16
PLEASE CONTACT ARTIST DIRECTLY

CORNING, NY
FAX 607-936-2488
607-936-8707

HELEN C. BUNCH
See page 126

ANN ARBOR, MI
313-741-8516

<table>
<tr><td>THE PHOENIX AT NEPENTHE</td><td>BIG SUR, CA
408-667-2347</td></tr>
<tr><td>ACCENTS WEST</td><td>BOZEMAN, MT
406-586-4185</td></tr>
<tr><td>AN AMERICAN CRAFTSMAN</td><td>NEW YORK, NY
212-243-0245</td></tr>
<tr><td>ANDY SHARKEY GALLERY</td><td>ROYAL OAK, MI
810-546-6770</td></tr>
<tr><td>CRAFT CO. NO. 6</td><td>ROCHESTER, NY
716-473-3413</td></tr>
<tr><td>FALLING WATERS</td><td>ANN ARBOR, MI
313-747-9810</td></tr>
<tr><td>FIREWORKS</td><td>SEATTLE, WA
206-682-8707</td></tr>
<tr><td>OFFERINGS</td><td>KATONAH, NY
914-232-9643</td></tr>
</table>

SUSAN EILEEN BURNES
See page 116

BRECKSVILLE, OH
FAX 216-526-0874
216-838-5955

<table>
<tr><td>GORDON BEALE FRANK GALLERY</td><td>CLEVELAND, OH
216-421-0677</td></tr>
<tr><td>RAINBOWER GALLERY</td><td>HUDSON, OH
216-467-0259</td></tr>
</table>

CAROL GREEN STUDIO
See page 41
PLEASE CONTACT ARTIST DIRECTLY

PERRYSBURG, OH
FAX 419-872-0589
419-872-0589

R. BRUCE CARPENTER
See page 30
PLEASE CONTACT ARTIST DIRECTLY

ALBUQUERQUE, NM
505-265-4503

WARREN CARTHER
See page 64
PLEASE CONTACT ARTIST DIRECTLY

WINNIPEG, MB
FAX 204-453-2496
204-956-1615

CYNTHIA CHUANG AND ERH-PING TSAI
See page 121
PLEASE CONTACT ARTIST DIRECTLY

FOREST HILLS, NY
FAX 718-575-9480
718-793-4225

HOLLY E. CHURCHILL
See page 107
PLEASE CONTACT ARTIST DIRECTLY

PORTLAND, ME
207-780-8068

CIRCLE 'ROUND THE MOON
See page 106

CAMDEN, ME
207-236-8124

<table>
<tr><td>CAMDEN JEWELERY</td><td>CAMDEN, ME
207-236-8124</td></tr>
<tr><td>CLAY POT</td><td>BROOKLYN, NY
718-788-6564</td></tr>
<tr><td>JENSEN - STERN</td><td>KETCHUM, ID
208-726-2361</td></tr>
<tr><td>PHILIP DAVID</td><td>WEST HARTFORD, CT
203-232-6979</td></tr>
<tr><td>SILVERSCAPE DESIGN</td><td>AMHERST, MA
413-253-3324</td></tr>
</table>

MARC COAN
See page 56

ALBUQ, NM
FAX 505-877-1676
505-877-5707

<table>
<tr><td>MARIPOSA</td><td>ALBUQ, NM
505-842-9097</td></tr>
<tr><td>OFF THE WALL</td><td>SANTA FE, NM
505-983-8337</td></tr>
</table>

COLE STUDIOS
See page 62

ANDOVER, NY
FAX 607-587-9683
607-587-9644

<table>
<tr><td>NANCY MARGOLIS</td><td>PORTLAND, ME
207-775-3822</td></tr>
<tr><td>CHIAROSCURO GALLERY</td><td>CHICAGO, IL
312-988-9253</td></tr>
<tr><td>DEL MANO GALLERY</td><td>PASADENA, CA
818-793-6648</td></tr>
</table>

CONSTANCE KENNEDY DESIGNS
See page 125

SAN FRANCISCO, CA
FAX 415-585-3038
415-333-7391

<table>
<tr><td>THE GALLERY</td><td>BURLINGAME, CA
415-347-9392</td></tr>
<tr><td>ATELIER SAINT-HONORE</td><td>PARIS, FRANCE
42-66-03-83</td></tr>
</table>

JANA COOPER
See page 119

SEATTLE, WA
FAX 206-523-5311
206-523-0694

<table>
<tr><td>MADE IN WASHINGTON STORES</td><td>SEATTLE, WA
206-728-0838</td></tr>
<tr><td>HEARTS EASE</td><td>CAMBRIA, CA
805-927-1420</td></tr>
<tr><td>REAL MOTHER GOOSE</td><td>PORTLAND, OR
503-223-9510</td></tr>
</table>

JEFFREY COOPER
See page 59
PLEASE CONTACT ARTIST DIRECTLY

PORTSMOUTH, NH
603-436-7945

SHIRLEY NOVELLA POST COX
See page 62
PLEASE CONTACT ARTIST DIRECTLY

SANTA ANA, CA
714-664-0915

STEPHAN J. COX
See page 21

RIVER FALLS, WI
FAX 715-425-6668
715-425-7006

<table>
<tr><td>NEW GLASS GALLERY</td><td>NEW YORK, NY
212-431-0050</td></tr>
<tr><td>CHRISTY TAYLOR</td><td>BOCA RATON, FL
407-750-4389</td></tr>
<tr><td>EVENTS</td><td>HOUSTON, TX
713-520-5323</td></tr>
</table>

(Listing continued)

SIGNATURE GALLERY	BOSTON, MA 617-227-4885

CREATIVE CONNECTIONS
See page 80
PLEASE CONTACT ARTIST DIRECTLY

SHERMAN, CT
FAX 203-355-1120
203-355-1129

AFTER THE RAIN	NEW YORK, NY 212-421-1044
APPALACHIAN SPRING	WASHINGTON, DC 202-342-5578
FREE FLIGHT GALLERY	DALLAS, TX 214-720-9147
GALLERY ONE	NAPLES, FL 813-263-0835
HAND OF THE CRAFTSMAN	NYACK, NY 914-358-3366
HANSON GALLERIES	HOUSTON, TX 713-984-1242
MOONSTONES	CAMBRIA, CA 805-927-3447
THE GLASS MENAGERIE	CORNING, NY 607-962-6300

GRACE CROWLEY AND GWEN WEINBERG
See page 83

SEATTLE, WA
FAX 206-789-2181
206-783-1189

FIREWORKS	SEATTLE, WA 206-682-8707
KATE'S PAPERIE	NEW YORK, NY 212-941-9816
POSITIVE IMAGES	AUSTIN, TX 512-472-1831
TWIST	PORTLAND, OR 503-224-0334

BOOTS CULBERTSON
See page 32
PLEASE CONTACT ARTIST DIRECTLY

SARASOTA, FL
813-355-3604

DANCING FIRE STUDIO
See page 31

NEWNAN, GA
404-251-7876

RED DOOR GALLERY	CARROLLTON, GA 404-830-0025
PANOPLY	NEWNAN, GA 404-251-4557

DAVID M. BOWMAN STUDIO
See page 46
PLEASE CONTACT ARTIST DIRECTLY

BERKELEY, CA
510-845-1072

DEBRA DEMBOWSKI
See page 123
PLEASE CONTACT ARTIST DIRECTLY

MILWAUKEE, WI
414-541-3085

DESIGNS IN LEATHER
See page 87

MINERAL POINT, WI
608-987-3607

FREE FLIGHT GALLERY	DALLAS, TX 214-720-9147
RUMORS	NEW ORLEANS, LA 504-525-0292
THE MOLE HOLE	BOULDER, CO 303-440-9131

RON DIEFENBACHER
See page 66
PLEASE CONTACT ARTIST DIRECTLY

ST. LOUIS, MO
314-966-4829

JUDY DITMER
See pages 55 and 116
PLEASE CONTACT ARTIST DIRECTLY

PIQUA, OH
513-773-1116

CAROLE ALDEN DOUBEK
See page 92
PLEASE CONTACT ARTIST DIRECTLY

SALT LAKE CITY, UT
801-487-1410

DON DRUMM
See page 51

AKRON, OH
FAX 216-253-4014
216-253-6268

HANSON GALLERIES	HOUSTON, TX 713-984-1242
ARTIFACTS GALLERY	MEMPHIS, TN 901-767-5236
J. HOWELL GALLERY	DENVER, CO 303-820-3925
SELDOM SEEN	FT. LAUDERDALE, FL 305-522-7556

JEROME R. DURR
See page 82
PLEASE CONTACT ARTIST DIRECTLY

SYRACUSE, NY
FAX 315-478-1767
315-428-1322

EKO
See page 97

SIGNATURE GALLERY	BOSTON, MA 617-227-4885
ABACUS HAND CRAFTERS GALLERY	BOOTHBAY HARBOR, ME 207-633-2166
SHAXTED	CHICAGO, IL 312-337-0855
SPECTRUM OF AMERICAN ARTISTS	BREWSTER, MA 508-385-3322

LINDA SUE EASTMAN
See page 81
PLEASE CONTACT ARTIST DIRECTLY

WINONA, MN
507-454-7435

JILL ELIZABETH
SCOTT MACLAREN
See page 124
PLEASE CONTACT ARTIST DIRECTLY

EAST STROUDSBURG, PA
FAX 717-421-7833
800-531-9992

JESSICA FELIX
See page 113
PLEASE CONTACT ARTIST DIRECTLY

OAKLAND, CA
510-547-2420

RONA FISHER
See page 113
PLEASE CONTACT ARTIST DIRECTLY

PHILADELPHIA, PA
215-627-3848

MICHAEL JON FLORES
See page 69

CLEMENTS, CA
209-763-5713

MICHAELJON, WOODWORKER	WALLACE, CA 209-763-5713

AUDREY FORCIER
See page 117

DOWNERS GROVE, IL
708-969-4116

VOLCANO ART CENTER	VOLCANO, HI 808-967-7511
CHIAROSCURO	CHICAGO, IL 312-988-9253
FLYING SHUTTLE	SEATTLE, WA 206-343-9762

KATIE GINGRASS GALLERY — MILWAUKEE, WI / 414-289-0855

NOHEA — HONOLULU, HI / 808-596-0074

SARAH FREDERICK
See page 41 — **LOUISVILLE, KY** / **502-897-1298**

SWANSON CRALLE GALLERY — LOUISVILLE, KY / 502-452-2904

BENNETT GALLERIES — KNOXVILLE, TN / 615-584-6791

KENTUCKY ART & CRAFT FOUNDATION — LOUISVILLE, KY / 502-589-0102

KEVIN FULTON
See page 22 — **BEND, OR** / **503-382-8636**

SEEKERS COLLECTION & GALLERY — CAMBRIA, CA / 805-927-8626

EMERALD CITY GALLERY AT THE SHERATON — SEATTLE, WA / 800-626-4648

GREGORY'S — SALADO, TX / 817-947-5703

PURPLE PELICAN — SEASIDE, OR / 503-738-5743

RARE DISCOVERY — CANNON BEACH, OR / 503-436-0119

SAXON'S — BEND, OR / 503-389-6655

THE EMERALD CITY GALLERY — SEATTLE, WA / 800-432-0090

THE HOST — SEATTLE, WA / 206-433-5122

SUSAN GARDELS
See page 89 — **DES MOINES, IA** / **515-265-2361**

GRACE CHOSY GALLERY — MADISON, WI / 608-255-1211

PIECES LTD — HIGHLAND PARK, IL / 708-432-2131

GINNY'S EAR•NEST
See page 58 — **PORTLAND, OR** / **FAX 503-230-9049** / **503-231-8744**

TABRA — NOVATO, CA / 415-883-1001

19TH STREET GALLERY — VIRGINIA BEACH, VA / 804-425-8224

BROCKTON ART MUSEUM — BROCKTON, MA / 508-588-6000

HEARTLAND GALLERY — AUSTIN, TX / 512-447-1171

JADE GUNNARSON JEWELERY — SAN FRANCISCO, CA / 415-861-1419

JOHN MCLEOD LTD. — WILMINGTON, VT / 802-464-3332

MINDSCAPE GALLERY — EVANSTON, IL / 708-864-2660

P.M. GALLERY — COLUMBUS, OH / 614-299-0860

H.C. FINE METAL WORK
See page 47 — **PORTLAND, ME** / **207-780-8068**
PLEASE CONTACT ARTIST DIRECTLY

MICHAEL K. HANSEN
NINA PALADINO CARON
See page 18 — **SACRAMENTO, CA** / **FAX 916-925-9370** / **916-925-9322**

OVERWHELMED! — BOCA RATON, FL / 407-368-0078

ARTFUL HAND GALLERY — BOSTON, MA / 617-262-9601

ATLAS GALLERIES — CHICAGO, IL / 800-423-8702

GLASS CANVAS GALLERY, INC. — CAMBRIA, CA / 805-821-6767

INTERNATIONAL VILLA — DENVER, CO / 303-333-1524

MARTIN LAWRENCE GALLERY — LAHAINA, MAUI, HI / 808-661-1788

MINDSCAPE GALLERY — EVANSTON, IL / 708-864-2660

PETRI'S — SAUSALITO, CA / 415-332-2225

JOHN HEIN
See page 68 — **HOPEWELL, NJ** / **609-466-8121**
PLEASE CONTACT ARTIST DIRECTLY

STEVEN HENSEL
See page 45 — **SEATTLE, WA** / **FAX 206-633-2346** / **206-547-7706**
PLEASE CONTACT ARTIST DIRECTLY

BARBARA A. HIRSCHFELD
See page 112 — **KINGSTON, NY** / **914-331-1114**

AMERICAN CRAFT MUSEUM — NEW YORK, NY / 212-956-3535

ART EFFECT — CHICAGO, IL / 312-664-0997

HANSON ART SOURCE — KNOXVILLE, TN / 615-584-6097

JERGER JOHNSON JEWELERS — HIGHLANDS, NC / 704-526-4511

N.W. BARRETT GALLERY — PORTSMOUTH, NH / 603-431-4262

THE AMERICAN HAND — WESTPORT, CT / 203-225-8883

THE ARTFUL HAND — BOSTON, MA / 617-262-9601

THE BACK DROP — ARLINGTON HEIGHTS, IL / 708-255-1965

BRUCE HOSKINS
See page 56

G. WEBB GALLERY — GATLINBURG, TN / 615-436-3639

ART LEAGUE OF MARCO ISLAND — MARCO ISLAND, FL / 813-394-4221

EAST BAY GALLERY — CHARLESTON, SC / 803-723-5567

RIVER GALLERY — CHATANOOGA, TN / 615-267-7353

RIVERWORKS CRAFT GALLERY — SAVANNAH, GA / 912-236-2012

THE FRAME UP — BREVARD, NC / 704-883-2385

VARIATIONS BY VICTORIA — KNOXVILLE, TN / 615-688-4920

FINDING THE ARTWORK

HOYMAN/BROWE STUDIO
See page 29

UKIAH, CA
FAX 707-468-1212
707-468-8835

TWIST — PORTLAND, OR — 503-224-0334

AMERICAN HAND — WESTPORT, CT — 203-226-8883

ARTISAN CENTER — DENVER, CO — 303-333-1201

ARTISAN SHOP — WILMETTE, IL — 708-251-3775

CLAY PIGEON — SEDONA, AZ — 602-282-2845

CLAY POT — BROOKLYN, NY — 718-788-6564

PEWABIC POTTERY — DETROIT, MI — 313-822-0954

PINCH POTTERY — NORTHAMPTON, MA — 800-732-7091

JOAN E. SCHECKEL: CERAMIC ARTIST
See page 38

PHILADELPHIA, PA
215-927-2821

LANGMAN GALLERY — WILLOW GROVE, PA — 215-657-8333

A STEP ABOVE GALLERY — SARASOTA, FL — 313-955-4477

ART EFFECTS — BALA CYNWYD, PA — 610-668-0992

CBL FINE ART — WEST ORANGE, NJ — 201-736-7776

HANSON GALLERIES — HOUSTON, TX — 713-984-1242

OUT OF THE ORDINARY — ST. LOUIS PARK, MN — 612-938-5743

SOMETHING UNIQUE — BLOOMINGDALE, IL — 708-894-6282

TRADITIONS - GRAND VILLAGE SHOPS — BRAMSON, MO — 417-336-7235

JOHN DODD STUDIO
See page 68

CANANDAIGUA, NY
716-229-4444

WILLIAM ZIMMER GALLERY — MENDOCINO, CA — 707-937-5121

CREATIONS FINE WOODWORKING GALLERY — YORKLYN, DE — 302-234-2350

IRON, GLASS & WOOD HANDMADE FURNISHINGS — PITTSBURGH, PA — 414-661-7550

PRITAM AND EAMES — EAST HAMPTON, NY — 516-324-7111

K DAHL GLASS STUDIOS
See page 73

CRAWFORD, CO
FAX 303-921-4595
303-921-6160

STEINHARDT GALLERY — HUNTINGTON, NY — 516-549-4430

CLAY POT — BROOKLYN, NY — 718-788-6564

DISCOVERIES — READING, PA — 215-372-2595

ENCHANTED FOREST — NEW YORK, NY — 212-431-1045

THE ARTFUL HAND GALLERY — BOSTON, MA — 617-262-9601

KALLIMA JEWELRY
See page 109
PLEASE CONTACT ARTIST DIRECTLY

LANCASTER, PA
FAX 717-299-9507
800-835-3331

CRAIG KAVIAR
See page 70

LOUISVILLE, KY
FAX 502-561-0377
800-500-3890

MIND'S EYE CRAFT GALLERY — SCOTTSDALE, AZ — 602-941-2494

ART MECCA — CHICAGO, IL — 312-935-3255

BARBARA BAKER'S ONE ROOM AT A TIME — DARIEN, CT — 203-866-7978

CARRIBEAN DESIGNS INTERNATIONAL INC. — NORTH MIAMI BEACH, FL — 305-824-3200

CYRNA INTERNATIONAL — CHICAGO, IL — 312-329-0906

LEGENDS A GALLERY OF AM. ARTISANS — SONOMA, CA — 707-939-8100

MAGPIE — MANHATTAN BEACH, CA — 310-546-5132

MATERIAL POSSESSIONS — CHICAGO, IL — 312-280-4885

KEVIN RAGALLER STUDIOS
See page 72

FLAGSTAFF, AZ
602-774-9025

AUSI GALLERY — TUBAC, AZ — 602-398-3193

GALLERY FOREST — SEDONA, AZ — 602-282-2744

BETSY KING
See page 111

OCEAN CITY, NJ
609-398-8824

HELEN DRUTT GALLERY — PHILADELPHIA, PA — 215-735-1625

SUSAN CUMMINS GALLERY — MILL VALLEY, CA — 415-383-1512

KOWALSKI CLOCKWORKS
See page 85
PLEASE CONTACT ARTIST DIRECTLY

BERKELEY, CA
FAX 510-548-2187
510-548-2185

ED KOZLOWSKI, JR.
See page 22
PLEASE CONTACT ARTIST DIRECTLY

PINELLAS PARK, FL
813-545-4451

KROMA
See page 125

SANTA FE, NM
FAX 505-989-1782
505-989-1744

RILEY HAWK — CLEVELAND, OH — 216-421-1445

AMERICAN PIE A LA MODE — PHILADELPIA, PA — 215-922-2226

ARTFUL HAND GALLERY — BOSTON, MA — 617-262-9601

COLLECTOR'S FINE ART — KOLOA, HI — 808-742-8331

DEL MANO GALLER — PASADENA, CA — 818-793-6648

IMPULSE — PROVINCETOWN, MA — 508-487-1154

MERRILL CHASE — BUFFALO GROVE, IL — 708-215-4900

REAL MOTHER GOOSE — PORTLAND, OR — 503-223-9510

SILJA LAHTINEN
See page 86
PLEASE CONTACT ARTIST DIRECTLY

MARIETTA, GA
FAX 404-992-8380
404-992-8380

ITALA LANGMAR
See page 91
PLEASE CONTACT ARTIST DIRECTLY

KENILWORTH, IL
708-259-0427

LIBRUS STUDIO
See page 93
PLEASE CONTACT ARTIST DIRECTLY

SARASOTA, FL
FAX 813-922-2367
813-921-5421

MARILYN MACGREGOR
See page 70

ROSS, CA
FAX 415-457-4377
415-457-8444

FINE WOODWORKING
SAUSALITO, CA
415-332-5770

ANIMALIA
SAUGATUCK, MI
616-857-3227

MARK EHRMANN JEWELRY DESIGNS
See page 114

S. SAN FRANCISCO, CA
FAX 415-583-5069
800-537-2902

THE HARRY MASON DESIGN STUDIO
SAN FRANCISCO, CA
415-558-9771

CASA RODRIGUEZ
ST. AUGUSTINE, FL
904-824-2305

GOLDEN PALET
CRIPPLE CREEK, CO
719-689-3041

MASTERWORKS OF HELEN
HELEN, GA
706-878-2352

MASTERWORKS OF HIGHLANDS
HIGHLANDS, NC
704-526-2633

RARE DISCOVERY
CANNON BEACH, OR
503-738-5786

STEINBECK LADY
MONTEREY, CA
408-649-1814

SUNDANCE
LAHASKA, PA
215-794-8871

GEORGE MARLOWE
See page 39

MARINA DEL REY, CA
FAX 310-301-0058
310-821-7725

GALLERY RODEO INTERNATIONAL
BEVERLY HILLS, CA
213-273-2105

DAVID MARSON
See page 120

FAYETTEVILLE, AR
501-444-0300

PLEASURES
PARK CITY, UT
801-649-5733

BIER POTTERY
CHARLLEVOIX, MI
616-547-2288

BLUESTEM MISSOURI CRAFTS
COLUMBIA, MO
314-442-0211

DAVLINS
MINNEAPOLIS, MN
612-378-1036

EXPRESSLY WOOD
EVANSTON, IL
708-869-7060

JOHNSTON GALLERY
MINERAL POINT, WI
608-987-3787

SABLE V FINE ART GALLERY
WIMBERLEY, TX
512-847-8975

THE CLAY PIGEON
SEDONA, AZ
602-282-2845

MARY BETH ROZKEWICZ JEWELRY
See page 110

MARK MILLIKEN GALLERY
NEW YORK, NY
212-534-8802

BENNETT GALLERIES
KNOXVILLE, TN
615-584-6791

SAN FRANCISCO MUSEUM OF MODERN ART
SAN FRANCISCO, CA
415-357-4035

SANDRA AINSLEY GALLERY
TORONTO, ON
416-362-4480

ZONA
NEW YORK, NY
212-925-6750

STEVEN MASLACH
See page 21

BAINBRIDGE ISLAND, WA
FAX 206-842-9212
206-842-9212

JOANNE RAPP GALLERY
SCOTTSDALE, AZ
602-949-1262

BRENDON WALTER GALLERY
SANTA MONICA, CA
310-395-1155

SIGNATURE GALLERY
BOSTON, MA
617-227-4885

THE RACHEL COLLECTION
ASPEN, CO
303-920-1313

PETER MAYNARD
See page 67
PLEASE CONTACT ARTIST DIRECTLY

SOUTH ACWORTH, NH
FAX 603-835-2969
603-835-2969

NANCEE MEEKER
See page 37

RHINECLIFF, NY
914-876-3119

THE WORKS GALLERY
PHILADELPHIA, PA
215-922-7775

RICK MELBY
See page 75

TAMPA, FL
813-248-1899

GALLERY I/O
NEW ORLEANS, LA
504-581-2113

MESOLINI GLASS STUDIO
See page 19

BAINBRIDGE ISLAND, WA
206-842-7133

NEW GLASS GALLERY
NEW YORK, NY
212-431-0050

LE CHERCHE-MIDI
NANTUCKET, MA
508-228-7600

LE CHERCHE-MIDI
NAPLES, FL
813-263-7999

MATERIAL POSESSIONS
CHICAGO, IL
312-280-4885

MATERIAL POSESSIONS
WINNETKA, IL
708-446-8840

MESOLINI & AMICI
SEATTLE, WA
206-587-0275

OPUS 5 GALLERY
EUGENE, OR
503-484-1710

JANE METZGER
See page 88

PHOENIX, AZ
602-863-1212

TEMPE ARTS CENTER GALLERY SHOP
TEMPE, AZ
602-968-0888

EDWARD MORDAK
See page 96

SAN FRANCISCO, CA
FAX 405-931-4515
415-621-7121

ABBY MORRISON
See page 65

ROCKLAND, ME
207-594-1448

HARBORSQUARE GALLERY/GOOD HANDS
CAMDEN, ME
207-236-8700

(Listing continued)

FINDING THE ARTWORK

DEL MANO GALLERY	LOS ANGELES, CA 310-476-8508
ETHAN ALLEN CORPORATE COLLECTION	DANBURY, CT 203-743-8500
MARK MILLIKEN GALLERY	NEW YORK, NY 212-534-8802

DONNA MURAKAMI
See page 115 — **SAN FRANCISCO, CA 415-252-0145**

SEDONNA	SAN FRANCISCO, CA 415-474-7152
ECLECTIA	SAN FRANCISCO, CA 415-255-3175
OUT OF HAND	SAN FRANCISCO, CA 415-826-3885

LENN NEFF
See page 75 — **ST. PETERSBURG, FL 813-823-3919**

FLORIDA CRAFTSMAN GALLERY	ST. PETERSBURG, FL 813-821-7391

NETTLES AND GREEN THREADS
See page 100 — **BERNE, NY 518-797-3163**

AFTER THE RAIN	NEW YORK, NY 212-431-1044
CALICO CAT	BALTIMORE, MD 410-944-2450
LUMA	COLORADO SPRINGS, CO 719-634-7711
MIMA'S	WARWICK, NY 914-986-3399
NOTHING IN MODERATION	OAK PARK, IL 708-386-9750
RUSTICA	DANIA, FL 305-922-2517
STUDIO 40	WHITE SULPHUR SPRINGS, WV 304-536-4898
THE POLLITT SELECTION	FAYETTEVILLE, NC 910-487-9100

DAVID NEW-SMALL
See page 20 — **VANCOUVER, BC FAX 604-681-6730 604-681-6730**

ANIMALIA	SAUGATUCK, MI 616-857-3227
LINDSEY GALLERY	OAK PARK, IL 708-386-5272
NEW ORLEANS SCHOOL OF GLASS	NEW ORLEANS, LA 504-529-7277
SABLE V FINE ART GALLERY	WIMBERLEY, TX 512-847-8975

CRAIG NUTT
See page 65 — **NORTHPORT, AL FAX 205-752-6535 205-752-6535**

CONNELL GALLERY/GREAT AMERICAN GALLERY	ATLANTA, GA 404-261-1712
EDGEWOOD ORCHARD GALLERIES	FISH CREEK, WI 414-868-3579
MARALYN WILSON GALLERY	BIRMINGHAM, AL 205-879-0582
MEREDITH GALLERY	BALTIMORE, MD 301-837-3575
SHOW OF HANDS	DENVER, CO 303-399-0201
THE ART OF THE TOY	SCOTTSDALE, AZ 602-423-2911

OAK RUN STUDIOS
See page 93 — **MOSIER, OR FAX 503-478-2269 800-346-3451**

THE ART OF THE TOY	SCOTTSDALE, AZ 602-423-2911

SUSAN M. OAKS
See page 98 — **SAN ANTONIO, TX 210-656-8440**
PLEASE CONTACT ARTIST DIRECTLY

GENE OLSON
See page 51 — **ELK RIVER, MN FAX 612-441-5846 612-441-1563**

JOHN MATTER ARTS	MINNEAPOLIS, MN 612-332-0676

KEVIN OSBORN
See page 36 — **TUCSON, AZ 602-624-2756**

RALEIGH GALLERY	DANIA, FL 305-922-3330
CROSS-HARRIS	NEW YORK, NY 212-888-7878
ELECTRIC GLASS	HAMPTON, VA 804-722-6300
MANDEL & CO	CHICAGO, IL 310-652-5025
ROCHE BOBOIS	PHILADELPHIA, PA 215-972-0168
SUZANNE BROWN GALLERY	SCOTTSDALE, AZ 602-945-8475

ANN WHEAT PACE
See page 30 — **HOUSTON, TX FAX 713-526-4103 713-529-7715**

HENRI BENDEL	NEW YORK, NY 212-247-1100
2 SUSANS	PHILADELPHIA, PA 215-242-0533
AMEN WARDY HOME	ASPEN, CO 303-920-7700
COMIN	WEST HARTFORD, CT 203-273-4522
GUMPS	SAN FRANCISCO, CA 415-982-1616
JOSEPH MASSIMINO	WAUKESHA, WI 414-821-6900
LA RUCHE	BOSTON, MA 617-536-6366
LIONS PAW	NANTUCKET, MA 508-228-3837

PEGGOTTY HANDPAINTED SILK
See page 101 — **PHOENIX, AZ FAX 602-548-8988 602-548-8988**

GALLERY FIVE	TEQUESTA, FL 407-747-5555

PHOENIX STUDIOS
See page 71 — **HARMONY, CA FAX 805-927-0724 805-927-4248**

VAULT GALLERY	CAMBRIA, CA 805-927-0300
BELLARDO LTD.	NEW YORK, NY 212-675-2668
CAROL JAMES GALLERY	ROYAL OAK, MI 313-541-6216
DALE TIFFANY INC	MOONACHIE, NJ 201-507-1515

DISCOVERIES — ELLICOTT CITY, MD — 410-461-9600

E.M.I. — VISALIA, CA — 209-732-8126

JOHN CHRISTOPHER GALLERY — STRONG BROOK, NY — 516-367-3978

MOLE HOLE OF FORT MYERS — FORT MYERS, FL

VICTORIA POTROVITZA
See page 100

GALLERY FIVE — TEQUESTA, FL — 407-747-5555

CHANGES — PORTLAND, OR — 503-223-3737

DREAM WEAVER — SARASOTA, FL — 813-388-1118

ORIGINS — SANTA FE, NM — 505-988-2323

RAM'S HEAD FORGE — TYLER, TX
See page 48 — FAX 903-581-4774
PLEASE CONTACT ARTIST DIRECTLY — 800-581-4774

JAYNE REDMAN — PORTLAND, ME
See page 47 — FAX 207-871-1343
207-871-1343

ROBIN RENNER — FARMINGTON, NM
See page 40 — 505-632-0182

DEARING GALLERIES — TAOS, NM — 505-758-8229

ART FOCUS — HAMILTON, MT — 406-363-4112

HIGH SPIRITS — WENATCHEE, WA — 509-663-7798

HUMAN ARTS — OJAI, CA — 805-646-1525

KINKOPF GALLERY — BRECKENRIDGE, CO — 303-453-9095

LINDSEY GALLERY — OAK PARK, IL — 708-386-5272

OLD TOWN GALLERY — FLAGSTAFF, AZ — 602-774-7770

REZWARE — NEW YORK, NY
See page 32 — 212-966-3595

AVENTURA GLASSWARE — NEW YORK, NY — 212-769-2510

AMEN WARY HOME — ASPEN, CO — 303-920-7700

CLAY ANGEL — SANTA FE, NM — 505-988-4800

CROCK-R-BOX — PALM DESERT, CA — 619-568-6688

SILVER CREEK OUTFITTERS — KETCHUM, ID — 208-726-5282

RINGS OF PASSION — PALATINE, IL
See page 122 — 708-359-2273

GILLMORE'S FINE JEWELERY — EVANSTON, IL — 708-328-3128

LA MAISON DE NICOLE — CHICAGO, IL — 312-943-3988

ONCE IN A BLUE MOON — BARRINGTON, IL — 708-381-7525

RITA BAKER DESIGN — ALLENTOWN, PA
See page 109 — 610-434-3464
PLEASE CONTACT ARTIST DIRECTLY

TIMOTHY ROSE — SAUSALITO, CA
See page 88 — FAX 415-331-5041
PLEASE CONTACT ARTIST DIRECTLY — 415-332-9604

BETSY ROSS — BEARSVILLE, NY
See page 36 — FAX 914-679-4780
914-679-7964

CROSSHANDS FINE CRAFTS — NEW YORK, NY — 212-888-7878

PERIMETER GALLERY — HOUSTON, TX — 713-521-5928

THE GOLDEN EGG — LAGUNA BEACH, CA — 714-376-0063

ROUX ROUX — BROOKLYN, NY
See page 50 — FAX 718-625-0581
718-875-4858

THE STORE NEXT DOOR — NEW YORK, NY — 212-606-0200

DEBORAH SABO — RIVERHEAD, NY
See page 115 — FAX 516-288-0551
516-369-9225

MINDSCAPE — EVANSTON, IL — 708-864-2660

ANGELHEART — NEWTOWN, PA — 215-968-1614

FIREWORKS — SEATTLE, WA — 206-682-8707

FREEHAND — LOS ANGELES, CA — 213-655-2607

KARL AND KRIS SACKSTEDER — SEATTLE, WA
See page 54 — 206-463-0978

ED HIGA CERAMICS — HONOLULU, HI — 808-943-8680

DEXTERITY — MONTCLAIR, NJ — 201-746-5370

SOMETHING UNIQUE — BLOOMINGDALE, IL — 708-894-6282

SOPHIA ST. STUDIOS — FREDERICKSBURG, VA — 203-372-3459

LOIS S. SATTLER — VENICE, CA
See page 40 — FAX 310-305-9229
310-821-7055

SIGNATURE IN ACRIVOE — WEST HOLLYWOOD, CA — 213-655-0554

BOBI LEONARD INTERIORS — SANTA MONICA, CA — 310-399-3251

GOLDEN EGG GALLERY — LAGUNA BEACH, CA — 714-376-0063

HUMAN ARTS — OJAI, CA — 805-646-1525

INTERIOR ACCENTS — HONOLULU, HI — 808-523-5553

TESORI — LOS ANGELES, CA — 213-273-9890

TOPS MALIBU GALLERY — MALIBU, CA — 213-456-8677

VIVANT INTERIOR — RANCHO MIRAGE, CA — 619-321-1515

MICHELE SAVELLE
SEATTLE, WA
206-233-0433
See page 19

ZYZYX!	BALTIMORE, MD / 410-486-9785
CBL FINE ARTS	WEST ORANGE, NJ / 201-736-7776
COURTYARD GALLERY	NEW BUFFALO, MI / 616-469-4110
MIND'S EYE GALLERY	SCOTTSDALE, AZ / 602-941-2494

KREG SCULLY
VIRGINIA BEACH, VA
804-496-8654
See page 110

KENT GALLERIES	SANTA FE, NM / 505-988-1001
AMETHYST LANE	CLEVELAND, OH / 216-231-7711
MARK LOREN DESIGNS LTD.	NAPLES, FL / 813-261-9135
MARK LOREN DESIGNS LTD.	FT. MYERS, FL / 813-482-4664
MINATA JEWELERS	CHAPEL HILL, NC / 919-967-8964
ROBERT BENTLEY CO.	NEW YORK, NY / 212-302-4846

LYNN SHANSKY
LEGGETT, CA
707-984-8797
See page 120

WOLFORD & CO.	SANTA ROSA, CA / 707-542-7426
BEADS OF PARADISE	PAIA, HI / 808-579-9459
SILVERADO JEWELRY	COTATI, CA / 707-795-9357

SHATSBY BRONZE
LEWISBURG, OH
513-962-4102
See page 50

SELDOM SEEN	FT. LAUDERDALE, FL / 305-522-7556
CALLAWAY GALLERIES	ROCHESTER, MN / 507-287-6525
CUDAHY'S	RICHMOND, VA / 804-782-1776
DIAMOND TANITA GALLERY	CRESTED BUTTE, CO / 303-349-0940
EARTHLY DESIGNS	INDIANAPOLIS, IN / 317-580-1861
NEW MORNING GALLERY	ASHEVILLE, NC / 704-274-2831
SAFARI COLLECTION	NEWPORT BEACH, CA / 714-720-9448
TAMARACK GALLERY	OMENA, MI / 616-386-5529

ALISON SHEAFOR
See page 118

VETRO MARMO ARTE GALLERY	GAHANNA, OH / 614-476-2211
GALLERY BUBACCO	VENICE, ITALY / 041-522-5981

SUSAN M. SIPOS
PHILADELPHIA, PA
215-482-5681
See page 33

ARGOSY, LTD.	WAUKESHA, WI / 414-821-6900

EXIT ART	LONGBOAT KEY, FL / 800-833-0894
OWEN PATRICK GALLERY	PHILADELPHIA, PA / 215-482-9395
THE MANGO TREE OF NEW YORK	NEW CITY, NY / 914-638-9668

SLEDD/WINGER GLASSWORKS
RICHMOND, VA
FAX 804-644-2837
804-644-2837
See page 23

EASY STREET	ANNAPOLIS, MD / 410-263-5556
GROVEWOOD GALLERY	ASHEVILLE, NC / 704-253-7651
J. FENTON GALLERY	WILLIAMSBURG, VA / 804-221-8200
WILD GOOSE CHASE	BROOKLINE, MA / 617-738-8020

GAEL A. SLOOP
OKLAHOMA CITY, OK
405-842-3295
See page 107
PLEASE CONTACT ARTIST DIRECTLY

SMITTY BLANKETS
FARMINGTON, MI
810-442-2269
See page 99
PLEASE CONTACT ARTIST DIRECTLY

MARGARET SOUTHWELL
FANWOOD, NJ
908-889-8512
See page 39

LEO KAPLAN, LTD.	NEW YORK, NY / 212-535-2407

THE CENTURY GUILD
DURHAM, NC
919-598-1612
See page 66

SANSAR	WASHINGTON, DC / 202-244-4448

CHRISTIAN THEE
COLUMBIA, SC
FAX 803-787-1459
803-787-1459
See page 69

HAVENS GALLERY	COLUMBIA, SC / 803-256-1616

CHARLIE H. THOMPSON
EL PASO, TX
FAX 915-591-3535
915-877-2257
See page 63
PLEASE CONTACT ARTIST DIRECTLY

CHRISTOPHER THOMSON
RIBERA, NM
FAX 505-421-2618
505-421-2645
See page 49

JOHNSON-BENKERT	SANTA FE, NM / 505-984-2768
BEYOND HORIZONS	SCOTTSDALE, AZ / 602-596-9234
DAKOTA	TELLURIDE, CO / 303-728-4204
FORM AND FUNCTION	SANTA FE, NM / 505-984-8226
GALISTO	SAN FRANCISCO, CA / 415-861-5900
LA MESA OF SANTA FE	SANTA FE, NM / 505-984-1688
MONTANA EXPRESSIONS	KALISPELL, MT / 406-756-8555
MOUNTAIN HOUSE	JACKSON, WY / 307-733-4227

KATHLEEN TOTTER-SMITH
See page 87 — **MEDINA, OH** · **216-725-8985**

GIFTED HANDS	SEDONA, AZ · 602-282-4822
A SHOW OF HANDS	NORTH OLMSTED, OH · 216-777-2143
A SHOW OF HANDS	CINCINNATI, OH · 513-421-7119
CHELSEA GALLERY	BEACHWOOD, OH · 216-591-1066
DON DRUMM STUDIOS	AKRON, OH · 216-253-6268
EXPRESSIONS GALLERY OF ART	MEDINA, OH · 216-723-6767
LUMA	COLORADO SPRINGS, CO · 719-550-9291

ANGELIKA TRAYLOR
See page 73 — **INDIAN HARBOUR BEACH, FL** · **FAX 407-779-3612** · **407-773-7640**
PLEASE CONTACT ARTIST DIRECTLY

TREE OF LIFE ART WORKS
See page 121 — **CANTON, IL** · **FAX 309-647-2737** · **309-647-2725**
PLEASE CONTACT ARTIST DIRECTLY

RICHARD TUCK
See page 34 — **CHURUBUSCO, IN** · **219-693-9596**

SCHNEIDER GALLERY, INC.	CHICAGO, IL · 312-988-4033
ARIANA GALLERY	ROYAL OAK, MI · 810-546-8810
ARTIFACTS GALLERY	INDIANAPOLIS, IN · 317-255-1178
COLUMBUS MUSEUM SHOP	COLUMBUS, IN · 812-376-2559
DEAN MOSS GALLERY	DECATUR, GA · 404-377-4705
FIORI-OMNI GALLERY	CLEVELAND, OH · 216-721-5319
FT. WAYNE MUSEUM OF ART SHOP	FT. WAYNE, IN · 219-422-6467
FUMIE GALLERY	CHICAGO, IL · 312-726-0080

GARY UPTON
See page 74 — **GRASS VALLEY, CA** · **FAX 916-273-0619** · **916-273-1449**

TERCERA GALLERY	LOS GATOS, CA · 408-354-9482
GALLERY FAIR	MENDOCINO, CA · 707-937-5121
SHARON PARK GALLERY	MENLO PARK, CA · 415-854-6878

GISELA VON EICKEN
See page 123 — **NEW YORK, NY** · **FAX 212-475-4102** · **212-780-0840**

PEIPERS & KOJEN	NEW YORK, NY · 212-744-1047
AMERICAN CRAFT MUSEUM	NEW YORK, NY · 212-956-3535
MAIN STREET GALLERY	SAG HARBOR, NY · 516-725-9884

TIM WALKER
See page 90 — **MADISON HEIGHTS, MI** · **FAX 810-543-1942** · **810-543-3232**
PLEASE CONTACT ARTIST DIRECTLY

PAULETTE J. WERGER
See page 104 — **MADISON, WI** · **FAX 608-258-1416** · **608-251-1897**
PLEASE CONTACT ARTIST DIRECTLY

ERNEST WILMETH II
See page 33 — **ALBUQUERQUE, NM** · **505-266-0391**
PLEASE CONTACT ARTIST DIRECTLY

JONATHAN WINFISKY
See page 17 — **CHARLEMONT, MA** · **413-339-8319**

ARTFUL HAND GALLERY	BOSTON, MA · 617-262-9601
BARUCCI GALLERY	CLAYTON, MO · 314-727-2020
SEEKERS COLLECTION & GALLERY	CAMBRIA, CA · 805-927-8626
STEIN GALLERY	PORTLAND, ME · 207-772-9072

WM. B. SAYRE, INC.
See page 67 — **EASTHAMPTON, MA** · **FAX 413-527-0502** · **413-527-0202**

SOCIETY OF ARTS AND CRAFTS	BOSTON, MA · 617-266-1810
SANSAR	WASHINGTON, DC · 202-244-4448
SKERA GALLERY	NORTHAMPTON, MA · 413-586-4563

TOM WOLVER
See page 35 — **WATSONVILLE, CA** · **408-724-8436**
PLEASE CONTACT ARTIST DIRECTLY

TOMOCO YAMADA
See page 105 — **LOS ANGELES, CA** · **FAX 310-473-8455**
PLEASE CONTACT ARTIST DIRECTLY

NANCY J. YOUNG
See page 91 — **ALBUQUERQUE, NM** · **FAX 505-299-2238** · **505-299-6108**

| WEEMS GALLERY | ALBUQUERQUE, NM · 505-293-6133 |
| LA FUENTE GALLERY | SEDONA, AZ · 602-282-5276 |

LARRY ZGODA
See page 23 — **CHICAGO, IL** · **FAX 312-943-9987** · **312-943-9978**

CHICAGO ART MUSEUM-GOOD DESIGN STORE	CHICAGO, IL · 312-251-0175
ECLECTIC JUNCTION	CHICAGO, IL · 312-342-7865
GALLERIE STEPHANIE	CHICAGO, IL · 312-880-0995
ILLINOIS ARTISAN'S SHOP	CHICAGO, IL · 312-814-5321
LINDSEY GALLERY	OAK PARK, IL · 708-386-5272
TOUCHÉ INC.	CHICAGO, IL · 312-433-0188
VALE CRAFT GALLERY	CHICAGO, IL · 312-337-3525

INDEX OF ARTISTS AND COMPANIES